MAINSTREAM SPORT

BLUE MOON

DOWN AMONG THE DEAD MEN
WITH MANCHESTER CITY

MARK HODKINSON

MAINSTREAM
PUBLISHING

EDINBURGH AND LONDON

Blue Moon is dedicated to the memory of my grandmother,
Eveline Duffy (12 September 1915 to 14 December 1998).
'How do you remember all those words, Mark?'

First published in Great Britain in 1999 by
MAINSTREAM PUBLISHING COMPANY (EDINBURGH) LTD
7 Albany Street
Edinburgh EH1 3UG

ISBN 1 84018 207 5

A catalogue record for this book is available from the British Library

Typeset in Garamond
Printed and bound in Finland by WSOY

Contents

Introduction

A Summer Birdcage

Back then, I didn't properly understand how you got from here to there. The world was confused and disconnected. It was streets and streetlights, cars and buses, fields and houses, and suddenly you were there. We made it to Maine Road, somehow. City drew 1–1 with Sheffield United. It was 1971 and I was six years old. A bus ride, and we were back home. I don't remember the game, only the noise, the overcoats, the rich green of the pitch, the overwhelming magnitude of the event – that people gathered together like this and sang and cheered and created something so much bigger than themselves.

Twenty-five years later. My first match report commissioned by a national newspaper. It could have been at any ground between Derby and Newcastle, such is the approximate patch of a northern football correspondent. It was Maine Road, obviously. It rained. The sky was thick with clouds, the match was dire. City drew 1–1 with Coventry City. Alan Ball, City's manager, provided the 'line' without really trying. At the after-match press conference he almost drowned in his own peculiarly random agitation. He coloured a grey day red, and we were all rather grateful he had. The report is included in this book, since it preceded City's downfall.

Thereafter, I did not return to Maine Road until the beginning of the 1998–99 season. I had spent the previous season as *The Times* quasi writer-in-residence at Oakwell, Barnsley, from where I had filed a weekly bulletin. Barnsley, after 110 years in football's backwater, had been promoted to the FA Carling Premiership. In short, it was a small club suddenly thrust into the big-time. Adopting reverse logic, *The Times* asked me to take on City in 1998–99, and relate the fortunes of a big

7

club in the small-time. This famous club – with two League Championships, four FA Cup wins, two Football League Cup wins, one European Cup-winners Cup win – was at its lowest point ever, the third tier of English football.

Initially, I had reservations. A season in the life of a football club is a long haul. I had lived the Barnsley experience. They were with me always: awake, asleep, stalking thoughts and dreams. A football club from close-up is consuming, it blocks out the view and life gets bent out of shape. As well as the interviews and the writing, there are the books, programmes, newspapers and fanzines to read. When the phone rings, they – friends, colleagues – talk about the club; another opinion, another insight, another snippet of news. And then the matches, the supporters' club meetings, the letters of complaint (or praise!) about last week's column. It becomes a loop, and real life becomes a half-life with indistinct edges. But this was City, Manchester City. The club of my home city. My grandad's club. My first love, my second-favourite team.

I spoke for some time with Keith Blackmore and David Chappell at *The Times*. They sold me the project. We were in a quiet room, blinds drawn, late summer afternoon. They are good motivators, they listen and then cajole. Half-way through the meeting I became ashamed of my reticence. This was one hell of a story, and I knew they would allow me to relate it without interference, but with encouragement and support.

I wanted the column to have a cinematic or literary title, 'Down and Out in Millwall and Colchester', 'Kick Out the Blues' or something similarly wide-screen. Over the course of a few weeks, 'Blue Moon', the club's unofficial theme song, became quietly but defiantly insistent. It is the supporters' song, and sums up everything about Manchester City. It is a lament, a torch song for the bruised, the last swig of hope for the sentimental. When City are playing well and winning, it becomes a heady, uplifting force. It breaks the heart. It is not a chant, but a sweet refrain offered to the sky and whatever lies above it. We called the column 'Blue Moon'.

Of course, it is perfectly legal to write about a football club without its express permission, though it is judicious and good form to ask first. I met the club's PR man, Chris Bird, late in July 1998. Over the season, I was to have more contact with Bird than anyone else at City – he was the official first-port-of-call. He was relatively new to the club, a protégé of the City director and ex-player, Dennis Tueart. They are alike in many ways. Drawn from traditional working-class backgrounds, they are straight-ahead, flinty characters. The drive and ambition is immediately noticeable in them both and they make no attempt to conceal it or dress it up. As we spoke in the reception area at Maine Road, Bird seemed a man suddenly flushed by power. He has a smile that can appear condescending but, as I later discovered, it is ingenuous, the real thing.

I was sure Bird would decline to co-operate, but he phoned the next day and said the club would be happy to help in any way it could, within reason. He said he had done some 'research' on me. Barnsley had told him I was a 'good lad', which, to a journalist, is both a compliment and a criticism. Was I a good lad because of my integrity or my compliance? 'In the end, we'd rather have you pissing from the inside than the outside, if you know what I mean. At least we can have some control over you that way,' said Bird. He was often direct and candid; I liked him for it. Too often, PR people couched their language in unctuous jargon. Bird spoke like a football man – told it like it was.

Manchester City, as everyone is aware, have what is typically known as a 'colourful' history. They have, down the years, become a stereotype of reckless profligacy and magnificent failure, usually in comical circumstances. I was determined that the columns would not dwell too much on the past, or the stereotype. The club had been held hostage by it for too long. Occasionally, I did seek out former personnel, but primarily for a slant on the club's current fortunes or, quite simply, because they were characters whose shadow still fell over the club. If anyone would like to place the 1998–99 season into a truly historical context, they should seek out Gary James's *Manchester The Greatest City*, a benchmark work by which other club histories should be measured. Likewise, the calamitous recent past is documented in Ashley Shaw's *Cups for Cock-Ups*, a breathless, if sketchy, resumé of Francis Lee's tenure as club chairman.

The season coincided with Manchester United's most successful campaign. They did the treble, winning the European Cup, FA Carling Premiership and the FA Cup. It would have been negligent not to mention United at certain points but, again, I wanted to avoid viewing the two clubs in parallel. It has become a futile comparison, since most clubs in England now trail United by some distance, such is their domination.

I have kept the news items between the columns as succinct as possible. Although City's league status was low, they remained a continual source of gossip and news. The club was based in a city with a high media presence, and stories, many of them speculative, emerged on a daily basis. They were linked with literally scores of players, and listing them all would have soon become tedious. In the columns I sometimes made reference to the most pertinent news items. Occasionally, this has led to the odd spot of repetition through the book since the 'news' is relayed as a snippet, and then commented upon in a column: please bear this in mind.

The columns published here are not strictly identical to those printed in *The Times*. In some cases, pressure of space necessitated either subtle or swingeing cuts – the versions here are unexpurgated. The additional comments underneath the pieces were written at the end of the season, after the event as it were, with the benefit of hindsight. Obviously, these are more direct because they were not – unlike the columns – laid before the club every Saturday morning in *The Times*. I hope no one at City will regard these after-words as vengeful, a sadistic dig-in-the-ribs once I had left their vicinity. I have assiduously followed the maxim of trying to write fairly, accurately and without malice.

It was magnanimous of City to open their borders to a prying journalist during such a baleful period of their history. Football clubs are changeable places: when a team is successful, the mood lightens dramatically and everyone is welcome aboard. Alternatively, when a team is struggling, they contract, draw in on themselves. In City's case, they had also been the subject of much damaging ridicule in the media. This led to intermittent bouts of paranoia and mistrust but, generally, the club was welcoming and generous. Everyone gave their time freely, and a time-limit was rarely placed on interviews. The only person to ask for payment was their former coach and manager, Malcolm Allison, who abruptly ended our telephone conversation when he learned none would be forthcoming. On the subject of City old boys, I made 17 calls to Francis Lee's office, spoke to him once and got a half-promise of an interview on the day of which he departed for Holland on business.

I did not attend every City match throughout the season. I wanted to stay at a reasonable distance, to remain as impartial as possible. I already had an emotional attachment to them and did not want to compromise my position further. Towards the end, though, rational, cool-headed thought regularly collided with partisanship.

Many people have contributed to this book. The original idea belonged to *The Times*'s Sportsdesk, chiefly Keith Blackmore and David Chappell. Support was offered from other quarters at *The Times*, namely Richard Whitehead, Mark Herbert, Kevin McCarra, Peter Dixon and Gertrud Erbach. Bill Campbell of Mainstream Publishing was forthright and committed enough to commission the book within days of our initial conversation. Paula Ridings generously allowed me compassionate leave and confined the commotion made by our two young sons, George and Alec, to other parts of the house. She also provided valued sustenance in a hundred other ways. Thank you.

Stephen Hewitt was a consistent source of information and gave invaluable assistance with the manuscript. Ann Hewitt kindly undertook a fair amount of word-processing. Other journalists, especially Mike Barnett, Mike Grime, Guy Raynor, Richard Burgess and David White (not the ex-City player) supplied phone numbers or a perspective on the City enigma, as did City-supporting friends Tony Kerr, John Wallace, and Steve Harrison – who also welcomed me into his executive box at Maine Road. Fred Eyre was always willing to offer an insight or two. Richard Lysons and Guy Patrick were a source of inspiration. John Maddocks was willing to double-check facts and figures, and Graham Williams kindly proof-read an early draft of the book.

The editors of the various City fanzines – Noel Bayley (*Bert*

Trautmann's Helmet), Dave Wallace (*King of the Kippax*) and Tom Ritchie (*City 'til I Cry!*) – were all helpful and supportive. City supporters have the fanzines they deserve: informed, heartfelt and intelligent, though each with its own idiosyncratic perspective. While I undertook the project, David Cooper, Rob Kerford, Ursula Lumb, Joanne Mortimer and Sarah Aspinall took care of business.

Within the club itself, everyone was polite and courteous. Chris Bird was consistently helpful. Calls were returned promptly and he often pieced together interviews at only a few hours notice. David Bernstein was accessible – he gave me his mobile phone number soon after meeting, for instance. Joe Royle was good company, and Willie Donachie too. In fact, all the backroom staff – Jim Cassell, Paul Power, Alex Stepney and the others – were kind and trusting with information.

Finally, the supporters. At the beginning, I was keen to challenge the stereotype of City's support. It had been portrayed as the most loyal in the country to the point of tediousness. Surely this masked some kind of conceit and vanity. I was determined to take a reactionary view and, since I was looking for it, I found the solidarity impeached by touches of arrogance, bitterness and martyrdom. They were only touches, mind.

The most perceptive comment on the subject came from Professor Cary Cooper, a City fan and psychologist, whom I interviewed at the end of the season. This erudite man had come to quite a simplistic conclusion, that City supporters were a cause of real celebration. They had remained loyal and committed, in it for the duration, when all around them was fickle and transitory. He plotted this to their working-class roots, Manchester's industrial past, the legacy of trade unionism and a cohesion born from a common adversary – United. His comments will be viewed by the sceptical as rather fanciful and romantic, but City *does* feel like a community and the supporters carry with them something that is extraordinary, something special.

Blue moon
You saw me standing alone
Without a dream in my heart
Without a love of my own

Blue moon
You know just what I was there for
You heard me saying a prayer for
Someone I really could care for

And then there suddenly appeared before me
The only one my arms will hold
I heard someone whisper please adore me
And when I looked to the moon it turned to gold

Blue moon
Now I'm no longer alone
Without a dream in my heart
Without a love of my own

And then there suddenly appeared before me
The only one my arms will ever hold
I heard somebody whisper please adore me
And when I looked the moon had turned to gold

Blue moon
Now I'm no longer alone
Without a dream in my heart
Without a love of my own

Blue moon
Now I'm no longer alone
Without a dream in my heart
Without a love of my own

One

Great Expectations

BALL BRINGS PASSION TO DRAB TALE OF TWO CITIES
(match report, *The Times*, Monday, 22 January 1996)

Alan Ball, face on fire, glass of beer in shaking hand, played the press with the same dearth of finesse that his side had shown in a bleak 1–1 draw with Coventry City. 'You lot write what you want to write. You all want to say it's doom and gloom and panic, but I was really pleased with the team,' was his crabby reply to the mildest of queries. Ball's invective, delivered in his famous tinder-dry shrill, was the most passionate interlude on a wretchedly cold afternoon of non-football.

The first half was supremely desolate, with only Niall Quinn supplying some levity as he twice sent stewards scampering to retrieve a ball which should have been in Coventry's net. Georgi Kinkladze, as usual, played as if on a magic carpet but his team-mates were strictly terrestrial; in fact, some of his prods and stabs were clearly Russian to the journeymen at his heels.

The draughty stands at Maine Road rang with groans and moans at half-time, the seagulls circling overhead providing a greater spectacle. Both teams had played ambitiously enough but basic inaptitude had so often ravaged their best-laid plans.

Ball was later to claim that young Martin Phillips had 'lit up Maine Road' when he came on as a substitute but it was, in truth, more 40-watt than 100. Phillips, at least, gave them shape, as John Salako did for Coventry when he raised suffi-cient valour to run for goal in earnest.

A double act which had hitherto bordered on comedy, Quinn and Uwe Rosler, suddenly found a punch-line of a goal so tidy that it served to amplify the previous disarray. Rosler impudently removed his shirt, waved it at the crowd and, like waking from a dream, soberly pulled it back on as Coventry waited to kick off.

Coventry's Dion Dublin, who had revealed in the programme that he shaved his head twice a day, pierced the home side's new poise when he put his burnished dome to a consummate cross from Hall. It was barely deserved. Coventry had been dogged, Dublin and Burrows especially, but torpid outside their own half of the field.

Afterwards, Ron Atkinson, their manager, was wonderfully agreeable. A smile, a wink to the press posse, another chew of the gum. 'We've had four points out of City this season, and they could be big, big points at the finish. We played intelligently, we sealed off the little spaces.' He was candid enough to admit that avoiding defeat had been the objective.

Ball, meanwhile, maintained his petulance. Did he think Nigel Clough would improve the team? 'He won't make any difference,' he answered sarcastically. Then why did he sign him? Ball looked skywards, lips pursed. 'That's one of the most ridiculous questions of all time. He's top quality, he's a good player, what do you expect me to say?'

Manchester City were better than their manager's public relations, and a good deal less edgy. Sometimes their play is a pastiche of 'total football', but some guile to complement the graft could make a wealth of difference. Ball will be discreetly making plans for Nigel.

MANCHESTER CITY (4–4–2): E. Immel, N. Summerbee, K. Curle, K. Symons, I. Brightwell, S. Lomas (sub: M. Phillips, 51 min.), G. Flitcroft, G. Kinkladze, M. Brown, U. Rosler, N. Quinn.

Sunday, 5 May 1996

On the last day of the 1995–96 season, City found themselves level with Southampton and Coventry City on 37 points with only one relegation place still unresolved in the Premiership.

City, playing against a distinctly indifferent Liverpool, found themselves 2–0 down before retrieving the game with goals by Uwe Rösler (a penalty) and Kit Symons. Rumours spread that

Coventry were losing against Leeds United and City, apparently under the orders of Alan Ball, began time-wasting tactics. The rumours were erroneous and Coventry defeated Leeds at Highfield Road to send City into Division One.

Sunday, 4 May 1998

Once more, City went into the final day of the season caught up in a frantic relegation battle. Reading had already been relegated and the other two spots were between City, Bury, Port Vale, Portsmouth and Stoke City.

Despite beating Stoke 5–2 with goals by Shaun Goater (two), Paul Dickov, Lee Bradbury and Kevin Horlock, they were still relegated. Portsmouth and Port Vale recorded victories at Bradford City and Huddersfield Town respectively. Portsmouth were managed by the ex-City manager Alan Ball.

City supporters at Stoke turned their second relegation in three years into a defiant party, chanting, 'Are you watching, Macclesfield?' 'I'm devastated. It's going to hurt for a very long time but we'll secure promotion next season for the fans,' said Jamie Pollock. 'This time next year we'll be singing and dancing.'

Tuesday, 6 May 1998

Joe Royle was given a contract to remain as City's manager for the next three years. Willie Donachie, the head coach, accepted a two-year extension.

Comedian and City fan, Eddie Large, said City would, 'go through the Second Division like a dose of salts'. Former City hero, Rodney Marsh, said it was 'unbelievably sad' to see the club so far down the League.

Friday, 15 May 1998

As expected, Georgi Kinkladze, the supporters' hero, finally left City and joined Ajax for £5.5 million.

Wednesday, 27 May 1998

Manchester bookmakers Fred Done made City 6–4 to win the Second Division title. They were the shortest odds ever offered for a Football League side at the start of a new season.

Paul Hince, chief sports writer on the *Manchester Evening News* and a former City player (seven appearances in the 1960s), promised to walk down Deansgate in Manchester city centre wearing just his boxer shorts if City did not gain promotion.

Monday, 1 June 1998

City, the official club magazine, lightened the mood by listing 'reasons to be cheerful' about relegation. Among them were 'fun weekends at a variety of coastal resorts like Blackpool and Bournemouth'; 'red-hot Lancashire derbies against grand old names of English football like Burnley and Preston North End'; and 'the chance to snuggle up together in the "cosy" stands that we'll be visiting on our away trips'.

Friday, 5 June 1998

City-supporting viewers of Sky TV's Bravo Channel were delighted when an episode of *Italian Stripping Housewives* was punctuated by a performance of 'Blue Moon', sung by the show's presenter.

Friday, 17 July 1998

Jamie Pollock revealed that he had lost a stone in weight over the summer months. 'The manager had told me I should lose some weight and I feel a lot better for it.' Pollock was among the full squad which began pre-season training with a stint at HMS Raleigh, the Royal Navy's training base in Cornwall, where they also played games against Torpoint Athletic and Newquay.

Tuesday, 21 July 1998

Dennis Tueart, a City director and former player, revealed several cutbacks for the 1998–99 season, among them fewer overnight stops for away games. 'It's a question of ensuring fans' money is spent properly and not wasted. For instance, we have worked out the games where we don't need to stay in a hotel the night before.'

Tuesday, 28 July 1998

The official launch of City's new away kit was postponed when suppliers, Kappa, delivered just a quarter of the ordered adult shirts and no junior sizes. 'We are extremely angry and frustrated by Kappa's failure,' said Mike Turner, the club's chief executive.

Friday, 31 July 1998

City striker Shaun Goater told the press: 'This will be my best ever season. I have set myself a target of 25 goals. I am putting my head on the block, but nobody should be in any doubt of my intentions.'

Tuesday, 4 August 1998

Joe Royle announced that 19-year-old Nicky Weaver would start the season as City's first-choice keeper, making his début in Saturday's game against Blackpool at Maine Road. 'I'm confident he won't let anyone down,' said Royle.

Several former City players were included in a list of '100 Soccer Legends' announced by the Football League to celebrate its centenary season. Denis Law, Colin Bell, Bert Trautmann, Peter Doherty, Frank Swift, Trevor Francis and Billy Meredith were listed. Many were surprised by the omission of Francis Lee and Mike Summerbee.

Thursday, 6 August 1998

Mike Turner revealed that the club had sold 13,771 season tickets and more than 28,000 match tickets for Blackpool's visit.

City began the season with just two new signings, Danny Tiatto from FC Baden of Switzerland (£300,000) and Danny Allsopp (£10,000) from Port Melbourne Sharks. Tiatto's father had played in Italy's Serie 'A'.

Friday, 7 August 1998

A new City fanzine, *City 'til I Cry!*, marked its first issue with the editorial: 'Our hopes and ambitions for the season are trivial and undemanding: 100 points, 100 goals and win the Auto Windscreen Shield before a fullhouse at Wembley. The voices of reason might call for consolidation, stability and realism. Well, bollocks to that!' It also placed City's relegation into context: 'Women say there's nothing more painful than childbirth – they've obviously never seen their team get relegated.'

Bert Trautmann's Helmet, meanwhile, pondered: 'Even City couldn't balls this season up, could they? No, don't answer that!'

ALL TOGETHER NOW, IT'S TIME TO START SINGING
THE BLUES
(*The Times*, Saturday, 8 August 1998)

Number eleven would have been more practical. Two thin pieces of cloth in parallel would have spared my mother a whole evening at the sewing machine, and most of the next morning too. In truth, it was not even open to discussion: it had to be number eight. Colin Bell wore number eight and he was the most important man on earth.

This shirt business had dragged on for some time. Back then, football clubs and merchandising were just nodding acquaintances. Clubs fretted that anything more than the obligatory enamel badge, plastic pennant and woolly scarf amounted to memorabilia overload. Replica shirts were almost non-existent. Eventually, a sky-blue Manchester City shirt was located, neatly pressed in a wooden drawer at a shop in Moston Lane, north Manchester.

The shopkeeper ran his fingers across it lovingly, as if it held the healing properties of the Golden Fleece. A City shirt really meant something in those days. A rough number eight was cut out of a piece of cloth. Sewing it on to the shirt took hours and, though I daren't admit it at the time, I was disappointed with the finished item. The number leaned and the two circles were twisted and pulled. Colin Bell's number eight was neat and orderly, mine was drunk and disorderly.

Manchester City were my grandad's club. They were made for each other. United, as he saw it, were brash and full of themselves, while City were perpetual underdogs. He had a pathological dislike of United's Bobby Charlton, though they shared the same haircut. On windy days, he would grumble that the breeze was 'disturbing his Bobby Charlton' as strands broke loose at will. 'All he can bloody do is kick it and run after it,' he said of this footballing great. He liked dribblers, players who could fool opponents with a trick of the instep or a shimmy of the hips.

City had these in abundance, he claimed, and they were usually small men with out-size hearts. We went on long walks, across railway tracks, over wasteland. City this, City that; players he had seen down the years. He would skip past a discarded shopping trolley, dummy an oil can. All the time: 'Don't be like everyone else. Don't do the obvious. Don't support United.'

Among work-mates and neighbours of a United persuasion, he felt there was no greater statement than holding aloft the blue flag. It was never nasty, though; his heart was big enough to embrace 'the other lot', as he called them. George Best was a good 'un; Nobby Stiles ('He went to school just over there,' he would say, pointing towards Collyhurst) was a battler; but Bobby Charlton, dear me, shake of the head: kick and bloody run; OK, he had a decent shot on him.

He took me to my first ever game, a 1–1 draw against Sheffield United at Maine Road. I wanted to leave after 15 minutes because my ears hurt from the sheer volume. Afterwards we went home on the bus and the windows steamed up. A lad of about 12 said he was going to sleep and asked my grandad to wake him up about two miles into the journey. He forgot, and that urchin in an anorak probably ended up at a bus depot in Bury or Oldham.

When I was 10 we moved away from Manchester. So, like a childhood friendship, I drifted apart from City. We went our separate ways. At first I watched their deterioration with concern, but my new club, Rochdale FC, to whom my loyalty has remained steadfast for 25 years, became an obsession. There was precious little emotional fuel left to generate more than a passing interest in another club.

City have been woefully mismanaged for nearly two decades.

Only the fans have remained constant, as players, managers and directors have passed through, heavy on promises, light on achievement. A fellow reporter, one who has to visit Maine Road on a regular basis, summarised the malaise at Moss Side. 'It's a cross between the Polit Bureau, *Fawlty Towers, Hi-De-Hi* and *One Foot in the Grave*,' he laughed, before coming over all serious and all but suggesting that the ground emanated a deadly blue mist. 'Don't go near there,' was his final counsel. The wind howled and curtains trembled.

Blackpool are the visitors today as City begin their campaign in Division Two of the Nationwide League. City supporters accepted a good while ago that their club is a Picasso painting (during his blue period); upside down, back to front, anyway you like, so they find nothing unusual or surreal about a league game against Blackpool. Perhaps when Macclesfield, Walsall, Gillingham, etc. pull on to the club car park, they might have a real sense of out-thereness.

They go into the season with a new chairman, David Bernstein, who has promised to restore stability, though there has been the habitual backroom personnel changes through the summer. 'Stability is a crucial aspect in our future success,' he said this week. He then added, imprudently: 'I cannot envisage circumstances where the relationship between Joe [Royle] and Willie [Donachie] will break down.'

City fans might suggest a few circumstances, though they would rather not. They are looking to a future of resounding wins and a team that passes and dribbles and tackles. They want their club to rediscover its nobility among the journeymen of the third best division of English football or, put another way, the second worst.

Fortunately, Colin Bell is on hand. After a messy, bundled exit under Franny Lee's reign as chairman, he has been reinstated in an 'ambassadorial role'. He no longer wears number eight; the sportsmanship, tact and dedication he personified, do not need a number. They can move through the corridors and dressing rooms of a football ground in a suit and tie, sweater and slacks; dignity does not need dressing up.

Saturday, 8 August 1998
Manchester City 3 Blackpool 0

Goals from Shaun Goater, Lee Bradbury and defender Kakhaber Tskhadadze inspired City to a comfortable win in front of 32,134 supporters. The attendance was the largest in England's Third Division for 20 years.

Tuesday, 11 August 1998
Notts County 0 Manchester City 2
(Worthington Cup First Round, First Leg)

Second-half goals by Tskhadadze and Danny Allsopp gave City the advantage for the return leg at Maine Road.

Thursday, 13 August 1998

Police warned City officials that the club's new away strip, a fluorescent yellow/green colour, might clash with those worn by stewards and emergency services.

Joe Royle gave permission for transfer-listed Nigel Clough to train with Birmingham City as he searched for a new club.

The latest squad count revealed 39 players, compared with 54 when Royle arrived six months earlier. David Bernstein said the rationalisation would continue.

Friday, 14 August 1998
Fulham 3 Manchester City 0

A poor performance by City was made even worse by the early departure of the in-form Tskhadadze. The Georgia captain twisted his knee and damaged ligaments after landing awkwardly in a challenge with Fulham captain Chris Coleman. 'It felt like an explosion in my leg,' said Tskhadadze. His wife, Tiniko, and 10-year-old son, Bacho, were in tears after seeing the incident back home in Manchester on Sky TV.

An estimated 3,500 City supporters saw goals from Peter Beardsley and German striker Dirk Lehmann (two) secure Fulham's victory.

Noel Gallagher of Oasis watched the game from an executive box but reportedly had his drink confiscated when he began to yell abuse at home supporters.

CYNICISM AND DEVOTION REMAIN AS CITY ADJUST TO THEIR ALIEN TERRITORY
(*The Times*, Saturday, 15 August 1998)

An assortment of dudes, suited-up and burly, stand guard at the entrance. 'Two quid, mate,' says the one with a neck the width of a fire extinguisher. The official car parks were full at 2 p.m., and all that remains are patches of roped-off wasteland with signs reading: 'Safe Parking'. In a rush, kick-off time looming, we'll believe anything.

It is the first day of the season and Manchester City supporters, as ever, are joyous in the pain. Relegation, ineptitude, a bi-weekly change of personnel (on and off the pitch), they just love it. These are people who eat three Shredded Wheat and skip on the milk, just to make breakfast a whole lot less fun.

Division Two is supposed to be a seaside resort out of season, creaky, in need of a lick of paint, and populated by die-hards in duffle coats, but Maine Road still feels big-time, Las Vegas in Accrington brick. People everywhere. A blur of electric blue is disgorged from narrow sidestreets to jostle for space among the police horses, fanzine sellers, burger stalls and face-painters.

Inside the ground, City's MC (Madam of Ceremonies) is orchestrating support, and a proper little madam she is too. She sashays across the pitch, with all the big-grin, thigh-slapping pizazz of someone born to star in pantomime, in exotic locations like Ashton-under-Lyne or Pocklington. She has no respect for syntax, no respect at aaaaall. Words are there to be stretched until they almost snap under the strain. 'You're looooking good, Maine Road,' she tells the crowd. As the team finally runs out, she shrieks: 'Go wild, go crazy, it's the start of a new season.'

The City players stare at the crowd in disbelief: 32,134 fans have assembled to watch them play Blackpool, in Division Two. They have ghostly, bloodless expressions that transmit the collective thought: 'Are we the lions, or the Christians?' The crowd starts to fidget after 24 minutes of aimless football. Suddenly, City score. Shaun Goater, a yard from the goal-line, stubs the ball straight at Blackpool's keeper. The referee, after a quick glance at his assistant, rules that it crossed the line. Maine Road goes wild, goes crazy.

Goal celebrations will prove enigmatic this season for City. Since they are perceived as infinitely superior to their rivals, it might be wise if goalscorers simply hold aloft a forefinger and nod sagely, in the manner of a Scout Master testing the wind direction before a six-mile hike. No chance! The players punch the air, punch their chests, punch Goater. A goal is a goal, and it feels good, or gooood, as the lady would say. And does, at half-time.

Mark Radcliffe and Marc Riley of Radio One are summoned from the crowd to draw the raffle. They hare on to the pitch and Radcliffe jumps up and down, throwing out his arms and legs in the manner of a starfish wired to the mains. The MC is dancing, knees bent, hair bobbing, with Moonchester, City's peculiar alien mascot thing. City are winning, aliens have landed, the whole world's gone mad.

Two more goals secure the win and the tension dissipates amid the communal singing. We love you City, they declare, before coming over all swoonsome with 'Blue Moon', which is, sniff, sniff, the most beautiful, sentimental song ever written, ever, ever, boo-hoo. At the final whistle, the results from Division Two are announced to the crowd. They carry on talking, barely noticing. One supporter, hurrying down the aisle, stops abruptly. 'Hey, this is our division, isn't it?' His mate nods. They both laugh.

In the press room, the league tables flash up on the television screen. City are top, and everyone chuckles. The football had been frantic, the players gripped by a form of agoraphobia, a fear of running into space, of holding the ball for more than a second. Where there was once a poetry about Manchester City, a sweet rhythm that even ran to their names – Bell, Lee, Summerbee – their game is now as fluid, as pleasing on the ear and eye, as the choppy, stroppy prose of Tskhadadze, Tiatto and Dickov. Still, at least it is effective, as wins against Blackpool and at Notts County in the Worthington Cup on Tuesday testify.

Give him a win, and Joe Royle is your genial Uncle Joe. A

defeat, and he can barely lift his head. Hands in his pocket, smile in place, he was Uncle Joe on Saturday, chuffed as little mint balls. 'We mustn't get too excited,' he said. Another smile. He was keeping his emotions in check, but his body language mocked the downbeat tone of his words. He shuffled from foot to foot, rolling his shoulders. 'There's a long way to go.' Big grin. 'We must carry on working hard.' If City still top the league next May, we may find Uncle Joe issuing these paeans to prudence and modesty while tap-dancing on the tables, singing 'Blue Moon' even.

● The scoreline flattered City. They did not play particularly well. Few players were comfortable on the ball and only their sheer strength of will carried them to victory. The supporters were relieved though – the result would resonate favourably in football circles and make City look the part. In their hearts, they were fearful. Blackpool, a solid but uninspiring Second Division team, had matched them for long periods of the game.

Sunday, 16 August 1998
The defeat at Fulham had sent City hurtling down the division and fans woke up to newspapers carrying the first published league tables of the new season. They were thirteenth, the lowest position in their history.

Monday, 17 August 1998
Fears over the severity of Tskhadadze's injury were confirmed. He had torn the cruciate ligaments in his left knee. 'I really feel for him. He was absolutely devastated after the match,' said Royle. Despite several attempted comebacks, he did not play again for the rest of the season.

Wednesday, 19 August 1998
Manchester City 7 Notts County 1
(Worthington Cup First Round, Second Leg)
Gary Mason opened the scoring before Paul Dickov celebrated the second anniversary of his arrival at Maine Road by scoring twice and laying on two more. The other scorers were Shaun

Goater (two), Lee Bradbury and Jim Whitley. Mason's mother, Liz, had put £1 on him to score the first goal at 20–1.

Sam Allardyce, County's manager, described his team's performance as a 'joke'. Joe Royle enthused, 'The fans have not seen a result like this in years. It's been a long time coming and I hope they enjoyed it.'

Thursday 20, August 1998

David Bernstein formally opened the club's new indoor leisure centre, The Dome. The £2.2 million centre, housed at their Platt Lane training complex, was a joint venture between the club, Manchester City Council and the English Sports Council. It included an artificial football pitch, hockey pitch, a sports injury clinic and solarium.

STORY OF FOOTBALL'S MOST FAMOUS FAILURE
(*The Times*, Saturday, 22 August 1998)

Our man in a Panama is looking good. The sun is out, the shorts are on, and the garden is quite magnificent. 'The bloke from the local golf club does it for us,' explains Fred Eyre. And a good job he does too: lush rolling lawn, neat borders, majestic conifers, an apple tree in radiant blossom, fruit everywhere.

Fred. The name suits him. Unassuming, to-the-point, anachronistic. This is football's most famous loser, outside his huge house, with electric gates and a drive as long as a motorway slip-road. Where did it all go right, Fred? 'Aw, don't go on too much about the money and all that,' he pleads.

The opulence that surrounds him is like snow that has fallen overnight. He sits among it, unaffected. We could be sitting at a bus stop, or back in the council house where he was brought up in north Manchester. His eyes are covered by toffee-coloured shades, but there is no doubt that, beneath them, they meet yours square on. No messing.

The honesty he personifies has had much to do with his success as an author. His first, and most celebrated book, *Kicked into Touch*, was a bulletin from the largely unseen, unsweetened side of football. Eyre wrote of free transfers, midfield grafters, high hopes and high tackles, scrappers and cloggers. Injuries were treated with a sharp slap on the affected area and trainers ('Coaches were what we travelled to games on.') tucked their jeans in their socks, their forefinger in your ribs.

Among the broken promises and broken hearts, Eyre found humour and related it with remarkable candidness. It wasn't Steinbeck or Conrad but, then again, unlike him they hadn't played for Wigan Athletic or Lincoln City. 'I didn't sweat blood at three in the morning writing the books. It was so easy, it just came natural to me. I've got a good memory, and I'm not bad at telling a story,' he said.

Eyre was the footballer of which we rarely hear. He was a not-quite-made-it, someone else in the team, a 'trier' as he was described in the pen pictures of one match programme. Back in 1981, when *Kicked into Touch* was published, he had played for 20 clubs in 20 years, under the supervision of 29 managers. Since then, the nomadic lifestyle has continued. Most recently he was chief scout at Sheffield United.

Paradoxically, he was an outstanding schoolboy footballer, and was one of about 1,000 boys asked by Manchester City to attend a series of trials. Only two were invited to join the club and at 15 Eyre signed for his beloved City. 'I went to my first game at Maine Road when I was three years old. Our right-back had a bandage on his knee and I asked my dad what it was for. He told me it was to stop his leg falling off!'

He joined as a ground staff boy but, along with a handful of other young players, he became an apprentice professional when the scheme was introduced in the 1950s. By virtue of his surname beginning with 'E', he was the first to receive an apprentice's contract. 'I was the first, and no one can say any different, not that anyone but me gives a damn,' he said.

His City career was stymied just four years later on a spring afternoon in Manchester. City's A team was drawing 1–1 with Bury when Eyre volunteered a leg to a loose ball in the centre circle. He met a defender at the wrong end of a one-way street tackle and the ligaments in his knee twanged like a 'guitar instrumental' (to use his own words). A few weeks later, he was given a free transfer. He had expected as much, not merely because of the injury, but also because, quite simply, he was not good enough.

Thereafter he eked out a living from football, while simultaneously setting up his own stationery business which expanded at an inverse rate to his sporting efforts. At the age of 37, he decided to log his experiences of football's underworld. 'I was living in a nice house with a nice business, a lovely wife; the world was rosy. I knew I was writing from a position of strength. I had worked hard at my football but it never quite took off. The luck was with me on the business side, it was as simple as that.'

He co-funded his book and it quickly became a success with constant reprints. He was the footballer we might all have been – all heart, effort and honesty, but without the requisite skill. The eye for detail and the ability to relate it succinctly, however, was with him at all times – in the dressing rooms, on the team coaches. He took us there and populated his books with characters that tackled hard but (usually) fair. Shining through each of them was the absolute love of football, this beautifully cruel game.

He has written five books and is unsure of how many they have sold, though he accepts 250,000 would be a fair estimate. It has galvanised a career for him as an after-dinner speaker. Where he once struggled to control a bouncing ball, he is now the master of the anecdote, a Johan Cruyff of the sprightly tale.

Surprisingly, despite his expansive knowledge of the game and his renowned business acumen, he has never returned to Maine Road in an official capacity. 'I've been dismayed at what has happened there. I thought Franny Lee would be absolutely fantastic for the job. I was amazed when it went even worse under him. It proves what a big job it must be to turn the club around,' he said.

It is not difficult to surmise that Eyre's pragmatism might not sit comfortably within the hush-hush communality of a football club. He is too much of his own man. Anyway, he has a garden to watch over, a business to run, jokes to tell, a hat to wear.

Saturday, 22 August 1998
Manchester City 0 Wrexham 0

The first ever league meeting between these two clubs was dubbed by one newspaper as a '0–0 massacre'. A combination of poor finishing and inspired goalkeeping by Wrexham's Mark Cartwright frustrated City. Joe Royle reassured the fans: 'It's a long season so there is no reason to panic. A lot of teams will come here and play as though they are in a cup final.'

The attendance, the fifth highest of the day at 27,677, was larger than at Upton Park where West Ham United played host to Manchester United.

Tuesday, 25 August 1998

A group of City fans from Cheadle hired a mini-bus and parked it outside Maine Road for the evening while they toasted the ground's 75th anniversary. After downing a few cans, they sang 'Happy Birthday' in the general direction of the famous stadium.

Meanwhile, winger Martin Phillips became the 22nd player to leave City since Joe Royle's arrival. His £100,000 move to Portsmouth saw him reunited with Alan Ball. He cost City £500,000 in November 1995 and made just three full first-team appearances. Ball had predicted he would become 'Britain's first £10 million footballer.'

LAKE FINDS NEW HORIZONS
(*The Times*, Saturday, 29 August 1998)

Throw us the ball back, mister. And when he does, we are all 12 years old again, worried about nothing much, apart from being home late for tea or slicing a shot into the porch window.

A ball at our feet, and there is joy in our hearts, a boy in our shoes. Imagine, then, possessing an abundance of skill. You're the best player in your neighbourhood, the best in town. The game becomes your livelihood. At 18, playing for your home-town club, you are fêted, everyone knows your name. It is spoken reverentially and already has a stately ring to it, the rhythm of a legend-to-be: Paul Lake.

Imagine, then, that all this is taken away, slowly, painfully, irredeemably, and at the age of 21 you are left shipwrecked on dreams, made old before your time, limping when you should be dancing.

Paul Lake played 125 league and cup games for Manchester City between 1987 and 1992. He was an England Under-21 international and a member of the initial squad for Italia '90. Tall, broad-shouldered, he was both strong and skilful. He read the game well, two moves ahead of most opponents, two yards quicker. 'He was our Duncan Edwards,' say City supporters. This is shorthand for a player of great talent and dignity, a maturity beyond his years and, also, an unfulfilled potential.

History has it that Lake's career ended in September 1990 when he twisted his right knee in a game against Aston Villa and heard 'a kind of crunch'. 'You'll be playing again in a week,' said his surgeon. The 'week', in fact, equated to the rest of Paul Lake's life.

The knee, though Lake refused to accept it at the time, had been seriously damaged 18 months earlier. City were playing Bradford City when Lake galloped forward and, side-stepping tackles, tore down on goal. At the end of his heedless, youthful charge was Mick Kennedy, Bradford's then record signing – bought, according to the match programme, to 'stiffen' the side.

The challenge left Lake with ligament damage. It was the beginning of the end. 'I was pushed back into playing just four months after surgery. The job was not done properly, the underlying problem of the cruciate ligament was not addressed,' he said.

The injury was exacerbated against Villa when Lake ruptured the cruciate ligament further. Thereafter, he joined the shadowland of the injured sportsman, cut off from the pack, alone among his own kind, a hospital appointment where there was once a training session, hope where there was once a guarantee. The injured are slapped on the back, encouraged, but they remain in purgatory, haunted by themselves. 'You get obsessed with your injury,' explained Lake. 'It takes over your whole life. From waking in the morning, you are flexing the affected area, tensing up, kidding yourself that you are getting better.'

Lake did not get better. He made several abortive comebacks but the knee was 'a bag of bolts'. Finally, in January 1996, he retired from the game. At this point, he was losing 18–1: 18 operations to one full first-team appearance in the six years since sustaining the injury. Surgeons were talking of completely replacing the knee, and still are.

'I sometimes take my 10-month-old son in the back garden and we play around with a plastic football. That's about as exacting as my football gets these days,' he said. Lake is an honest man, and what he has lost in the pleasure of playing the game, he has perhaps gained in sensitivity and wisdom. 'I've had some bad times, seriously bad times. I was so depressed I had to see a counsellor once or twice.' Most footballers would not make such an admission; was this information off the record? 'No, it's what happened. It's a hell of a thing to come to terms with. Football was the focal point of my life and I was playing for City, my team, the team I have always supported.'

City granted him a testimonial against Manchester United last October. His son, Zachary, was born on the same day. Lake took the ceremonial kick-off in front of nearly 25,000 supporters at Maine Road, a remarkable turn-out for a player who had not played regular first-team football for over seven years. The memory had clearly lingered.

He wore a knee-brace on the day to avoid aggravating the injury or causing it to lock as he jogged on to the pitch. Afterwards he overheard a comment to the effect that it was a good idea since it garnered him even more sympathy. He shakes his head at the callousness of this remark and can recall, if pushed, similar examples of crass thoughtlessness. 'It's not all bad though,' he laughed suddenly. 'I met some really funny people in football, some great people. I'd say the ratio is about 80/20 in favour of good people.'

Appropriately, he is now training to become a chartered sports physiotherapist. He has been there, suffered it, and wants to help others. 'It's not the same as playing, but it really pleases me to help other lads back to fitness,' he said. He has parted company with City to complete his university studies. 'City was too much of a security blanket for me. I want to achieve something in my own right,' he explained.

While he looks to the future, he is a man finally coming to terms with his past. 'All right, my career ended very early, but I did something thousands dreamed of. I sometimes think back to what it was like in the dressing-room before a match. I'd put on my City shirt, smear the Vaseline on my eyebrows, look into the mirror . . .' The words tail off. You are with him, among the shin pads and liniment, for ever 12 years old, and up for the cup.

Saturday, 29 August 1998
Notts County 1 Manchester City 1

A goal in injury time by Shaun Goater earned City a point after Notts County had taken the lead from the penalty spot when Kevin Horlock was judged to have handled the ball.

Jamie Pollock was dismissed for dissent after telling referee Terry Heilbron that giving the penalty was 'an absolute holocaust of a decision.' City were in fourteenth position.

Two

The Heart of Darkness

Tuesday, 1 September 1998

After just six senior appearances, 18-year-old midfielder Gary Mason won a call-up to the Scotland Under-21 squad for their European Under-21 Championship match in Lithuania. He had been recommended by Willie Donachie, himself a former Scotland international with 35 caps.

Mason's elevation was remarkable. During the previous season he had barely made the club's reserve team, playing just two matches. It was a typical example of a footballer being in favour with a particular manager. Similarly, Nicky Weaver had been the club's third-choice goalkeeper during Frank Clark's regime.

Wednesday, 2 September 1998

Manchester City Council announced it would build a £90 million stadium to house the Commonwealth Games of 2002. The stadium would be financed by a £77 million lottery grant and the remainder supplied by the city council. Situated a mile from the city centre, it would be built in two phases, with 21,000 covered seats for the Games, rising to 48,000 to accommodate football matches. City, subject to approval from shareholders and supporters, would be invited to take over the stadium as their new home in time for the 2003–04 season.

Wednesday, 2 September 1998
Manchester City 3 Walsall 1

Goals from Shaun Goater (two) and Paul Dickov sealed a comfortable victory. Andy Rammell hit a late consolation goal for Walsall. City climbed six places to eighth – seven points behind leaders Stoke City.

CITY FORTUNES LACK RHYME AND REASON
(*The Times*, Saturday, 5 September 1998)

First World War soldiers had the poets Wilfred Owen and Siegfried Sassoon at their side, men able to proffer words of compassion and empathy among the monstrous anger of the guns.

Manchester City supporters, who know plenty about dodging flak, have turned to a famous Scottish bard in their darkest hour. Rabbie Burns, no less, is quoted in the latest issue of the City fanzine, *King of the Kippax*: 'To see her is to love her, and love her forever. For nature made her what she is, and will support her evermore.' The line with the most resonance and relevance is: 'For nature made her what she is.' Nature, damn it, made City capricious, foolhardy, a club that stares at the stars but crashes into a lamp-post, ouch, while its gaze is averted.

This season has been typical, painfully typical. Pundits foretold that they would storm through the division, scoffing at the cloggers at their heels, chuckling in their laser blue. City fans remained silent. They know that Maine Road is Heartbreak Hotel, or, better still, Bates Motel, a place where the strange is commonplace.

Among their supporters, nothing is taken for granted. Too often City feels like the kind of place where cursed skulls are tossed around like frisbees and black cats are culled on a weekly basis. If City lined up against the Red Lion Second XI they would create 47 goalscoring chances, miss them all and concede a goal, an own goal at that, in the 90th minute.

A month into the new season, they have played five league matches, won two, drawn two and lost one, which, sad to say, is patently not the form of league champions elect. They beat Walsall with ease on Wednesday night, but they are still only in eighth position. In short, it is not going to be a stroll, but more of a brisk walk with a stone in your hiking boots.

Once more, a litany of fiendish ironies has beset them: different division, same curse. They lost heavily against Fulham, so thousands decided to sit-out the next match against Notts County – admittedly it was in the Worthington Cup – when they went on a goal frenzy and won 7–1. Seven-bloody-one, and two thirds of City's following missed it. Fists were pounded on tables, ornaments hurled across the room.

Never mind, they cried, for another home game loomed, against Wrexham, just three days later. Oh, such fun; poxy Wrexham, a team containing Ian Rush, the only player in the league older than the Queen Mother. This was a case for the League Against Cruel Sports, a lurcher let loose in a hen coop. Dutifully, 27,677 skipped merrily to Moss Side, calculators in their rucksacks. Oh, such pain – a 0–0 draw. Now we know why Ken Barnes from Ashton-under-Lyne sent the club a photo of himself by the Wailing Wall in Jerusalem for inclusion in the match programme. Move along Ken, there are another 27,676 jostling for space.

Perhaps the proposed move to a new £90 million stadium in east Manchester will allow City to rid themselves of their famous ill-luck. Fans have been asked to vote on the move, pencilled in for 2003. Club officials have already declared their support. 'I believe this is a unique opportunity for the club as we go into the 21st century,' said David Bernstein. He strenuously denied that the stadium's site was chosen merely because a four-leafed clover had been discovered in a nearby field.

Since the departure of Georgi Kinkladze, City fans have become restless in their pursuit of a new hero. Their rush to deify young players such as Nicky Weaver, Gary Mason and Nick Fenton is rash, and inadvertently reveals their desperation. 'I got my first glimpse of not one, but two raw youngsters who are going to make the whole of English soccer sit up and take notice,' sang Paul Hince of the *Manchester Evening News*. Steady on, haven't we been here before?

Three years ago, Martin Phillips, then 19, joined City from Exeter City. 'He will become Britain's first £10 million player,' said Alan Ball, the City manager at the time. In the week that Fenton, Mason, *et al*, were prematurely acclaimed, Phillips, quietly, was sold to Portsmouth. The fee? Just £100,000, one per cent of the amount predicted by Ball. The teenagers in the present City side are promising, but they need time to gel as a team. Great players emerge from good teams, and good teams take time and patience to build. Joe Mercer would have confirmed as much.

Monday, 7 September 1998

Gerard Wiekens, City's Dutch defender, revealed that a reunion with his dog, Joey, might have been behind his return to form. The golden retriever had been in quarantine for six months in Crewe where Wiekens had travelled to see him four times a week. 'I don't know if it affected my football but I do know I'd have felt a whole lot better if I'd had Joey with me,' he said.

Tuesday, 8 September 1998
Manchester City 2 Bournemouth 1

Danny Allsopp, making his full début, scored a headed goal before half-time. Steven Fletcher equalised for Bournemouth before Paul Dickov scored his fourth of the season.

City legend Colin Bell was introduced to the crowd who as told he had returned formally to the club in an ambassadorial role.

Friday, 11 September 1998

A survey conducted by the club revealed that supporters were overwhelmingly in favour of a move away from Maine Road. A *Manchester Evening News* phone poll among supporters was four-to-one in favour of the switch. 'I am delighted that the response has been so positive. The new stadium is a very exciting development,' said David Bernstein.

MUIR THE MERRIER FOR STORMY 30-YEAR AFFAIR
(*The Times*, Saturday, 12 September 1998)

A family portrait, of sorts. The camera homes in. Faces are picked out from the grainy monochrome. Middle row, centre:

middle-aged man, suit, glasses, benign expression. Front row, far right: stocky, fair-haired sportsman, steely, 'up-for-it' look. At this point, the film director spatters blood over the picture and we recognise the code: family at war; along this way will pass hostility and cruelty.

The photograph, a team shot of Manchester City taken in 1969, hangs in the living room of Chris Muir's home. Muir, now aged 69, is in the photograph. He is the man in glasses and the fair-haired man is Francis Lee. 'Do you know what is unusual about this photograph?' he asks. He embarks upon a story about the silverware placed conspicuously in the foreground. He is, of course, missing the point. What *is* unusual is that it depicts a football club with the capacity to make the rise and fall of the Roman Empire seem like a toga party that turned nasty.

Muir was a director of Manchester City for nearly 30 years. He has a silver salver to commemorate the fact. A war medal might have been more apt. 'I can tell you a few stories,' he begins. And he can. A theme will soon fall into place – of manipulation, betrayal, egotism, vanity, rashness, bloody-mindedness. 'All this stuff that's happening at United [the ill-fated takeover bid by Rupert Murdoch's BSkyB]. It's been part of football for years. It's just that the stakes have got higher and the media profile so much greater.' Indeed, in the week that United are valued at £623 million, City have an overdraft of £10 million.

United. Always United. For Muir, and indeed City, they were there in the beginning, there at the end. 'When I first came to Manchester from Scotland, everyone told me United were the greatest football club in the world. I was a rebel looking for a cause. I found it at City.' Born in Leith, his work in the stationery business brought him to Manchester and, in the early '60s, he was attracted by the sullied charm of City as they withered beneath the bloom of United. He formed a pressure group designed to oust the old guard at the helm. 'They were very old-fashioned, a group of freemasons who had fallen behind the times,' he says.

Back then, City's share issue ran to just 2,000 and Muir

started to buy as many as possible. Most were kept as quasi souvenirs by fans, tucked away in cupboards and shoe boxes. 'I have a nice smile and a pleasant Scottish accent. They thought if I was mad enough to buy them, I must have the club's interest at heart.' He became an agent provocateur, goading supporters to campaign against the board. In his own grand terms, he was a 'swordsman of the revolution' and, such was his drive, sentiment did not impede his progress. He probably knew, even then, that one day he too would be put to the sword.

In 1967, he duly became a director. Joe Mercer and Malcolm Allison were two years into their managerial reign and the club was entering a successful era. 'If ever two people needed each other, it was those two. Malcolm was the man of a thousand ideas, many of them born from fantasy, but some were sheer genius. Joe had the ability to pick out the gems,' he says.

Muir was the Mr Fix-It. He fixed it for the club lottery to make noteworthy profits and he oversaw the youth policy. His brief also ran to the unusual: remonstrating with a player who thought it was a good idea to urinate over the side of the open-top bus as they paraded the League Cup in 1970; explaining to office staff why a member of the coaching team required numerous guest tickets for young, attractive girls. He will put a name to a story, but he would rather it did not appear in print. He is discreet, a wheeler-dealer of the old school. He says that in and around the club there were 'phenomenal womanisers, bloody lunatics – all manner of life'.

In the early '70s, another power struggle saw Muir briefly lose his position. He formed an alliance with Peter Swales, then the chairman of non-league Altrincham. The public image of Swales was later cruelly lampooned – small man, crimson complexion, hair intricately weaved to conceal an obvious baldness. Muir saw him as 'a man who could lead City to greatness'. He admired the tact, the sleight of hand, the charm and the cunning of Swales. He was a master of well-placed gossip, a schemer, always out for the best deal. Whether this was for City or himself, well – 'that was a matter of opinion, but he had the blue blood of City in his veins,' Muir avers.

Swales became chairman in 1973 and reappointed Allison during the close season of 1979. He wanted the magic of old, but the 'Hold on, pal' discernment of Joe Mercer was missing and Allison's ego, along with City's spending – most of it ridiculously speculative – went awry. 'Swales was trying to keep up with Manchester United. Whenever Allison wanted a player, Swales found the money.' Although City enjoyed qualified success, they began to trail United by some distance and Swales, as the club's figurehead, was blamed.

In September 1993 Francis Lee led a consortium determined to seize power. 'He appeared at Maine Road and was seen as the knight in shining armour,' says Muir. The ensuing battle was fierce and dirty. 'Oh Christ, it was savage,' recalls Muir. 'They were throwing things at Swales's house, shouting abuse at his 80-year-old mother. I think it had a serious effect on his health.' Swales resigned as chairman in November 1993 and was replaced by Lee three months later. Muir, inevitably, was asked immediately by Lee to leave the board. 'I was completely shattered and heartbroken.'

Sitting underneath that infamous photograph now, Muir looks across at the silver salver. It seems rather small and insignificant. 'No, at least it's some kind of recognition. It's a memento of a large part of my life, half of my life.' Beneath the glasses, there is still a twinkle in his dark eyes. It might have been a bloody and breathless life in football, but it was – make no mistake – also fun, a life lived to the brim.

Saturday, 12 September 1998
Macclesfield Town 0 Manchester City 1

A record league crowd of 6,381 at Moss Rose witnessed City's first ever visit in a competitive match. Just three years previously, five divisions had separated the clubs when City were in the FA Premiership and Macclesfield the Vauxhall Conference League.

As expected, in the days leading up to the match, the media made great play of the difference between the two clubs. Tickets proved extremely scarce and many City supporters had queued in the early hours when they went on sale three weeks earlier.

One die-hard waited from before midnight until 9 a.m. when the ticket office opened.

Shaun Goater scored in the 87th minute. It was the first time City had won three consecutive league games since February 1997.

Wednesday, 16 September 1998
Derby County 1 Manchester City 1
(Worthington Cup Second Round, First Leg)

Derby County took an early lead through Rory Delap but Danny Tiatto pounced on a rebound from a free kick to equalise. Jamie Pollock, returning after a one-match ban, was sent off again after an off-the-ball incident with Francesco Baiano. He was suspended once more, this time for four matches. A week earlier, Royle had been pushing Pollock's case for inclusion in the full England squad. 'When I look at some of the players in England's squad, some of them have no more natural talent than Jamie,' he said.

FALLEN BENEATH THEIR DIGNITY
(*The Times*, Saturday, 19 September 1998)

Posters for church galas and village fêtes were still affixed to trees and gate-posts throughout Cheshire. Occasionally the sun found a splinter of space between the clouds and set the rain on fire, but more usually the air was cold, thick, heavy and sluggish.

The summer had dallied a while, but had now finally departed, the rain washing away the detail of the posters. Cars clogged the roads through Macclesfield. Engine fumes drifted across puddles made fluorescent by car headlights.

Inside their cars, Manchester City supporters had an irksome accompaniment to their afternoon in the heart of darkness. Radio phone-ins were singing the song of Manchester United. The words formed a mantra: success, money, ambition, profit, as if anyone needed reminding. Suddenly, a City supporter was given air-time as he shouted into his mobile phone. 'I tell you what,' he told the presenter. 'There's plenty of pubs in Macclesfield, there's one on every corner.'

They skittered out from these pubs, zipped up their anoraks, dodged the rain, and made their way to Moss Rose, the home of Macclesfield Town. Many had parked their cars in farmers' fields, the mud already ankle deep. A few years ago, City fans referred to matches against Oldham Athletic as 'donkey derbies'; this was beyond such a sobriquet, beyond a joke. David Bettany, the chairman of Macclesfield's supporters' club, had earlier volunteered the understatement: 'This is going to be a massive culture shock for City and their fans.' And some.

City were supplied with just 1,600 tickets, and such is their masochistic streak that many were bartering for more on the streets around the ground. Inside the club office, Harry Armstrong, a director, was patiently issuing complimentary tickets. The bundle was getting thinner, the queue at the window thicker. A City fan pushed his way through and jabbed his mate in the ribs. 'Look, you could just reach over and grab them, couldn't you?' He kept repeating this to himself, thinking aloud, unable to believe that a football club could be so naïve, so trusting. Next time he visits, there will be reinforced glass across the office.

With a certain inevitably, my ticket was missing. Harry wrote me a note which I was to show to the person in my seat. In fact, there was no one sitting in it, just a puddle of water. The steward, resolutely uninterested, pointed vaguely towards the soaked seat and watched to see if I was stupid enough to sit directly beneath a leaking stand.

On the terraces, supporters mixed freely. It is widely accepted that Macclesfield contains more Manchester City supporters than followers of its own home-town club, so the support was roughly divided into two equal halves. The game's historical significance, which had been proclaimed to the point of numbness beforehand, was lost in the downpour. The grave business of trying (but failing) to stay warm and dry on uncovered terracing tended to wash away any sense of disbelief that this game was actually taking place.

Moss Rose, though it might be a fond home to a certain sector of the Cheshire sporting public, is a place from where only misanthropists would want to send a 'Wish You Were Here' postcard. While some lower league grounds are neat and quaint with a certain pleasing symmetry, Moss Rose fits perfectly into the Heart of Darkness theme. Admittedly, it's not quite the Belgian Congo, but it has a distinctly portside feel with its squat, angular stands dotted around randomly like broken teeth; grey portable caravans; matchstick pylons; seats covered by billowing canvas roofs – City will have left the engine running on the team coach.

A football club, of course, is fundamentally about its people, not its architecture. Macclesfield fans were granted a long, long time to prepare their big-match repartee. In fact, they have waited a lifetime, and a forebear's lifetime, to play City on an equal footing. Under the circumstances, then, we might have expected a better standard of insult. 'Shitty City!' shouted one. His friends roared. Paul Dickov, City's diminutive striker, was caught off-side and let fly a disgusting volley of swear words to the referee's assistant. 'Hey, Dickov, stand up, we can't see you!' responded a middle-aged man who was himself of no great stature. The same man, round-shouldered and hunched, spent the rest of the game chunnering in the rain. 'City . . . ' he bellowed, 'You're crap.' More riotous laughter.

At least the programme editors were subtle in their mockery. 'You did not have to support Man City to appreciate the skills of Ball, Lee, Summerbee and Colin Bell,' read the introductory notes. Bell, Lee and Summerbee, are, indeed, *bona fide* City legends, but Ball? There has never, in the club's 104-year history, been a first-team player with the surname of Ball. There was, however, in more recent times, a chap fond of combining flat caps and track suits, a certain Alan Ball, who was briefly a manager at Maine Road. His 'skills' are still the subject of much discussion in many parts of the north-west.

The game was as wretched as the slow soak of dampness through your clothes or the ache of pushing your car through squelchy, clinging mud in some cut-up farmer's field. City won, just, and there was a hearty cheer, but as the City fans trudged from the terraces at the end, many will have muttered: 'We won't be coming to a place like this again.' Whether their team secure promotion or not, they should remain true to their word. Sometimes, it's a question of dignity.

Saturday, 19 September 1998
Manchester City 1 Chesterfield 1

David Reeves scored for the visitors before Lee Bradbury, the subject of much transfer speculation, equalised. Thereafter, stand-in goalkeeper Andy Leaning frustrated City with several excellent saves. Chesterfield's Jamie Hewlett was sent off for handling the ball on the goal-line. Leaning saved Shaun Goater's penalty.

After the match, Joe Royle said he was looking for another striker to bolster the attack: 'We have got to be more clinical up front.'

Wednesday, 23 September 1998
Manchester City 0 Derby County 1
(Worthington Cup Second Round, Second Leg)

A deflected shot by Paulo Wanchope settled a closely fought cup tie. Steve McClaren, Derby County's coach, said afterwards that he had been impressed by City and had put a £50 bet on them to gain automatic promotion. Later in the season, McClaren left Derby to become Alex Ferguson's assistant at Manchester United.

Thursday, 24 September 1998

City's annual report showed they had made a pre-tax loss of £6.3 million for the year ending 31 May 1998. The loss on transfers was £1.9 million and the total wage bill, including players and staff, was £8.7 million, an increase of £1.5 million on the previous year. 'Turnover is up 20 per cent to £15.3 million but we have an unacceptable level of expenses, mainly from the size of the playing staff,' said David Bernstein.

Nick Fenton, City's 18-year-old central defender, signed a deal to keep him at Maine Road for the next four seasons. Fellow youngsters Gary Mason, Nicky Weaver and Leon Mike had already been made similar offers.

When Royle arrived at City he grumbled that too many

players were on long-term contracts. His own long-term sign-ings were, however, young players, most likely on lower salaries than the experienced professionals they replaced.

FORLORN FIGHT FOR THE BLUE CORNER IN A SWELLNG SEA OF RED
(*The Times*, Saturday, 26 September 1999)

'City or United?' The nurses used to ask at Booth Hall Children's Hospital in Manchester. At one end of the room was a poster of George Best while, at the other, Colin Bell, a vision in sky blue, was pictured gliding past desperate defenders. Choose your corner, choose your team. Back then, Manchester City and Manchester United were, more or less, equals.

The children who shuffled into Booth Hall in the 1960s, with their poorly tummies and broken arms, now have children of their own. They live in a very different city. On the playing fields and the street corners the ratio is much altered. Where it was once blue, red, blue, red, it is now red, red, blue, red. The kids are United.

Manchester City are a club in retreat. Their older supporters, to whom success is within touching distance (an FA Cup final defeat 17 years ago is as good as it gets), are like colonialists lamenting a glorious past. They sit among the ruins, incredulous to their plight. 'When I was a lad . . .' they lament. Son passes dad a hankie.

These supporters have been betrayed by the people entrusted to run their club. On the field and behind the scenes, there has been a succession of personnel to whom personal gain and self-aggrandisement has mattered more than the well-being of the club. In the absence of everything else, City supporters have been left with nothing else to celebrate except themselves.

Their loyalty has been acclaimed throughout the country. They are acknowledged as the supporters' supporters, the suffered of Maine Road. Within us all, however, there is the potential to martyrdom-by-football-club, and this has been fulfilled, perhaps dangerously so, at City. The defeats and the relegations have become addictive. They find themselves strengthened, emboldened by adversity. While their Stretford neighbours attract capricious lightweights, City fans are true men of steel, cut from character-building torment.

The basis of their support is erroneous. A football club should be supported for the joy it brings, not the misery. Love and hate for your team is always intertwined, but at City the hate is institutionalised, a seed of bitterness passed down the family line. Sometimes, following City must feel like a job of work, without any fag breaks or a lunch-hour. In their defence, they are at this apogee of dissatisfaction not out of choice, but because they have been made to walk the gang-plank by the mismanagement of the club.

At home matches, their cussedness and ardour foams like a restless sea. It makes players nervous. Perhaps, as it is at almost every other club, a natural wastage of support would have inadvertently helped their cause. The standard of football they proffer merits a crowd of, say, 10,000, not the 25,000-plus that regularly fills Maine Road. Those extra, edgy supporters tap on the shoulder of every player. A 25-yard pass is traded for a six-yard tap, a surging upfield run for a safe one-two: the City players are afraid of failure, wary of the moaning and the mocking.

The breathless success of Manchester United has run parallel to City's demise and it has turned warm hearts to stone. Many call United fans 'rags' or 'scum' and the hundreds who used to watch City and United on alternate weeks have drawn a metaphorical line in the sand. In return, some United fans are malevolent enough to wish the very worst on City, with plagues, boils and cup defeats by Derby County thrown in. Others, and this is perhaps a worst indictment, are completely indifferent to City; they don't believe they count.

Howard Wheatcroft, a United season-ticket holder and shareholder, wants the suffering to continue. 'I want to see City go down even further. I think it is fantastic. They would slaughter us if it was the other way round. Whenever I feel depressed, I goad a City fan and it makes me feel better.' Andy Mitten, editor of the fanzine, *United We Stand*, grew up in a divided city. 'City always had a healthy support when I was at school,' he said. 'They *are* a big club. I think they have more support than Newcastle, for instance, but they are their own worst enemies. They are obsessed with United. They have always talked big, but never justified it.' A typical example of this obsession with United is the autobiography of the film producer and City fan, Colin Shindler. The book's title? *Manchester United Ruined My Life.* It had to be.

In recent years, supporting City has had a social cachet by virtue of their association with Oasis, the rock group, and Kappa, one of the leading urban fashion houses. 'It makes me laugh, all that,' said Mitten. 'City fans are shell-suit wearers from Stockport and pie-eaters from Wigan. Check them out walking to the ground on match days.' City, remember, also boast a celebrity roll call of Eddie Large, Bernard Manning, Rick Wakeman and Kevin Kennedy – a list unlikely to interest the style gurus at *The Face* or *GQ.*

Many United fans are not without their own sense of dissolution. The club has become too big for its gilded boots. Its traditional Manchester-based support feels alienated, annexed by the world and its wife. 'The other week I was asked by this bloke, dressed in a United shirt, where the statue of Stanley Matthews was at Old Trafford,' said Mitten.

Only on derby days did Manchester feel at peace with itself in all the chanting, partisan chaos. 'It used to be a real buzz. It was a Manchester thing. A lot of the southern-based United fans saw it as just another game, something they weren't part of,' said Mitten.

City fans, it seems, are hurting because they are too much a part of it, United because they are not enough a part of it. Somewhere in between is the football supporter we all want to be.

Saturday, 26 September 1998
Northampton Town 2 Manchester City 2

A goal two minutes from time by Shaun Goater earned City a draw. It was his eighth of the season and a retort to the City supporters who had booed him off the pitch after his penalty miss against Chesterfield.

Northampton had taken the lead through Dean Peer. Paul Dickov equalised but Carlo Corazzin restored the home side's lead before Goater struck. 'You need to show courage to pick up points at tricky away fixtures like this one,' said Joe Royle.

Sunday, 27 September 1998

Joe Royle entered hospital for a hip replacement operation which would keep him away from the club for 10 days. 'I've known for a number of years I needed a new hip, but I hoped I could put off the operation until the end of the season. Unfortunately, it has deteriorated quite quickly since the summer,' said Royle.

Tuesday, 29 September 1998
Millwall 1 Manchester City 1

The match was marred by violence both on and off the pitch. Referee Matt Messias issued six yellow cards and two red as Millwall's Paul Shaw and City's Tony Vaughan were sent off after a mass brawl involving 18 players.

There were several pitch invasions during the game and afterwards Millwall fans fought with police in the streets around the ground. More than 2,000 City supporters attended and were praised for their good behaviour. They had to remain in the stadium for an hour afterwards while police cleared the streets outside. 'The violence was absolutely horrifying – the worst I have seen for a long time,' said Chief Inspector Christopher Miles of the Metropolitan Police.

A police officer suffered a broken arm and there were 18 arrests, 15 of them Millwall fans and three City. 'I cannot believe what I have seen tonight. It was a disgrace. If we had scored another goal in that atmosphere, I don't think we would have got out alive,' said Joe Royle.

Neil Harris gave Millwall the lead a minute into the second half. Lee Bradbury levelled in injury time.

Wednesday, 30 September 1998

City 'til I Cry! ventured once more into the intriguing interior life of the club. It questioned the summer departures of Ian

Niven (director), John Clay (public relations manager), Joanne Parker (match programme co-ordinator) and various members of the office staff. 'Were these replaced because of their very close (almost intimate?) links with the previous regime?' it asked.

It also highlighted the growing number of ex-Oldham Athletic employees now working at City. Aside from Joe Royle and Willie Donachie, the academy/coaching staff included Jim Cassell, Terry Cale and Frankie Bunn, all formerly of Oldham. Also, Richard Jobson had been signed from Oldham on a two-year contract at the age of 34 after suffering a serious knee injury. ' . . . it seems odd that some of the replacements [for the various departing employees] are Joe Royle's cronies from his Oldham days,' pondered the fanzine.

Three

The Go-between

GONE BUT NOT FORGOTTEN
(*The Times*, Saturday, 3 October 1998)

So, finally, a parking space. Within seconds, the attendant is at my window. 'You can't leave it here, mate.' He sees the despair in my eyes as I look out at all these cars, bumper to bumper. 'I tell you what . . . ' he says. I sense immediately that this is a once-in-a-lifetime offer: 'Park it over there, in one of the disabled spaces. I'll come and get you if it needs moving.'

Five minutes later, the longest Mercedes in the world pulls on to this same hotel car park. Its owner brings it to rest in front of the reception area, straddled across enough yellow paint to colour in the sun. He is soon on his feet, wonderfully indifferent to the chaos around him as drivers circle repeatedly, sweating in the sunshine.

The name's Bond, John Bond. You must remember him. He was the big-time manager before football even went big-time. He looks much the same as he did in his glory days of the 1970s: immaculate hair, Rolex watch, top-notch suit, a certain sophistication. This is the man who was big enough to take on Manchester City. He lost, of course, but it was a decent match, all blood and thunder, toil and trouble. 'It took me three weeks to realise what a nonsense job it was at Maine Road. I knew more or less straight away what a fool I'd been in going there,' he said.

In the 1970s, Bond was hot property after propelling Norwich City to the top flight and a League Cup final. The soundbites were tasty, the coats large and furry, and the football wasn't too bad either. Glamour and East Anglia were on nodding terms for the first time ever and Bond knew the best camera angles. Inevitably, ambition got the better of him and in October 1980 he broke a 10-year contract (*10 years*) to replace Malcolm Allison at Manchester City.

'Norwich was one big happy family. Everyone got on with each other and mixed really well. At City there were so many undercurrents and such a lot of back-biting,' he said. Back-biting is a misnomer since some directors had no qualms about attacking from the front. 'At my first board meeting, Peter Swales asked whether the directors were in support of my appointment. This should have been a formality, but one said – and I can remember the actual words – "I'm withholding my feelings because I have not yet seen the messiah who can take over from Malcolm Allison."' Diplomacy 0, Antagonism 1; let the battle commence.

Maine Road, he claims, was awash with whispers and conspiracies. 'There were a lot of ex-players walking straight into the club, making themselves cups of tea. They were all picking the team for me, saying so-and-so should be in and someone else shouldn't be. A football club is a very private place, people shouldn't be able to just walk in off the street. Can you imagine something like that happening at the Arsenal?'

In his first season in charge, City finished twelfth in the top division and were finalists in the centenary final of the FA Cup, losing to Tottenham Hotspur after a replay. In 1981–82 they were tenth but in January 1983, following a 4–0 FA Cup defeat at Brighton, Bond resigned. He accepted the manager's job at Burnley who were themselves embroiled in boardroom upheaval. In hindsight, he feels he should have waited; he had earlier been linked with managerial vacancies at Benfica and Manchester United. Thereafter, he tumbled down the leagues and now, at 64, finds himself director of football at Witton Albion of the UniBond League.

'We get an average crowd of about 300 people. I absolutely love it. I'm every bit as keen as I used to be,' he said. He means it too, the passion for football still burns, and the charm evidently remains. The hotel staff recognise him and we are ushered through to the restaurant where tables are being prepared for lunch. The waiter looks perplexed. 'I have to set these tables out,' he grumbles. The manager is soon upon us with free coffee. He apologises that his staff might be disturbing us: Bond, John Bond.

Back in his early days as manager of Bournemouth, a chance remark led to speculation that George Best was about to join the club. 'And that's on the record,' was his catchphrase among journalists. Might he have been too media-friendly for the liking of Manchester City? 'I am a person with opinions and I'm not frightened to express them. It's all part and parcel of the game.'

Bond is one of a long tradition of managers able to exercise authority by sheer strength of personality. The downside is that this submerges a footballing antecedence that, in his case, stretches back nearly 50 years to his days as a teenage player with West Ham United. He laments his early exit from the big-time he helped invent. 'I do have my sad moments. I might be driving along the motorway and thoughts come into my head. They are very sad and not something I want to delve too deeply into. I do wonder what would have happened if I'd waited for a bigger club to come in for me after City.'

Suddenly, the sheen of glamour falls from this tall, thick-set man. The suit, the watch, the hair, it is just camouflage, expensive scent thrown across the trail of another boy-man lost to the joy and cruelty of football. The waiters and the porters fall over themselves to bid him a fond farewell. He sets off for the small Cheshire town of Witton. Something doesn't quite add up here.

Saturday, 3 October 1998
Manchester City 2 Burnley 2

Shaun Goater's ninth goal of the season gave City an early lead, but failure to capitalise on chances cost them dearly. A poor back-pass by Nick Fenton was pounced on by Andy Payton who scored the equaliser. Burnley took the lead through Andy Cooke, but City substitute Danny Allsopp equalised five minutes from time.

Joe Royle listened to the match on the radio from his

hospital bed while Willie Donachie took charge in his absence. It was City's fourth consecutive draw and left them in eighth position.

Monday, 5 October 1998
Jamie Pollock went into hospital for a hernia operation. It was timed to coincide with his four-match suspension.

Former City striker Gerry Creaney criticised the club in a newspaper interview. 'I wouldn't go back to Maine Road if they paid me double. The whole experience at City brought me down to a level I didn't think I was capable of reaching,' he said.

Tuesday, 6 October 1998
Nigel Clough was released from his contract with nine months still to run. City agreed to a pay-off, reportedly £250,000. A £1 million signing from Liverpool by Alan Ball in January 1996, Clough made just 38 first-team appearances. 'It's very sad, but the club has made the decision to go with youth and give our young players a chance,' said Willie Donachie.

Wednesday, 7 October 1998
Nicky Weaver was put on stand-by for England Under-21s in their forthcoming match with Bulgaria. Weaver had played just ten league matches for City, and one for his previous club, Mansfield Town.

MAINE MAN CALLS CITY TO ACCOUNT
(*The Times*, Saturday, 10 October 1998)

It was only a tiny gate, more a piece of wood really. He might have placed it to one side for an underling to deal with later on, or tossed it away angrily when it stubbornly refused to rest on its hinges. Instead, David Bernstein, Manchester City's new chairman, tried patiently to slot it back at the entrance to the directors' box at Maine Road. Eventually, he succeeded.

Manchester City, until now, has been a magnet for the vainglorious. On the pitch and in the boardroom, they have talked it like they couldn't walk it. The egos have collided with one another and piled up like flash cars rusted to a standstill. Bernstein has resolved to pick his way through the debris, bolstered by a quiet determination to reinvent a club he has supported for more than 40 years.

'I am happy to keep a low profile. There have been too many statements made from this club. I want us to be realistic and absolutely honest from now on. I know the fans will be sceptical, but they are entitled to be. They must be utterly pissed off with what has happened,' he said. It is the only time he will swear during the interview.

His rise to eminence has been discreet, the low profile he talks of has really been no-profile. He is not borne from the three distinct groups of power-brokers within the Maine Road cabal. He is neither a celebrity, ex-player or local self-made businessman. He joined the board in 1994 as financial director at the request of Francis Lee, who had usurped Peter Swales as chairman after a 21-year tenure. When fan-power forced Lee to resign, Bernstein became vice-chairman and then chairman in March of this year. He is a chartered accountant and looks the part. The dress is formal, the manner prudent and attentive. He is the man from the insurance company you would want to see the day after your house burned down.

When Francis Lee took office, his vindictiveness spilled forth immediately. The fallen members of City's previous hierarchy were described variously as 'reptiles', 'the enemy within' and 'little shits'. This street talk is anathema to Bernstein; he is a peacemaker, heavy on forgiveness and conciliation. 'I like to be able to relate to people in a positive way. I think I have a certain pragmatism. I get things done and I am happy to delegate,' he said.

His subtle diplomacy and skill with words have been noted among the few Manchester journalists who have seen him at close quarters. 'It's obvious straight away that he is not on some kind of ego trip,' said one. 'It is probably in City's favour that he is so low-profile. He is willing to answer questions, though I think he is a bit like Tony Blair. When you actually dissect his answers, I'm not sure that they say a great deal.'

Many feel he is *in situ* precisely because he is an antidote to the recent past. Where there has been hyperbole and profligacy, he will bring realism and stability. 'It was like wading through treacle,' he volunteers when asked about the club's infamously muddled financing. Some feel he is a bridge between the past and future, someone reflective and calm to hold court until he is superseded by someone drawn from the ruthlessly charismatic breed that drive football clubs to absolute glory. 'He will bring an air of respectability to the place, and that's been missing from Maine Road lately. Everyone says how nice he is, but bland people rarely make great football clubs. There is always a point where you have to stop being nice,' said an insider.

Aside from the administration of City, Bernstein holds directorship with several multi-national companies. His laid-back, thoughtful style of management may be misconstrued among the hurly-burly men of football. It probably masks a degree of implacability that would surprise the sceptics. Tea and biscuits are on the table, followed by a civil chat, but more than a few have been informed of their redundancy before the custard creams have left the plate.

Supporters are invariably suspicious of the personnel entrusted to run their clubs, and Bernstein's background has been appropriately scrutinised. The hard facts do not bode well. He was born in St Helens in 1943 but has lived most of his life in north London. He is not, then, either a Mancunian nor has he been a habitual attender at Maine Road. He developed a 'romantic attachment' to City in the 1950s and watched them play whenever they visited a London ground. Trips to Maine Road were an occasional 'pilgrimage'.

He is aware – as you might expect – that fans demand a chairman as smitten with the club as themselves, and more so. He must share the pain and elation. Every missed scoring opportunity must stab him in the heart, every victory send him dancing. He is popular with supporters, and is keen to develop fan forums which, for once, he promises will not be mere talking shops. For their part, supporters are pleased that he is not drawn from the club's murky past and they kindly overlook his links with Merseyside and London; Francis Lee was considered one of their own, and many view his chairmanship as a spectacular failure.

Bernstein sometimes over-emphasises his love of the club, perhaps apprehensive that his background will not ring true enough for the City faithful. At the end of our conversation he talks of City's last brush with success, the FA Cup final of 1981. Many remember Glenn Hoddle's equaliser for Tottenham Hotspur, deflected off the shoulder of City's Tommy Hutchison, but few will remember a miss by Kevin Reeves in the dying minutes. Bernstein recalls the moment. 'All he had to do was stick his leg out like this . . . ' he says, and directs his right foot towards the coffee table. He is not a man who has stood shoulder-to-shoulder on the Kippax, sipping Bovril and shouting his love of the club, but he still flickers with his own kind of passion.

He poses for our photograph sitting in the directors' box in the main stand. Afterwards, he comes across the gate that is not a gate as he moves down the aisle. In just a few seconds he shows the kind of patience and perseverance that has been long overdue around these parts. They've had a bellyful of bravado.

● The ideal football club chairman is an amalgam of many qualities, some of them contradictory. He must be sympathetic yet decisive, eloquent yet direct, diplomatic yet forthright, speculative yet prudent. He must also be inordinately wealthy, foolhardy and a believer in dreams. Inevitably, these men are extremely scarce. David Bernstein was the chairman City required during a crisis.

Unlike many chairmen, he is not egocentric. He has no desire to be bigger than the club, indeed much of his actions appear genuinely altruistic. He does it for the love. In company he is reserved and discreet, but not without a kindly demeanour. He ponders over his words, almost with the solicitude of a lawyer. This understated but discerning approach has clearly served him well in business where he has become one of the UK's largely unseen, yet potent corporate power-brokers. Conspicuously, he has both Dennis Tueart and Chris Bird at his side, men with the sixth-sense gleaned from living closer to street level.

During the season, some observers suggested Bernstein was little more than a stooge for the parties vying for power in the background. Tueart, many claimed, was in the shadows, allowing Bernstein to finally bring some class and poise – of the traditionally patrician variety – to Manchester City, before the club's stewardship reverted once more to the hustlers and self-made men that had served the club before with varying degrees of success. To bolster this theory, it would seem peculiar that Bernstein should take on such a fraught, demanding role on anything but a short-term basis. If it wasn't for his ego, or financial gain, why should he do it, especially when it necessitated many days away from his family in north London?

His laboured manifesto throughout was of stability and consolidation. On a purely business level, he undoubtedly brought some much needed pragmatism to the club's financial affairs. Most of it was common sense, but he also had an innate understanding of the financing of businesses. In laymen's terms, he was an accountant *par excellence.*

The plea for stability was a reaction to the erratic nature of the club's recent history. Supporters, and the club's staff, were convinced that City's failings were due entirely to its policy of continually changing personnel, both at boardroom and dressing-room level. Stability, in itself, however, was not necess-arily a prerequisite of success. It was certainly beneficial to the sense of well-being within a club, but it was meaningless if it became dogma and people remained when the club was clearly ailing. Stability was only relevant when all the key people had been put in place, otherwise it was stability for its own sake which was worthless.

David Bernstein's allegiance to Royle was, on a superficial level, commendable – he granted him a new contract just days after relegation to Division Two. While this was widely held to be a statement of honour and faithfulness, others saw it as an example of the benign nature of the club's hierarchy, supportive whatever the circumstances. Royle had been appointed with enough time to avoid relegation during the previous season but had failed to motivate the team sufficiently. Their early form at the new lower level was also patchy and unconvincing. Whether he and Donachie, and the players they chose or discarded, were appropriate was a matter of opinion. In the prevailing climate of a search for permanence, counter-opinion was discouraged and stifled; in fact, it was seen as disloyalty. Royle and his boot-room team were granted a rare immunity from meddling and criticism. It was all down to trust.

Bernstein was extremely popular with supporters. They liked his self-effacing personality and the fact that he arrived at the club without any 'history'. He was often waylaid by City fans on train journeys to and from London. He regularly sat among them, sharing opinions, outlining his plans. He was not the man-of-the-people to which Francis Lee aspired, but he was approachable, friendly, a gentleman.

As is so often afforded to men of finance and business, little was known of his background. To ask him is to invoke a convoluted list of directorships where one company is a subsidiary of another, where the trading name is not the recognised name, where one company amalgamates with another and, before the end, the biographical thread is lost amid the complexities. He was, therefore, taken pretty much on face value; football supporters have little choice but to accept the caricature presented to them. In this respect, Bernstein was judicious, well educated, well groomed, good with money ('A jew *and* an accountant: could City have a better man looking out for them?' – Stuart Hall), and the antithesis to Francis Lee. What more did they need to know?

Saturday, 10 October 1998

Kevin Horlock played for Northern Ireland as they beat Finland 1–0 in a Euro 2000 Championship qualifier.

Monday, 12 October 1998
Manchester City 0 Preston North End 1

Former chairman Francis Lee returned to Maine Road for the first time since relinquishing overall control of the club. Lee, still a major shareholder, witnessed a woeful performance by

City. A second-half penalty from Gary Parkinson saw them slump to their first home defeat of the season.

The team left the field to boos. 'We have no arguments because we were crap. We didn't deserve anything and we didn't get anything,' said Kevin Horlock. City had collected just four points from their last five matches.

Michael Brown, the 1997–98 player of the season, made his first full appearance of the season after falling out of favour with Joe Royle. He was subsequently left out of the side again, and did not return until nearly two months later, during which time there was much speculation about his future at Maine Road.

Tuesday, 13 October 1998

Cheeky City fans wrote to the Queen complaining that she should not have signed a Manchester United football on her visit to Malaysia. They were surprised to receive a reply stating: 'Her Majesty is well aware that there is more than one football club in Manchester.' *City 'til I Cry!* claimed to have seen the message scrawled on the ball by the Queen. They reprinted it in issue five: 'Why doesn't one naff orrfff and support one's local team? City 'till one dies – Elizabeth R.'

Friday, 16 October 1998

The club's AGM was held in Manchester's Bridgewater Hall. Back after his hip operation, Royle heard the views of fans distressed to see the club struggling in ninth place. 'I also hate this division,' he said. 'It drives me mad. We've got to get out of it this season.'

David Bernstein received an unsolicited vote of confidence from the shareholders. Several remained unconvinced, one insisting that the team were 'garbage', and another claiming that only Merlin the magician could bring promotion to Maine Road.

DEFINING THE EXTENT OF DISASTER
(*The Times*, Saturday, 17 October 1998)

Eventually, frustration gets the better of him. He speaks quickly, very quickly, without a pause for breath. 'I'm sick of my dad and his mates going on about Colin Bell and Francis Lee and all that lot. It all happened years ago. I'm 24 and all my life I've been fed . . .' He tails off suddenly, his voice shrill: 'Shit, 20 years of shit.' He is almost screaming now.

The panel – each of them connected in some way to Manchester City – is momentarily apoplectic. Chris Bird, City's combative PR man, is the first to counter: 'Look, we're all frustrated, but shouting and swearing will get us nowhere.' The disgruntled fan shuffles in his chair, and tries to speak again but his voice has gone, evaporated. He has given his all.

After this impassioned interruption, the supporters' club meeting returns to form as the fans have their say: grumble; nostalgia; a joke at Alan Ball's expense; the 5–1 win against Manchester United in 1989; another grumble; another Alan Ball joke; thank you and goodnight. May all your nightmares be blue, laser blue.

The season is more than a quarter of the way through and clubs can no longer claim that the league table is merely a directory of participants. Each team in Division Two has played 11 or 12 games. This is more than enough football to deduce which teams are playing well, and which teams are not. City, in ninth place, are not playing well.

They lost at home in midweek against Preston North End and the verdict on their current form ranges from execrable to abysmal. Richard Burgess, the sports reporter who covers City for the *Manchester Evening News*, used the words 'trash', 'abject' and 'ghastly' in his match report, and this from a man who must maintain a certain level of diplomacy since he has to knock on the door at Maine Road every day of his working life.

Now, damn it, City were supposed to storm through this division. It was proclaimed as a glorified bonding session. They would put their arms around one another, flatten all oncomers. In the league, they have inflicted just one heavy defeat, a 3–0 win against Blackpool on the opening day of the season. The scoreline was delusive; in the flesh it was a nervy affair, more a St Vitus's dance than a glorious hokey-cokey.

On the other three occasions when they have won, fans have

muttered the old cliché that their team has not fired on all cylinders or is stuck in second gear. They are deceiving themselves. City are a rusty Fiat Panda left standing for two weeks in the January frost. There's an engine in there somewhere, but it sounds like death. Second gear would be an achievement.

It is widely accepted that there are two ways of escaping the lower reaches of English football. The first is via a slick, passing game, a metaphorical laugh in the face of the broad-shouldered athletes snapping at your ankles. The other is to embrace the mêlée of elbows, knees and shin pads and slug it out defiantly. City are doing neither.

Willie Donachie made matters significantly worse by comments he made prior to the match against Preston North End. Football people should trust the vocabulary of physical expression, deed above dialogue, especially in crisis. Writing in the match programme, he proffered: 'I feel there is too much negative criticism of the team. Maybe it stems from years of failure. We have the most loyal fans in the country and their support is unwavering. But there are too many critics who want to emphasise the black side of everything here.'

He felt that four successive draws should have been viewed positively since they formed part of a nine-match unbeaten league run. He complained that some saw it as a 'disaster'. City fans, to their eternal credit, have the wisdom to look beyond mere results. They care little for statistics, and know they can be dressed up. They trust, above all else, their eyes and hearts and they see and sense a City team out of sorts, providing football on the edge of a nervous breakdown. Three consecutive home draws, against – wait for this – Bournemouth, Chesterfield and Burnley, followed by a defeat against Preston, is not in itself a 'disaster' but their frenetic, aimless football is.

The worry among supporters is that their club is set to become a Burnley or, indeed, a Preston; a footballing giant that is not so much sleeping but distinctly comatose. They can currently count on support that is four times greater in numerical terms than their two Lancashire rivals. A few seasons among the grafters and grapplers of the lower two divisions will, surely, cause this support to wane.

Joe Royle has spent the last two weeks in hospital after a hip-replacement operation. By all accounts, he has been in jovial mood and is enjoying the rare privilege of a life without constant, nagging pain. Within the game, Royle is renowned for his generosity of spirit. He has the necessary ruthlessness, but he is fundamentally a relaxed, blithe character. It will take time for this to permeate the team. There will be more scrappy draws and ignominious home defeats, but Royle's record suggests there will also be flamboyant 4–2 away wins, and players confident enough to hold the ball and skip past desperate tackles.

In the meantime, like his assistant, Donachie, he will talk the good talk in defence of his team. He knows, though, that they are floundering, that there is no joy in their play. A life of constant nagging pain is no life at all.

Saturday, 17 October 1998
Wigan Athletic 0 Manchester City 1

Torrential rain almost led to a postponement but referee David Pugh decided the pitch was playable. Shaun Goater's tenth goal of the season, a volley, gave City their first win in six games. Wigan hit the woodwork three times and afterwards complained that City had been lucky.

'It wasn't pretty, but there were lots of good things for us. It wasn't our greatest performance, but I think that's only the second game of the season we haven't totally dominated and we've got three points out of it. So maybe it's a good omen,' said Joe Royle.

Again, tickets for the game had been much in demand. Many City supporters had queued overnight in heavy rain for them. During the game, they were housed on uncovered terrace and cheered themselves with renditions of 'Singing in the Rain' and 'All we are saying is give us a roof'.

Tuesday, 20 October 1998
Lincoln City 2 Manchester City 1

City's defence twice fell victim to goals from set-pieces. Tony Battersby scored after four minutes following a long throw-in and Kevin Austen added another from a corner. An own goal by Steve Holmes eight minutes from time brought City a scrap of consolation.

The City backroom staff were upset by the reluctance of the Lincoln bench to shake hands after the match.

Friday, 23 October 1998

Nigel Clough was named player–manager of Dr Marten's Premier League side Burton Albion. At a press conference he chose not to dwell on his experience at Maine Road, commenting briefly: 'My time there coincided with an unhappy time in the club's history.'

BUILDING UP HOPE FOR THE ROYLE ASCENT
(*The Times*, Saturday, 24 October 1998)

The two giant projections quivered in the curtains and added a touch of eeriness to the mood of solemnity. It was raining heavily outside, the sky lost in a grey wash, and they walked from sodden streets like extras in a Fritz Lang movie.

Beneath the ghostly holograms, Manchester City's board of directors sat in silence while people settled into their seats, shaking the rain from their anoraks, nodding to acquaintances dotted around the hall. It felt like the last supper without any food, the last rites without a priest.

Inevitably, Chris Bird was asked to conduct the annual general meeting of Manchester City plc. Bird is nominally the club's PR man, but he appears to be fed on kryptonite or spinach, such is his capacity for work. In daylight hours he talks in good style for City, while after dark he tours supporters' club meetings, an evangelist for the Church of the Latter Day Blues.

While we all coughed those nervy, formal coughs, Bird donned a headset microphone, the kind normally the preserve of rock stars on their stadium comeback tour. His movements were a tad wooden, a tad Virgil Tracey in fact; someone might well have murmured, at the appropriate point: 'Thunder Bird Are Go!'

Before Bird invited the assembled shareholders to have their say, David Bernstein opened the meeting. He has been criticised previously for indulging in slick-speak – talking a lot, but saying very little. To his credit, he made no attempt to excuse another relegation and a trading loss of £6.3 million which has left City paying more than £21,000 in interest every week. In his written statement he summed up last season as 'nothing short of disastrous'; clearly, this was not the fey, soft-focus terminology of the politician. He is the type of man who will give you the measured formal treatise, then look you in the eye and add: 'You're up the creek, pal.'

The club has, he says, thrown money at its problems for too long. He wants a measured approach, stability, solid found-ations, more attention to detail; never has common sense seemed so astounding. There were almost sighs of glee among the audience. Most in the hall could boast only a handful of shares. To them a share is a souvenir, something more dis-tinctive and worthwhile than the fare sold at the club's superstore. It also allows them to stand, once a year, toe-to-toe with the board of directors.

City, despite an occasional tetchiness borne from their current dire position, remain a refreshingly open club. Questions from the floor were answered candidly and patiently. Joe Royle took the top-table less than two weeks after major surgery on his hip. He could easily have stayed at home 'recuperating'.

An old chap took to his feet to proclaim the club's new era of reconciliation in stirring fashion. 'The days of recrimination and criticism are over. We should all get behind the team and with a bit of luck, please God, we will get back to our good days, back to the Premier League.' The applause was magnificent.

Another had clearly not heard the chairman's message. 'Merlin the magician wouldn't be able to get us out of this divi-sion with the team we've got. We are not going to carry on year after year watching garbage. You have got to find money to buy new players now,' he said. Bernstein, kindly in the circum-stances, repeated his previous speech of prudence and stability.

After years travelling to Arsenal, Liverpool, etc. City supporters are palpably not enjoying their wet Saturdays in

Wigan, nor indeed – as in this week – their windy Tuesdays in Lincoln. 'This division is doing my head in,' said one shareholder. 'It really is driving me daft. Do you know what it is like to have to drive away from places like Northampton?'

Joe Royle, despite the hobble, was in top form. 'This division is driving me mad as well,' he admitted. He conceded that the team lacked composure and quality, but said he was looking to find better players. 'But I don't want anyone who is out to financially rape the club,' he added.

His tactics were questioned in detail. 'Why do we keep whacking the ball up to Paul Dickov who is only 4ft 2ins tall? Can't they pass the ball?' asked one exasperated fan. Dickov, as he would point out, is actually five feet five inches, though the point remains salient. Royle said he wanted more wide players and would return to a 4–4–2 system when he had settled on his final squad.

Among supporters there is belief in both Royle and Bernstein. They are seen as the end-of-the-line, the place where they have come to rest after all the futile swapping and changing. They are the men for a crisis – cool, thoughtful, shrewd, pragmatic, and with their own kind of differing charm. In pub terms, Royle would entertain them in the vault, while Bernstein holds court in the lounge.

'This club has had a charisma transplant. Let's get the fire in our bellies and sock it to them,' said one shareholder. For a few seconds, such was the emotion, they might have broken into a rendition of 'Blue Moon'. Instead, Chris Bird formally closed proceedings and while feet were shuffling and overcoats pulled back on, someone volunteered a vote of confidence in the manager and the chairman.

The bizarre club-crest of an eagle, three stars and a ship continued to drift across the curtains. Hopefully, the eagle will one day be superseded by a phoenix.

Saturday, 24 October 1998
Manchester City 0 Reading 1

The headlines told it straight: 'Royle Misery Continues', 'Sorry City Looking Down In The Dumps', 'Williams Sends City To A New Low'. A cheeky back-heeled goal after 56 minutes from leading scorer Martin Williams secured Reading's first ever win at Maine Road. It was City's second successive home defeat and their third loss in four games.

The dismissal of Danny Tiatto, City's fourth red card of the season, was the only spark of life in a drab game. He was involved in a scuffle with Bryon Glasgow who received a booking.

The defeat left City in eleventh position, already 10 points behind league leaders, Stoke City. 'My message to the fans is don't panic – we will get it right,' said Joe Royle.

For Glyn Chadwick, writing in *King of the Kippax*, it was all too much: 'As far as I can see we are deep in the shit. Unless somebody takes over the club and pumps some big money in, I think the only way is down and I for one am not going to shell out £300 to watch more of this crap.'

Monday, 26 October 1998

Midfielder Ged Brannan joined Scottish Premier League side Motherwell for a fee of £378,000. He had cost City £750,000 when he signed from Tranmere Rovers 18 months earlier.

Tuesday, 27 October 1998

City supporter Will Aldersley, travelling through north Vancouver in Canada, was surprised to find a signpost to 'Paul Lake'.

Thursday, 29 October 1998

Crystal Palace finally signed striker Lee Bradbury after doubts over a back injury had threatened to halt the deal. The fee was £1.5 million, rising to £2 million after a specified number of appearances.

Bradbury, a former England Under-21 International, had cost City £3 million when he joined them from Portsmouth. During his 15 months at the club he made 29 appearances and scored seven goals. As many newspapers pointed out, he had cost the club £135,000 per goal.

Joe Royle completed the loan signings of 20-year-old Everton striker Michael Branch and Huddersfield Town's 28-year-old defender Andy Morrison.

The club learned of the death of major shareholder Stephen Boler. Boler, 55, died from a heart attack on a business trip to South Africa.

CASSELL PERFORMS HIS CIVVY DUTY IN QUEST FOR BEST
(*The Times*, Saturday, 31 October 1998)

The telephone rings for the third time in the past hour. It's the same man who called on the previous occasions. Young feet pad quickly along the hallway to answer it. 'Dad, it's Joe again,' says 10-year-old James Cassell.

The door to the hall is left slightly ajar. After a cursory greeting, the two men talk football, serious football. 'He's good from set-pieces, I agree, but I'd be a bit concerned about his lack of pace,' says Jim Cassell, Manchester City's chief scout and director of academy.

Joe Royle and Jim Cassell have plenty to discuss. City have lost three of their last four home matches and are mid-table in Division Two. Supporters visiting their website have made their feelings known after an abysmal 1–0 defeat against Reading last Saturday: 'The team has little more talent than a pub side,' complained one, while another wrote from the heart: 'Gloom, gloom, gloom . . . I'm fed up of City ruining my weekend.'

With a certain inevitability, Royle has announced this week that he is on the look-out for new players. Of course he is, mutter City's army of sceptics. Where is he looking? On the golf course? At a sportsman's dinner held in the plush environs of somewhere south of Manchester? An hour or two spent in the home of Jim Cassell would reaffirm their faith, re-light their fires.

This is Cassell – and, indirectly, Joe Royle – caught unawares, caught off-side. It is tea-time on a wretched Wednesday night. The rain outside is falling downwards and sideways. The phone is white-hot: Joe asking Jim, Jim advising Joe, 4–4–2, 3–5–2, a sigh, a pause, another player assessed, another idea ignited. Twenty minutes later, it starts all over again. Along with Willie Donachie, the pair form the triad that effectively shapes Manchester City.

Within football, there is a disparaging term for those that draw a living from the game without having played it. They call them 'civvies'. Cassell's professional playing career lasted all of two full matches for Bury in the mid-1960s. Afterwards he worked as a scout and later chief scout for Oldham Athletic. All the same, he is, in effect, a 'civvy', not that he cares. 'Football is the most insular profession there is. They have created a jobs-for-the-boys logic. I think increasingly people realise that there needs to be a little more thought, preparation and compassion in the game,' he says.

Manchester City, perhaps more than any other club, has been populated in recent times by egos in tracksuits and pin-stripes. There has been a proclivity to self-preservation, thyself above all else. The notion no longer stands, however, that the man shouting loudest and longest will inherit the club. Jim Cassell, much like the chairman, David Bernstein, is proof of the fact. He is thoughtful and shrewd, candid and friendly, immaculate in a suit and tie and wire-framed glasses, the original Gentleman Jim. 'It's been said before now that I look a bit like a Roman Catholic priest,' he laughs. He likes the comparison.

Cassell's brief has been to restructure the club's youth policy. Appropriately, for a former book-keeper and local government officer, his approach has been fastidiously methodical. 'This has been missing at City. There was no one picking up the bits of paper off the floor, no one taking care of the detail,' he says. In the summer he presented a 51-page dossier to the board. It revealed a club run by people without real job specifications, where the hierarchical structure was muddled and essential facilities had to be borrowed, or were missing altogether. 'A football club is a bit like a hotel. You've got to get the structure in place and running properly before you can achieve anything,' he says.

The framework is now clearly defined – and funded to the tune of £500,000 – but Cassell and his team still face the problem of attracting promising young players to Maine Road, and ensuring that they remain. 'Parents are more aware that sport can give their boys a lucrative standard of living these days. We are totally up front with them, we don't try to kid anyone and we always stress that we put the welfare of their boy first.'

He concedes that parents, above all, want to see their sons connected to a 'winning club', which City clearly are not. The inducements might be fiercely homespun, but it would be foolish to underestimate his own role within the design. Parents will trust Cassell, view him as a man of his word, and this will be persuasive as the sport loses itself increasingly to greed and self-gain.

Cassell is on a five-year contract, and it will take at least that long for his young charges to work through to the first team. 'I know that I cannot fail. Failure is if you don't give everything to the job and we're working our socks off,' he says.

The phone goes again. He tells Royle he will have to cut short the conversation, he has to dash to see a reserves match between Oldham Athletic and Bolton Wanderers. It is still raining. Oldham's Boundary Park is so far above sea level it is submerged in the clouds. Only a fool or an obsessive would venture out on such a night. 'I always get a cup of tea off them when I go back to Oldham,' he says. That's fine, then.

● Of City's personnel, Jim Cassell came closer than anyone to typifying the good heart which has earned the club such widespread historical support. He was courteous, open, gentle, trusting; the consummate ambassador.

During our interview he was amazingly frank. He told me his salary and allowed me to borrow the report he had compiled on the club's youth policy. It would have been easy for me to generate a great deal of copy from this, but his is not the kind of trust easily betrayed.

I made light in the column of his 'civvy' status, but it is an issue within the club. Like most clubs, City has had its share of gritty, feisty characters to whom Cassell is an enigma. They like to portray him as the schoolteacher twit caught blinking in the hurly-burly of football. Certainly, they do not feel he is chief scout material, a role habitually undertaken by seasoned ex-pros, unafraid of breaching an unfamiliar dressing-room or resorting to subterfuge or duplicity to get their man. To their mind Cassell's decency is meekness, his politeness a cover for indecision.

While it was impossible to gauge his effectiveness or otherwise in the duality of his job, it was palpably a boon that City should have someone of such a kindly demeanour working with their young players. He was also the counterpoint to the very men who might try to undermine him.

Saturday, 31 October 1998
Manchester City 2 Colchester United 1

Loan signings Michael Branch and Andy Morrison made impressive débuts as City won at home for the first time in almost two months. They were booed off after a goalless first-half, but substitute Ian Bishop rejuvenated their play after the break.

Kevin Horlock gave City the lead with a 49th-minute penalty. Four minutes later, Horlock's corner was headed in at the near post by Morrison. Colchester pulled a goal back through Jason Dozzell. 'Morrison was strong-willed and proved a good passer. And at last we have someone who talks at the back,' said Joe Royle.

Four

A Talent to Annoy

Tuesday, 3 November 1998
David Bernstein wrote to all club employees informing them that the death of Stephen Boler would not affect the club's stability.

Wednesday, 4 November 1998
Supporters were surprised to learn that Kinkladze had returned to Manchester. The Kinkladze in question was a greyhound named after the former City player, a regular visitor to the city's Belle Vue stadium.

Friday, 6 November 1998
Andy Morrison completed his £80,000 move from Huddersfield Town, two days after issuing City with a 'sign me' plea.

City were linked with various wingers, among them Lee Sharpe of Leeds United, Joey Beauchamp of Oxford United and George Donis of AEK Athens.

THE WISDOM OF MR GRIMSDALE
(*The Times*, Saturday, 6 November 1998)

A football – a jazzy white one with green chevrons – makes the occasional cameo appearance. Otherwise, its middle-aged men eating, drinking, adjusting their ties, or photographs of empty dining-rooms, all starched napkins and sparkling silverware.

The brochure offering the 'very best in corporate and match-day entertainment' makes no mention of Manchester City's current league status. Imagine: 'Lovely meal, excellent wine, and what's for afters?' 'Hmmm, how about Macclesfield, distinctly hard-boiled, or Gillingham, new to the menu, and a bit of an unknown quantity?'

City, to their credit, have stayed resolutely in the corporate age, determined to view their form on the pitch as a mere blip, a side dish as they serve up lashings of new potatoes and goodwill in one of their three impressive suites, each with a suitably grandiose title – Millennium, Centenary and Silver. A new addition has been the facility to host full-scale marriage ceremonies. Funerals might be more tricky.

The club has 80 executive boxes in the Kippax and Platt Lane stands, the price for a season ranging from £8,500 to £14,000. Only a handful remain untenanted which means the club has raised more than £700,000 from these glasshouses dotted around the ground.

Traditionalists almost phlegm-up the words 'executive boxes' whenever they rue the state of the modern game. They are seen as final, indisputable proof that football has gone irredeemably limp-wristed. The flower-pressers are in the house, the real men have gone home to creosote the fence or sandpaper their teeth. They hold the view that the pleasure of a game of football is heightened to an almost sensual level only in bitter adversity. The ice has to freeze together extruding parts of your anatomy; the bloke in front must cough and wheeze through a pack of 20; the kid in the next-but-one seat, must scream, 'Come on, City,' every three seconds in a voice so high-pitched it makes Alan Ball sound like Barry White.

And so to the dilemma. It's Halloween, the air is cold, grey and damp and, behold, glamour-ghouls Colchester United are in town. City have lost three of their last four home matches. The home supporters have not had this much fun since their car broke down at the lights, in winter, in the rain, and no one stopped to help. So, what's it to be? Out in the cold, a man of the people, or in Executive Box Seven in the Kippax Stand? The ticket is in your pocket, your principles somewhere close to knee height, and falling.

'Hello sir,' is the welcome, and a free programme. 'Level

three, sir.' Everywhere there is the smell of coffee and the distant clip-clip sound of cutlery. Women in white shirts and black skirts whisk purposefully in and out of ante-rooms. It feels like a cruise liner about to set sail.

Box Seven is a good size and furnished with a family-sized pack of biscuits and a fridge stocked with beer and minerals. The television is showing a Norman Wisdom film. The cosy domesticity is only shattered when someone has the audacity to slide open the patio doors: bloody hell, there's a football match out there! The noise is like a sudden blast of heat, and then it is gone as the door is snapped shut. Norman has dropped a crate of milk bottles and is shrieking, 'Mr Grimsdale, Mr Grimsdale!'

The box comes complete with balcony seats, two rows perched behind a veranda in the – gasp, shiver – open air. This is perfect for leaning upon wearing a thoughtful, ever-so-meaningful expression à la Terry Venables when the *Match of the Day* camera pans up to the stands.

Before the match, there is consternation about the death just two days earlier of Stephen Boler. Boler owned almost 25 per cent of the club's shares and one might expect talk to focus on a potential power vacuum, or another period of boardroom instability. Not so. 'Do you think we should stand up, even though we're in a box, when they have a minute's silence?' asks someone in the corridor. 'Nah, shouldn't think so.'

The first half is aimless and hopeless, but it doesn't seem to matter when, behind you, the plate of biscuits is being replenished, a young girl is pouring coffee into cups, and Norman Wisdom has worked his way up to joint-owner of the dairy. The crowd boo on the half-time whistle. We cheer.

The football is briefly absorbing in the second half, especially when City score twice in quick succession but, with Norman now gone, there is the new distraction of scorelines flashed on the television from the other games. 'Stuart Pearce has been sent off at Newcastle,' proffers one member of the party on a return mission from the glasshouse to stock up on Budweiser and Nice biscuits. As the game falls into yet another lull, a discussion follows on Stuart Pearce. Is he tenacious and salt-of-the-earth or a muscle-bound clogger? The former is the consensus, though perhaps our minds should have been elsewhere, as Paul Dickov chips a 'pass' 10 yards over the head of Richard Edghill.

After the game, there is much ironic discussion about the forthcoming draw for the First Round of the FA Cup. 'We could be sat here [meaning in all this relative splendour] watching City play Marine or Bacup Borough – imagine that!'

The draw has actually paired City against Halifax Town next Friday evening, though no one has been laughing about this. Back in January 1980, Malcolm Allison took his team of expensive follies (Steve Daley, Michael Robinson etc.) to the Shay in the FA Cup and they lost 1–0 on a pitch of sand and mud. 'It has left a stain on our playing record that will take a long time to fade if, indeed, it is ever allowed to,' said Allison at the time.

The memory *has* lingered, from the executive boxes to the manager's dug-out, where Willie Donachie, a City player at the time – though he missed the game through injury – takes his position. People in glasshouses don't throw stones any more.

Saturday, 7 November 1998
Oldham Athletic 0 Manchester City 3

After 12 years as manager of Oldham Athletic, Joe Royle returned with another club for the first time. Two first-half strikes by Kevin Horlock gave City a lead that Oldham rarely threatened. Andy Morrison's superb volley, his second goal in two games, sealed victory.

'We were nowhere near our best but we scored three terrific goals, had one disallowed, hit the bar and didn't get a blatant penalty so I can't be disappointed. It could have been embarrassing, really, but I'm glad it wasn't – I still feel a lot for Oldham,' said Joe Royle.

Tuesday, 10 November 1998
Wycombe Wanderers 1 Manchester City 0

Wycombe Wanderers had their largest attendance for two years when 8,159 crowded into Adams Park, causing a delayed kick-off.

The home side were awarded a penalty after Richard Edghill was ruled to have fouled Andrew Baird. Michael Simpson scored from the spot. 'I spoke to the referee after the game and told him he had a good game but that he made a mistake with one vital decision,' said Royle. 'The two lads just collided, that was all. It was right in front of the linesman and he didn't give anything so I don't see how the referee, who was 20 yards away, can give it.'

Friday, 13 November 1998
Manchester City 3 Halifax 0 (FA Cup First Round)

Live coverage by Sky TV and a Friday evening kick-off contrived to reduce the attendance to just 11,108, the lowest ever FA Cup attendance at Maine Road.

Craig Russell, making his first full appearance of the season, hit two first-half goals and set up Shaun Goater who scored an easy tap-in. It was Goater's first goal in five games. 'It's nice to be in the next round, but we're still in the middle of a nightmare here,' said Joe Royle.

CHUCKLE HAS THE LAST LAUGH
(*The Times*, Saturday, 14 November 1998)

The ball hits the net and our principles become decidedly flimsy. No question about it, he was worth the money, and if he wants to drive a custard-coloured Lotus, that's his choice. Likewise, when the ball misses by some distance and the said striker tumbles to the turf we mock and jeer, begrudge him his every penny. We love them and we hate them, it's part of the fun.

Another tenet of this bizarre relationship is that it must be symbiotic: players must share both the joy and the suffering at precisely the same level as ourselves. If they are three goals down, and shuffling about impassively, we wish upon them a downpour, a veritable monsoon, hailstones as sharp as carpet tacks.

Apart from seriously inclement weather, there is another requital we covet for our anti-heroes. 'I hope the trainer puts them through it on Monday morning,' mutter the broken-hearted as they leave the ground. Step this way, Mr Baranowski. A Yorkshireman of Polish parentage, he is the kindly chap who makes supporters' dreams come true. Manchester City fans will take great delight to know that Baranowski, stop-watch in hand, frown on face, is waiting to give them the mother of all Monday mornings.

He has one of those faces that is, in one instant, stern and intimidating, and then open and comical. The hair is slicked back, he wears a neat, carefully tapered moustache. 'Some of the players have called me the Führer and Saddam Hussein,' he says. 'They also reckon I look a bit like one of the Chuckle brothers. I don't mind them taking the piss. I give it them back. I always remind them that it's me who decides how long they should run for and how fast they should go.' Still chuckling, brother?

Although he wears the obligatory tracksuit, Baranowski is as much scientist as football coach. The vocabulary gives him away: 'energy systems', 'nutritional intake', 'resistance training', 'exercise prescription', and this is just a warm-up before we move on to 'biomechanics', 'physiotherapeutic' and 'pharmacological'. Inevitably, he learned his trade in the United States, where fitness conditioners (the job title he gives himself) are seen as essential.

'They are years ahead of us in the States. Every college team will have a fitness conditioner. I have put into practice what I learned over there and made it soccer-specific,' he says. Baranowski and his staff work in peripatetic fashion, with Sheffield United, Leeds United and Lincoln City among their current clients, aside from City. He also spent six seasons with Blackburn Rovers and was called upon by Kenny Dalglish once more when he moved to Newcastle United.

Baranowski provides a bespoke training plan for footballers. They are assessed individually and then, via the stop-watch and heart monitor, they effectively compete against themselves in a series of regulated training sessions over the course of a whole year. It is the antithesis of the system that has served football for decades and, unsurprisingly, it is viewed suspiciously in some quarters. 'A lot of football coaches have the attitude that what worked for them as a player will work for anyone else. It is all volume and not quality. They think that if everyone is completely knackered after a session, it must have been worthwhile. They are missing the point completely.'

A fitness fanatic himself and a karate black-belt, he is not impressed by the level of fitness of most footballers. 'At City, when we first started working with them, I'd have given the squad six marks out of ten for their fitness level. We have worked with them from the first day of pre-season training and they have got on with the job without moaning. I know the results on the pitch haven't gone as well as everyone hoped, but there is a real sense that they know there is work to do.'

The best advocate for Baranowski has been Jamie Pollock. He was put on a specific six-week training programme in the summer and lost 10 lbs which many felt had honed his game noticeably. Unfortunately, a combination of two sending-offs and a hernia operation has limited his impact. 'Some things are out of our control,' rues Baranowski.

Baranowski makes no claim to be the authentic 'football man'. He did not play the sport to any level and although he has worked alongside the likes of Dalglish and Shearer, he has a markedly secular attitude to the game. During matches his gaze wanders continually from the ball: is the centre-back racing back to his position after moving forwards for a corner?; are the midfielders covering their counterparts' runs?; is the striker using his additional upper-body strength to shield the ball?; is the winger turning more quickly away from his marker using the footwork technique he was shown?

City, after two consecutive wins, lost at Wycombe Wanderers on Tuesday and, while their level of fitness was satisfactory, their level of finesse was once more lacking. Did Baranowski give them hell on Wednesday morning? Were they left mopping up the sweat with their wage packets? 'Funnily enough, we never mention the last result. By the time we get to the players, Joe and Willie have already had their say with them. It is a dead issue once we're on the training pitch.' Damn.

Sunday, 15 November 1998

Despite lying outside the play-off zone, bookmakers William Hill quoted City as third favourites to win the league, behind Fulham and Stoke City.

Saturday, 21 November 1998
Manchester City 0 Gillingham 0

Jamie Pollock returned for the first time in seven weeks but Gillingham, on their first ever visit to Maine Road, defended well. 'We have dominated the game, had a redundant goalkeeper, their keeper is man-of-the-match, everything flashes around the box and we've come away with a draw,' said Joe Royle. City had dropped 14 points at home already during the season.

Monday, 23 November 1998

Mike Turner, City's £100,000-a-year chief executive, announced that he was to leave the club 'to pursue other interests'. He had been with City for two years and resigned amid rumours that he was unhappy with the behind-the-scenes atmosphere. 'There is still a canker of back-stabbing within the club that seems to go on from generation to generation,' a 'close source' told the *Daily Mail.*

Thursday, 26 November 1998

Gareth Taylor, Sheffield United's 25-year-old Wales international, signed for City. The 6ft 2ins striker cost an initial £350,000, rising to £400,000 after a specified number of appearances.

Friday, 27 November 1998

A supporter discovered a counterfeit Manchester City kit on sale in a sports shop in Kampala, Uganda. It bore little resemblance to an authentic kit, replete with sky blue polka dots and huge shorts. 'The material appears to have come straight from Mike Baldwin's knicker factory,' said Steve Doohan. 'And the shorts! Even Jamie Pollock would struggle to fill them with his voluminous behind.'

TURNER TAKES FAMILIAR PATH OFF CITY ROAD
(*The Times*, Saturday, 28 November 1998)

Ladies and gentleman, today and for the rest of his life, Mike Turner will be pursuing other interests. He is not alone, for there are many others dotted around the north-west of England who are doing just the same after once pursuing the interests of Manchester City FC.

Turner resigned this week as chief executive of City after almost two years at the club. 'He has left to pursue other interests' said a club spokesman. 'Resigned', in Turner's case, is probably a misnomer. More likely, he was jollied along through the main door, both sad to go and glad to go – life's like that at City. The other recent snarl in the Maine Road boardroom was the death a month ago of Stephen Boler, the largest individual shareholder.

Since David Bernstein succeeded Francis Lee as chairman in March, the new regime has zealously portrayed itself as pragmatic, staunch and provident, an antidote to the profligacy and egocentricity of before. Bernstein has honest brown eyes and a gracious but assured manner. When he tells you something, you believe him. He is big on words like 'stability' and 'foundations', but sometimes he is like the television reporter speaking directly to camera: 'We are determined to bring stability to this club,' he avers. To his right, still within the shot, someone is making off with the desks, or holding up a placard reading, 'Don't Believe A Word'.

Manchester City will always be so, at least until it attracts an individual or organisation with the finance to secure overall control. The fragmented nature of the club's ownership dictates that a certain level of turmoil is a normal state of being. The best Bernstein can hope for is a manageable turmoil. He oversees a board comprising four main factions held in an uneasy but workable alliance: JD Sports, Greenalls Brewery, Goldenworld Ltd (Francis Lee's business interest) and the Limelight Group which is the generic name of Boler's former businesses incorporating Moben kitchens and Dolphin bathrooms.

Where power is so indistinct, it can be appropriated by those with no authentic right to it. A book published this week, *Cups for Cock-Ups* by Ashley Shaw, claims that the club hosts a malevolent force, the much-vaunted Fifth Column. Directors and managers are only allowed to change the club superficially while its administrative staff, who habitually remain at the club much longer, protect their own interests. In short, their jobs and salaries remain intact, sometimes to the detriment of the club itself.

In football an autocracy is much easier to administer. Across the city, for example, United have benefited greatly from the single-minded approach afforded by the secure ownership of the Edwards family. City suffer for their stifling pseudo-democracy. The talk is as plentiful as the paperwork, but sometimes they order peas instead of beans, full-backs instead of wing-backs. Even now, for all Bernstein's obsession with rationalisation, the club has a staff of 104 (excluding players) and an annual wage bill (including players) of almost £9 million. Macclesfield Town FC, of the same division, is run on a staff of 10 full-time officials.

There was little consternation at the news of Boler's death at Maine Road and no mention of a power vacuum; this is because the club has carried one for as long as anyone can remember. Turner's departure has been greeted with a similar shrug of the shoulders. He was brought in by Lee to administer much of the club's day-to-day activities on a weekly wage in excess of £2,000. He had previously been commercial manager at Liverpool FC and before that had worked for Puma and as a Rugby League administrator.

In the long-term, Turner will be seen as another legacy of the Lee era finally swept away. They will proffer the opinion that he was, like so often before, someone else's idea of a good appointment; football clubs are habitually run on such a whimsical basis. Paradoxically, Bernstein himself was invited on to the board by Lee. Nothing is black and white among the blue and white.

Officials claim Turner's departure does not mark a return to the club's infamous internal squabbling. 'I have talked a great deal about stability but you cannot legislate for everything,' said Bernstein. 'It was Mike's decision to go.' Some suggest that Turner was upset over the appointment of a new financial controller. He has also been heavily involved in several industrial tribunals with former club employees. Turner is on 'holiday' this week and has received a cash settlement from City so is unlikely to go public on why he has left such a well-paid job at a club he has supported since a boy.

Dave Wallace, editor of the City fanzine, *King of the Kippax*, reluctantly senses further boardroom disharmony. 'Whatever way you look at it, Turner was in a high-profile position. You can't pay someone that kind of salary and then claim he wasn't important in the scheme of things. It does throw up once more the question of stability and unity.'

Turner's exit, along with the death of Boler, will have alerted predatory outsiders with a declared interest in acquiring City, principally the solicitor Raymond Donn and businessman Mike McDonald. There has long been speculation about possible takeovers, but it would require a large amount of capital. Boler's shares alone have been valued at £8 million and collecting enough of the others to wrestle power would cross several entrenched political boundaries within the current set-up.

City fans, meanwhile, view the shenanigans with indifference. They've seen it all before and have learned repeatedly that it hurts to care too much. Generally, they trust Bernstein and Joe Royle, and there is a prevailing belief that they are the men of integrity to address the multitude of problems both on and off the pitch. Both, however, must be wary of the tackle from behind.

● My intuition on Chris Bird was correct. It was announced soon after Turner's departure that he was to become the 'chairman's assistant' while simultaneously undertaking his PR duties. It seemed a vague term, but carried with it significant authority and prestige. He immediately began to attend board meetings and his capacity for hard work and long hours meant he soon became City's 'Everyman' – the club's interface between the media, the supporters and the directors. He was known to everyone within the club. The tea ladies joked with him, the ground-staff would stop and talk. I remember a remark made by Colin Bell at the end of our interview. This footballing legend, a man who had travelled the world, met all manner of people, announced demurely: 'I asked Chris first, and he said it was okay to talk to you.'

I did not write a profile on Bird during the season because of the intrinsic risk. In his own right he wielded a degree of power, but he was also the emissary of Tueart, the director responsible for media relations. Unlike many in the PR profession, it was always manifest that Bird's remit would not limit itself to simply drafting the odd news release or issuing press passes. He was a man on the move, a man with plans.

Born in 1963, he left school with one 'O' Level and joined British Rail as a trainee signalman at Guide Bridge, Audenshaw. He worked nightshifts and spent his days running a market stall on Hyde Market. Even then, he rarely needed more than three or fours hours sleep to get by. He had been on the market since a young teenager, and patently had the gift of salesmanship. 'My dad always said I wasn't someone who had kissed the blarney stone, I'd swallowed it,' he said. He left British Rail to join his father, Patrick Bird, working at a local dye factory.

Wearing his work overalls, he responded to a job advertised in the *Ashton Reporter*. It wanted a representative to sell advertising space in the newspaper. He told them he would be the most successful rep they had ever employed, and was true to his word. 'I took to it like a duck to water. I'd walk up one side of the street and get all the shops to advertise, then walk up the other side and do the same all over again.' He was on a wage of £75 per week without any commission. The job did not include a company car, just a bus pass to all points in Ashton-under-Lyne.

His next move was into local radio, where he again sold advertising. It was the consummate job for his relentless personality. 'I suppose I *am* aggressive at times. I do not suffer fools. I cannot abide people who do not give everything. I think I am fair, but I can be cut-throat at times. If someone doesn't give it their best, boy do I let them know about it.' Within two years he had risen to the position of sales controller at Piccadilly Radio. He flourished in local radio, a famously hierarchical environment where the naïve or gullible were habitually put to the sword. Bird routinely dealt with media power-brokers like Owen Oyston and, evidently, knew how to connect with leadership and wrestle his own kind of influence. He was a hard-worker, someone who could see a project through. He was sometimes bullish, but he phoned everyone back, got the job done.

In 1990, he left Piccadilly Radio. 'I wasn't happy any more at the radio station. I wasn't sure whether people were buying into Chris Bird or Piccadilly.' He needed a broader stage, and set up the PR company, Bird and Wood, with the former Piccadilly DJ, Phil Wood. After seven years, Bird bought out Wood's share, and changed the company name to The Bird Consultancy, in a 90/10 per cent partnership with his brother, Peter Bird, nine years his senior. It boasted several notable clients, including the G-Mex Centre and Diadora.

Initially, City was merely another addition to the company's roster but Bird was soon perceived as *their* PR man. While he was sometimes criticised in the City fanzines for his attempts to stage-manage fans' forums, the wider issue of his sudden rise to eminence was barely addressed. Regardless of his enthusiasm and love of City, he was in a peculiar situation, seemingly without mandate from either shareholders or supporters. There were mutterings that he was in place solely through his friendship with Tueart and Bernstein, though, it had to be said, such arrangements proliferated in football.

While Bird's route into the heart of City drew some scepticism, few doubted the qualities he tendered. He did not have the subtlety and chicanery of a Sidney Rose, the club's life-president, or indeed a Peter Swales, but he was linear, determined, confident, dogged, a supreme foot-soldier for the Bernstein administration.

Saturday, 28 November 1998
Luton Town 1 Manchester City 1

Andy Morrison, captaining City for the first time, gave them the lead after 29 minutes with a header from a Craig Russell corner. Luton equalised when teenage substitute Gary Doherty, left unmarked at a corner, headed in at the near-post.

Monday, 30 November 1998

Michael Branch returned to Everton after completing his month-long loan period at Maine Road. The two clubs could not agree a fee.

Five

The Winter of Our Discontent

Tuesday, 1 December 1998

Letters appeared in the *Manchester Evening News* which were critical of City. 'We can see how far City's standards have dropped' – T. Knott, Droylsden; 'What is going on at the Moss Side Academy? It's football, but not as we know it!' – A. Menzies, Gorton; 'The team is poor, probably the worst City side ever' – A. Holland, Lytham.

Wednesday, 2 December 1998

Millwall were fined and warned by the Football Association after being found guilty of failing to control their spectators when City visited the New Den in September.

City were quoted as 1000–1 to win the FA Cup by Manchester bookmaker Fred Done. The odds were the longest in the club's history.

Friday, 4 December 1998

Darlington 1 Manchester City 1 (FA Cup Second Round)

Gary Bennett, Darlington's 37-year-old player–coach and an ex-City player, scored his first goal of the season. City were rescued from another FA Cup embarrassment by substitute Paul Dickov's late volley. Darlington's Steve Gaughan was dismissed for manhandling referee Barry Knight.

Willie Donachie complained that City supporters had shouted abuse at the team throughout the match. 'It left me feeling sick . . . I can honestly say it left me wondering why I bother,' he said.

The geeks are in town, better lock up your railway timetables and acrylic, star-patterned cardigans. Think again, for these are geeks with attitude, boffins with bite to match the bytes.

Manchester City have just held their second tribal gathering, a weekend of City-tinged frivolity for supporters who communicate via the Internet. From across the globe they trekked to Moss Side, Manchester, to press the flesh and share the pain with the similarly afflicted. It is a pilgrimage of grotesque proportions, akin to an assignment undertaken by the American writer P.J. O'Rourke, famed for his droll bulletins from various war zones around the world.

Through the cold, damp, rain-lashed streets, visitors from as far away as Hong Kong and Kenya, Pakistan and Moscow, travelled to a part of Manchester that is a no-go area for many of its own citizens. After their Friday night (anti-)social, their itinerary took in a trip along Rusholme's famous curry mile, a tour of Maine Road, a five-a-side tournament and, of course, a Manchester City match.

Since most Internet users have codenames, the introductions were more complex than usual. 'Hmm, are you Stan the Man or Son of Stan the Man?' asked one. 'Neither, actually, I'm Stockholm Blue; I think that's Stan the Man over there.' Similar conversations could be heard throughout the over-lit Oasis Suite which, appropriately, has the same decor as an airport departure lounge.

The guests of honour were five ex-City players boasting between them more than 1,100 games and 150 goals for the blues. Dennis Tueart, the former City striker famous for extravagant overhead kicks, was spotted first, standing by an extravagant Welsh dresser. A chant struck up immediately: 'There's only one Dennis Tueart, one Dennis Tueart.' He carried on his conversation, breaking off occasionally to acknowledge the noisy approval of a group in the corner of the room. 'They've been drinking all day, that lot,' he was told.

On the table by Tueart's side was a framed collection of his medals and an England international cap. It might have been a goodhearted gesture on his behalf, a compulsion to share his moments of glory with others. Alternatively, it might have been evidence of a monstrous ego. One supporter had no doubts: 'Look at that, he's only been here five minutes and he's got his bloody medals out. Talk about full of himself!' Ridiculed and deified simultaneously in the same room: only football can stir such a miscellany of opinions.

The other guests from City's glorious recent past were Willie Donachie, Gary Owen, Peter Barnes and Harry Dowd, their goalkeeper from 1958 to 1970. The club is currently on a mission of openness and similar forums are being held throughout the country. The procedure at each is identical. Fans submit written questions and a panel supplied by the club provide the answers and the anecdotes.

Within minutes, the irritable Interneters were expressing their discontent. They objected to the formulaic approach and wanted to fire from the hip, to ask questions as they thought of them. Chris Bird remained steadfast. 'We're lucky that these gentlemen have given up their time tonight . . .' he began, pointing towards the panel. He sounded disconcertingly patronising, and someone duly said it in unequivocal terms. 'You patronising bastard,' muttered the man on his feet at the corner table. 'Now then,' chorused the people around him, much in the manner of the midnight chip-shop queue trying to restrain a young buck determined to pick a fight with the middle-aged man next to him.

More agitation ensued when talk turned to the naming of City's new stadium. Several were disappointed to learn that the Joe Mercer Stadium was not among the early favourites from the various supporters' polls. Inevitably, there were suggestions of rigged voting. More shouting, a grimace from Bird. The cups on the dresser were starting to shake. The call for calm was heeded eventually, and the tension further assuaged by the first Monica Lewinsky joke of the evening. 'Let's call it the Monica Lewinsky Stadium, that way we can make sure we never go down again!'

Harry Dowd, a snowy-haired gentleman with a permanent

smile, hardly inspired the throng with the admission, part-way through, that he no longer watched football, or cared much about it. 'What's he come for then? A chicken wing at the end of the night?' came the stage whisper. City know how to treat their heroes!

The question–answer session over, more humour, this time from a professional comedian, would surely unite these troubled blues. The evening was to provide one more shock. 'Right then,' said the comedian. 'I was really pleased to see that a bloke from Lancashire won £7 million on the lottery the other week. Until I realised it was a Paki . . .' He was challenged immediately by several members of the multi-cultural audience. 'I'm only saying what you're all thinking,' was his bizarre response. Some left, some stayed and heckled. A bad time was had by all.

● The column was an attempt to relate the irritation and mistrust that City's poor form had engendered in supporters. Many had become cynical and humourless. The evening was awful – an argumentative party of people at one table, everyone else too shy to bridge the distance between one another. Beer was on sale, but the room was flushed with bright light as if we were specimens in a museum. It felt like something organised by the Parent–Teacher Association to raise money for a pony-trekking holiday.

Of course, I only attended one event, so perhaps should not have used it as an indicator for the entire Tribal Gathering which spanned the weekend. As I learned later, supporters rallied and the frigid opening evening was superseded by a renewal of the camaraderie and warmth of old. In effect, the supporters had regenerated themselves.

I was telephoned afterwards by Chris Bird, upset that I had accused him of patronising the fans. He had assembled the panel of ex-players as a favour to the Gathering. I didn't see that this had any correlation to his attitude on the night, but conceded that it was probably unfair to portray him as super-cilious when the event would not have taken place without his assistance.

After the article, I became a figure of disdain on the various web-postings. It seemed supporters were desperate for scapegoats, their frustration and spleen needed to be discharged. City, briefly, had started to feel like a different club. The famous good humour had become sarcastic rather than heartfelt; the losing was turning dissatisfaction to bitterness.

Peter Brophy's broadside, 'TG2 – Hack Just Behind The Times' was included on MCIVTA (Manchester City Information Via The Alps), the bulletin board visited by hundreds of City fans around the world. It was typical of the criticism that came my way. It was a little over-cooked, but he had a point . . .

TG2 – HACK JUST BEHIND THE TIMES

It occurred to me when I was flying home for TG2 that I must be mad. On the face of it, there seems little sense in making a 4,000-mile round trip for an event centred round a match against unglamorous opponents at a level to which, until a few short months previously, I never thought City would sink. Especially when you can't even rely on the team to go out, do a solid professional job and win. Sure enough, we didn't win, we couldn't even bloody score. And yet I flew back to Russia knowing I hadn't been mad at all. I'd do it all again – indeed I will do it all again. There's so much more to it than the football, you see.

As a non-attending Blue Viewer [another site devoted to City] remarked, those who've only seen the account which appeared in *The Times* newspaper probably picture an event which failed, marked by sniping at the panel of ex-players and uproar during the stand-up's act. Mark Hodkinson, author of the piece, focuses largely on the controversies of the Friday night event, which have already been aired in MCIVTA and on Blue View – a classic case of accentuating the negative.

Maybe there's just cause to criticise the club's consultation with fans over the new stadium, though I disagreed whether it was the right time and setting to question the process. It was certainly more than unfortunate that the comedian pandered to the worst prejudices of his stereotype of a group of football fans, ignoring that he had a rather more sophisticated, cosmopolitan audience to entertain. However, to claim that even the Friday night was ruined by these incidents would be inaccurate. I was in the Oasis Suite for six hours, and for more than five, Blues were sitting and talking, eating and drinking, singing and dancing or laughing and joking together.

That's to say nothing of the article's comments about the panel. Personally, I enjoyed the chance to meet and chat to the ex-players whom I, like many others, remember with great reverence; and they stayed round for photos with good grace. I was actually interested to see international caps and trophies brought along by Donachie and Tueart, not offended by the egotism of the display. Maybe a few people voiced the odd cynical aside – as if that's a surprise in a room filled with more than a hundred – but I'm pretty confident that this paragraph reflects the general mood better than the quotations produced in Hodkinson's piece.

Even for those who departed from the function in the Oasis Suite (and though I didn't, I understand why people walked out) I don't think it was more than a small blight on the weekend as a whole. Hodkinson lists the other events, but not in full – some played golf on the Friday or went out for a meal on the Sunday, for instance. How can he ignore the fact that these events and the 'trip along Rusholme's famous curry mile, tour of Maine Road, five-a-side tournament and, of course, Manchester City match' he mentions were all attended by many and by all accounts I've seen (more than he has, I'd wager), thoroughly enjoyed.

Or at least, all were enjoyed apart from the game. Of course, I'm used to seeing City struggle to break their opponents down, spurn a couple of chances, grow uninspired and achieve a disappointing result. I'm used to seeing some of the players appear possessed of a first touch which would have embarrassed any of the lads playing in the five-a-side on the Sunday. But it's worse now than it ever has been, because at least for most of our history we've been spurning chances and playing uninspired football and achieving disappointing results and showing poor first touch against top-flight opposition.

Yet I think the fact we follow a club with these characteristics brings us all closer together – we're all people who love what most football fans would regard as unlovable. I wouldn't be so trite as to say we're all a brotherhood. In most respects, we form a pretty disparate group. Maybe without City to bind it together, many of the component parts might not have much in common and one or two may even not like each other all that much. But this is irrelevant, because we do have City to bind us together, and that means we can gather and do what we did for most of the Friday night and for all the rest of TG2. And at the end of it, ask any one of us and we'll tell you we had a bloody great weekend.

In the light of this, when I read the piece from *The Times*, I was a little surprised. Indeed, if it hadn't cited a couple of events I'd witnessed I might have wondered if Hodkinson had attended a parallel TG2. As it was, I felt that the author had given a disproportionate focus to a couple of brief episodes to fit what he wanted to say irrespective of the truth. I live in Russia, and am old enough to have spent a fair amount of time here when it was still the Soviet Union, so I can recall how this approach was a journalistic staple here in those days. I really think Hodkinson was born out of time – he'd have made a fantastic pre-glasnost Pravda hack.

So next year, come November, I'll already have bought my ticket back to Maine Road for the next one, probably centred around a game against Wigan or Northampton or equally alluring opponents. I can understand why an onlooker might think it a crazy P.J. O'Rourke-style pilgrimage, but as for some smart-arse telling me I've not had a good time? Sod him! Roll on TG3.

Saturday, 5 December 1998

Television celebrity Paul Merton made himself unpopular with City fans after a joke on the comedy programme, *Have I Got News For You*. One of the guests, George Melly, commented on a recent Turner Prize-winner famous for making art from elephant droppings. 'There isn't much elephant shit to be found in Manchester,' he said. Merton butted in: 'Haven't you seen Man City lately?'

Tuesday, 8 December 1998
Manchester City 1 Mansfield Town 2 (Auto Windscreen Shield)
Since the club expected a low turn-out just one stand was opened, the Kippax, and in an eerie atmosphere supporters saw City put in a dire performance. Lee Peacock scored twice for Mansfield and Danny Allsopp pulled one back for City who left the field to boos and jeers. 'We were worse than poor,' said Joe Royle.

The attendance was 3,007, the lowest for a competitive game in the club's history. The previous lowest had been 4,029 for a Full Members' Cup match against Leeds United in 1985. 'We have always maintained our main priorities lie in the league,' said Jamie Pollock afterwards.

Wednesday, 9 December 1998
A match report of the Mansfield Town game in the *Daily Mirror* caused a great deal of ill-feeling at Maine Road. Underneath a colour photograph of a near-empty ground, ran the headline: 'Manchester United will play in front of 55,000 screaming fans at Old Trafford tonight. Meanwhile, at Maine Road . . .'

United were about to play a European Champions League match against Bayern Munich and the paper could not resist comparing the differing fortunes of the two clubs. The day before, the *Mirror* had carried a similar story under the headline, 'City Face New Low'. The club, and many supporters, maintained that the *Mirror's* coverage was unnecessarily vindictive.

MISFIT RELUCTANT TO PLEAD CLOUGH JUSTICE
(*The Times*, Saturday, 12 December 1998)

Ultimately, I just didn't have the courage. The opportunity arose several times, but I made a metaphorical shuffle to the touch-line, out of harm's way. I went as near as I dared, but always held back on the absolute truth. How do you tell someone that they are hated?

Now, away from the gaze of those keen brown eyes, the vitriol Manchester City fans hold for Nigel Clough can be related fully. He is, according to the City fanzine, *King of the Kippax*, a 'lazy, money-grabbing leech'. To further reinforce the point, a cartoon drawing of Clough shows him with a contemptuous smile on his face, a bundle of cash in his hand and the taunt, 'Suckers', on his lips.

Fanzines are habitually cruel and direct, so the attack in itself is nothing new or particularly disconcerting. The inky anger of the disgruntled fan-cum-writer is now an accepted constituent of football, but this demonisation of Nigel Clough has also suited others in and around Manchester City FC. In the cartoon world that is Maine Road, Clough is the black-cloaked baddie; admittedly not quite the boo-hiss anti-hero of Alan Ball, but running him fairly close.

Clough was signed by Ball so, to many observers, they form a heinous double act. Both men are seen as a reminder of a foolhardy, inglorious recent past, a time when the club fired from the hip with a wad of notes. When Clough left City two months ago, the *Manchester Evening News* painstakingly relayed how much he had cost per game, per goal, and the subtext was crudely apparent.

David Bernstein rejoiced that he had stymied this flow of cash – reportedly £6,000 per week – to a player not even on the fringes of a first-team place. Bernstein is a gentleman, a man to whom a deal is a deal, but in professing City's new-found pragmatism and parsimony, he inadvertently cast Clough as avaricious, another example of player putting himself before club.

Until Clough joined City in January 1996 for £1 million from Liverpool, he was – for a footballer anyway – a surprisingly popular figure. We had known him since a boy. He was the thin, dark-haired youth half-smiling on family photographs next to his famous dad. Secretly, we all felt a bit sorry for him. Brian Clough was great on television, but imagine him in your front room, every night! Nigel became a neat, intelligent professional footballer, while off the field he was patently not a chip off the old block. He spoke quietly and sensibly, without the extravagant gestures and rhetoric of his father.

City fans were delighted when he signed, because above all else they exalt the ball-player. They were also encouraged that he had taken a drop in wages (thought to be £2,000 per week) to join. He scored on his home début but thereafter his form was inconsistent. City were relegated in May 1996 and when Frank Clark replaced Alan Ball as manager he believed Gio Kinkladze and Clough were not compatible in the same team. Clough played just 19 games in the 1996–97 season and last season did not make one appearance for City, though he was loaned to Sheffield Wednesday and Nottingham Forest.

Clough has spent most of his life in close proximity to journalists. He is cautious, not rude or evasive, but vigilant. He had not been forewarned that we would talk at length about City. Clearly, he would rather we didn't. His eyes narrow, there is an invisible fire beneath his chair. 'I got on with most people at City. I would like to think that I could call Joe Royle tomorrow and he would sort me out with a match ticket if I wanted one,' he says.

He is oblivious to the ill-feeling that has developed since he left the club. He does not look surprised, or particularly upset. He has been in the game a long while, he knows the capricious nature of the supporter. A stern look suddenly falls across his face, perhaps he senses a set-up, that I want him to 'clear his name' and speak disparagingly about City. 'I'm not going to have a go at City,' he says.

Without ever sounding pompous, he says that he would not use a newspaper article to, as it were, 'tell his side of the story'. I inform him that he is among a minority of footballers who would feel this way. He shrugs his shoulders. He mentions his family, his friends at Maine Road, players he has worked alongside; it is their respect he covets the most. 'Supporters only get to find out so much . . .' he begins. And then ends, abruptly.

His reluctance to elaborate is frustrating, his politeness and quiet dignity infuriating. I push and push, he moves further away. It must have been distressing, as a relatively young man, to spend a whole season out of the first team, I proffer. Perhaps now, the catharsis will begin, we will learn of the ignominy, the misery. He is, inevitably, two moves ahead: 'When you're out of the team you just get your head down in training and get on with it. I am not the type to go hammering on the manager's door. I turned up every day at City and always made myself available for selection,' he says.

Eventually, reluctantly, he presents the facts: it took precisely one hour to negotiate his three-year contract with City. For once, the language is colourful and linear: 'It was done in no time, I didn't try to screw the club to the floor,' he says. He *was* unhappy to remain in City's reserves and asked the PFA several times to help find him another club. Unfortunately, no one wanted to sign him. He left City with a cash settlement which was significantly less than if he had remained and drawn his weekly wage.

He is now manager of Burton Albion of the Dr Marten's Premier Division. He has inherited a squad of about 50 players and smiles at the irony of having to shed some of his staff. Later, as he talks more of the club and enthusiasm washes over his prudence, his eyes dance and the smile becomes more frequent. It was a long time in coming, but well worth the wait.

Saturday, 12 December 1998
Manchester City 0 Bristol Rovers 0

An uninspiring game saw City booed off for the second time within a week. 'It was our poorest display of the season,' said Joe Royle. It left them 14 points behind league-leaders Stoke City. They had not won in their last five matches and had won just four times in 19 outings.

Before the game, supporters were handed invitations to an after-match Christmas pub crawl with the editorial teams behind three City fanzines, *Bert Trautmann's Helmet, Chips 'n' Gravy* and *City 'til I Cry!* The leaflet boasted: 'We will guarantee the much-loved sore head tomorrow morning, but who cares – you will probably suffer more this afternoon!'

During the match, an ugly scene developed in the press area when the freelance reporter covering the game for the *Daily Mirror*, Lindsay Sutton, was accosted by fans. 'We'll get you,

you're dead,' shouted one fan. A group of about 20 supporters laid siege to the press room at half-time and four people were ejected from the ground. Sutton, who did not write the original piece, was given a police escort from the ground.

Sunday, 13 December 1998
Masked thieves carrying baseball bats tied up staff at City's Platt Lane training complex and made off with 'a large amount of cash'.

Monday, 14 December 1998
The sports editor of the *Daily Mirror* took the unusual step of including an editorial in the paper defending its right to contrast City with United. 'The fact that a club of City's size and history is struggling is worth talking about,' he wrote.

City supporters were not appeased. Matches in the Auto Windscreen Shield habitually drew extremely low crowds and they were upset that the *Mirror*'s reports made no reference to City's renowned high league attendances. 'If they want to criticise the board or even the team at the moment I can understand it, but not the supporters,' said David Bernstein.

Tuesday, 15 December 1998
Manchester City 1 Darlington 0 (FA Cup Second Round Replay)
Another low crowd, just 8,595, saw an extra-time winner from Michael Brown. Both teams had been reduced to 10 men when Danny Tiatto and Marco Gabbiadini were involved in a scuffle. Darlington's manager, Dave Hodgson, was also dismissed and ordered to leave the dug-out area. 'I've got a right to get upset when a player nuts one of my men,' he complained.

Friday, 18 December 1998
A group of fans recorded their own City song in a bid to 'lift the doom and gloom from Maine Road.' 'Going Back' ('City 'til I Die') included the refrain: 'Blue blood flowing from my heart, waiting for a beginning and a brand-new start . . .'

David Bernstein issued one of a series of rallying calls via the *Manchester Evening News* under the headline of 'We Will

Succeed.' 'Ultimately I am totally aware of the need to win matches and get promoted,' was his closing address.

Club chaplain, Tony Porter, chipped in with his own manifesto for success. 'The thing I pray for above all at City is stability. If I'd had seven bishops in two years we'd be up the pole. I long for City to get away from this quick-fix idea,' he said.

CANDID TUEART MEANS BUSINESS
(*The Times*, Saturday, 19 December 1998)

The tea lady got the message. So did the photographer and the giddy supporter reckless enough to laugh out of turn. Dennis Tueart does not suffer fools. Not one bit.

Firstly, the indiscreet fan. Tueart had just given one of his typically direct responses while on the panel at a supporters' club meeting. Someone sniggered. 'What are you laughing for? he snapped, his eyes ice-cold and piercing. 'Have I said something funny?' 'No,' came the response. 'Well don't laugh then.'

Our photographer had asked Tueart to pose in front of City's trophy cabinet. He liked the light reflecting off the glass. 'You're not going to take the piss about it being empty are you?' asked Tueart. He was also reluctant about being pictured near the bust of Joe Mercer. 'We've had enough of all that past-glory stuff,' he grumbled. The tea lady arrived. She had been over-generous with the milk. Tueart pointed to his cup. 'I can't drink that, love.' Polite, but firm. Within seconds, another was placed before him. Thanks, love.

It has been a bad couple of weeks in the life of Manchester City. Their form in the league has remained disappointing: they recorded an all-time low home attendance against Mansfield Town in the Auto Windscreen Shield; and a replay and extra-time were required to see off Darlington in the FA Cup. 'We've had a few upper-cuts lately,' he says. 'You obviously feel frustrated by it, but you've got to play the percentages game. We try and do the right things at the right time and put in the commitment. If we do that, on the field and off it, we'll give ourselves the best possible chance of succeeding.'

Tueart played 259 games for City in two separate spells in the 1970s and early 1980s. He is best remembered for the stunning overhead kick which gave City victory in the 1976 League Cup final against Newcastle United, his home-town club. When he left City for the first time, in 1977, he joined New York Cosmos, to play alongside the likes of Franz Beckenbauer and Carlos Alberto. Off the field, the company he kept was also stately. 'You were more likely to find me in the sponsors' lounge after the game, than the players. I was very interested in the corporate side of the game, the way sport dovetailed into business.'

Back in the UK, he worked for a company specialising in launching products, usually against a sports backdrop. He would hire suites at football grounds to stage conferences, and he rightly saw football clubs as a natural focus for media interest. In 1988 he bought out a partner and launched Premier Events. He also has business interests in a travel agency and a property company. Clearly, he is equally at ease in a suit as he was a football kit.

His father was a fitter in the shipyards of the north-east and Tueart has the rugged edge of a working-class boy made good. He has been quick to learn, shrewd and single-minded. He tells a story of a conversation he had with a fellow apprentice-professional while he was with Sunderland in the late 1960s. Tueart asked him whether he would go easy on a challenge if the ball fell between them. It took some time before his friend responded. 'I wouldn't even have had to think about it . . .' said Tueart.

His vocabulary is peppered with business-speak. He rarely says 'me' or 'I', but talks of 'Dennis Tueart', what is good for Dennis Tueart, what Dennis Tueart believes. He has a brusque charisma, one could imagine him at a business seminar, drawing out the unbelievers, inspiring the indifferent. He is at the point where evangelism meets consumerism and pleased to be there.

He joined the board at City last December. His company had held an executive box at Maine Road and he maintained a keen interest in the club's fortunes. He was asked to provide expertise in his field of corporate hospitality and also to form a link between Joe Royle – with whom he played at City – and the board. 'I am not here through ego,' he says. 'I've come to City because I want to be part of a good spirit and an on-going development of the club. We've had a lot to sort out behind the scenes, but we are building foundations that will serve us well. I can understand that the fans are getting frustrated and edgy, but we are doing everything we can to progress.'

Noticeably, he is the same weight as he was as a player, though he is now 49 years old. He works out in the gym every day. His mobile phone rings, so does another phone in the room. He is quick to his feet, energetic and nimble. He seems like a man heading some place and others will gladly travel with him. This busy-busy aura is infectious, many will want to please him, to secure his approval.

Before the interview he had twice asked, 'What's your angle?' It is hard not to feel sorry for the off-field personnel at City and, of course, the supporters. They are the epitome of dedication and enterprise, yet the team on the pitch continue to play like 11 young men who met for the first time an hour before kick-off. The few spoil it for the many and a certain malcontent is inevitable. 'We've been knocked from pillar to post lately,' Tueart laments.

Some gossip-mongers have implied that Tueart is a potential club chairman, a natural leader. They suggest that after the tenure of the equable David Bernstein, City might require a more bullish approach, fronted by someone who has spent foggy mornings on training pitches and long evenings in the oak-panelled boardrooms of multi-national plcs. Tueart refutes the claim and laughs for the first time. Take that as you will.

● I had seen Tueart at close-quarters several times before actually meeting him. On the various supporters' panels, he emitted a forceful aura. City supporters were habitually rever-ential towards him and he appeared comfortable with this deference.

His fussiness about having his photograph taken was comical; he was convinced we were laying a trap for him. He was supposedly the club's expert on PR, yet his opening gambit was a major PR faux pas. He was immediately confront-ational and his ramblings about a possible set-up bordered on the neurotic. It suggested a vulnerability that would have hitherto remained hidden.

He commented on my clothes soon after we met. He said he had expected that I would dress more formally, to have worn a suit even. No one had said this to me before during my 15 years as a journalist. I asked him about his grown-up children and he was most proud that they had each secured a good education.

Close up, one-on-one, he is not particularly spiky or intimidating. He is trim, vigilant, sharp of movement and mind. He is also quite likeable, with a ready smile and laugh. He is best when recalling his playing days; the stories are rich and engaging, he tells them with a boyish enthusiasm. He becomes more direct and punctilious when he talks of his interest in corporate affairs. The child in him disappears. He seems a man who has read too many business self-help books, taken on capitalism with the zeal of a religious convert. He has learned the jargon, seen its rewards, but has no interest in that which is not fervent and linear – the subtleties, the softer edges, the emotional side.

Later in the season, I met one of his former team-mates. He asked me what I thought of Tueart. I told him and he smiled and said something along the lines of, 'He fooled you then . . .' I think he was implying that Tueart had adopted the posture of the assertive, abrasive businessman. It suited him, validated him in the circles in which he mixed. The brashness covered the tracks that lay to his resolutely working-class background. Underneath, though, he was a sympathetic character, less strident and sure of himself than he would like to appear.

When we parted after the interview, Tueart looked con-tinually over my shoulder. It was nightfall, it might have been a trick of the light, but I suspected he was trying to catch sight of my car, making an assessment.

Saturday, 19 December 1998
York City 2 Manchester City 1

City's season reached its nadir at Bootham Crescent on a bitterly cold afternoon. They dominated the match but lost to a goal by 18-year-old débutant Andrew Dawson four minutes before the end.

Gordon Connelly had given York an early lead before Craig Russell equalised. Veteran goalkeeper Bobby Mimms, who had been on loan to City a decade earlier, made a series of excellent saves.

Traditionally, league tables were said not to really count until mid-December. City were now twelfth, 15 points adrift of the pace-setters Fulham and Walsall. While they had briefly been in fourteenth position after the away draw at Notts County in August, with the season now half-completed, the club was indubitably at the lowest point in its history.

Sunday, 20 December 1998

Former City player Alan Kernaghan, now playing for St Johnstone in Scotland, was highly critical of the club in an interview with a Scottish newspaper. 'Four years of my prime were completely wasted at City,' he said. 'I still follow their results though, with a snigger.'

Monday, 21 December 1998

Richard Edghill, City's longest-serving player, was granted a new four-year contract. He had made his début back in September 1993 in a 1–0 defeat at Wimbledon.

In the various City fanzines he had received stinging criticism for his inconsistent form. 'I suppose the fans have got to pick on someone but I am not going to start sulking about it. I can take the abuse. My shoulders are big enough,' he said.

Meanwhile, Ray Kelly was released and returned to his native Ireland after five years at City. The 21-year-old had played just 45 minutes of first-team football in a 1–0 defeat at Huddersfield Town in 1997. 'I think Ray might have been the biggest victim of the stockpiling of players at City in recent years,' said Joe Royle.

Tuesday, 22 December 1998

Joe Royle, sensing the supporters' anger and frustration, made an impassioned plea. 'I am disappointed with our current position – there's no point in pretending otherwise,' said Royle. 'I know some supporters are starting to lose their faith, but I still believe this side will make a charge in the second half of the season. I honestly believe the team has improved since I arrived. I promise we will get things right.'

Supporter Andrew Waldon crystallised the sentiments of many City fans when he wrote an open letter to his son Daniel in *City 'til I Cry!*: 'I apologise for picking City as my team. I apologise for buying my season ticket. I apologise for buying all the merchandise. I apologise for supporting City through thick and thin (yes, Daniel and I were part of the 3,007 against Mansfield) . . . I am sorry Daniel!'

TRAPPED BY THE PICTURES OF THE PAST
(*The Times*, Saturday, 26 December 1998)

The ball fell between George Best and a defender. The United winger stuck out a leg randomly. It was one of his less graceful contributions to a game of football and the ball ricocheted into the crowd. The incident, meaningless in itself, was forgotten within seconds by everyone except two people in the ground. Dennis and Kevin Cummins, dad and lad, red and blue, would remember the moment for the rest of their lives. It left one with broken glasses, the other unable to suppress his joy.

'It was one of those big European Cup nights at Old Trafford in the '60s,' explains Kevin Cummins. 'When Best went in for this tackle the ball flew into my dad's face and broke his glasses. I remember thinking straight away, "Good, we can go home now." My dad was a big United fan and he took me a few times but it always left me cold.'

Cummins had already fallen in love with Manchester's other team. 'Straight away there was something magical about City. Maine Road always had a unique atmosphere. It would be pissing down, and we'd see these ghostly figures moving about the pitch. It was always foggy in Manchester in the '60s. I remember, at my first ever game, Bobby Kennedy did an overhead kick in the middle of the pitch, for no reason.'

If Cummins has an eye for the unusual or the extravagant, it serves him well in his profession as one of the UK's leading rock photographers. Since rising to eminence during the punk era, he has photographed a wealth of stars, from David Bowie to The Rolling Stones, The Sex Pistols to Oasis. His work has been heavily profiled in the *New Musical Express*, where he has contributed scores of cover shots.

In recent years his photographs of Oasis have become indelible rock images. 'I photographed them quite early on in their career. Their record label just said to me, "They're City fans from Manchester, you're bound to like them."' His first session with them was aborted when the band was refused entry into Holland after fighting broke out on the ferry carrying them across the North Sea. 'I had flown out the day before and was with Noel Gallagher waiting for the others. There'd been a punch-up or something with some Chelsea fans and they were sent straight back to England.'

Subsequent sessions were given a uniquely City theme. In London they were photographed in Flitcroft Street (in tribute to the former City player, Garry Flitcroft), while Maine Road was used as a backdrop when the Gallagher brothers donned their City shirts with the aptly named club sponsors, Brother, stamped across them. Unfortunately, the pictures were rejected as potential front cover shots by the *New Musical Express*. 'The editor told me that the paper was for winners, not losers.' Cummins's eyes narrow and his lips become pursed as he imparts this information.

Football has become showbiz in shin pads and Cummins has seen this at uncomfortably close quarters ('I've heard that Mick Jagger is trying to pass himself off as a Chelsea fan now,' he sighs), but to him it is a heartfelt, heartbreaking experience, nothing fey or whimsical. He was the only City supporter in an all-boys, all-United, Catholic school in Salford. His loyalty stretched to watching City reserves; he danced on the pitch at St James's Park, Newcastle, when City won the League

Championship on 11 May 1968 – he recalls the date as effortlessly as he might his own birthday.

Football, and City in particular, has given him, at different times, a sense of kinship, pride, joy, loyalty, defiance and, more recently, acute disappointment and unhappiness. 'Even when we win, watching City still spoils my weekend. There's no real joy in beating teams in this division. We should win every game. I have no pleasure in watching City play at all. It is like seeing an aged relative riddled with cancer, you go out of a sense of duty.' An overstatement, surely? 'My mother died of cancer 18 months ago, and coming up to see City does feel very similar. City have been part of my life for such a long time.'

He is a shareholder and attended the club's recent annual meeting where, among others, he was able to express his concern. 'I am upset and angry about what has happened to this club. Everyone is transient in football except the supporters. All these platitudes we are hearing now will mean nothing if we don't get promotion. The crowd will be halved next season if we're still in this league. People can't stand the heartbreak any longer.'

Cummins does not rate Joe Royle, with whom he had a bizarre encounter a few years ago. They met in a corridor at Goodison Park while Royle was still manager of Everton. Cummins, weighed down with camera equipment, was to take his picture for an interview piece in a football magazine. Royle misunderstood and thought he had breached the club's security to snatch a photo of their new signing, Andrei Kanchelskis. 'He just went for me and got me in a headlock shouting and swearing,' says Cummins. Fortunately, Royle was told quickly of his mistake and was deeply apologetic.

'Royle is not the man to lead us to the Premiership – and this isn't because I've still got a grudge against him. I don't think his track record is particularly good. It's too much a case of jobs for the boys. It's some bloke with a cigar saying, "Now, who shall I get now, my old mate Alan Ball, or my old mate Joe Royle?"'

Cummins attends matches with his 12-year-old daughter, Ella, who is equally fanatical about City. She first became interested in football during the 1994 World Cup while they were on holiday in Italy. They watched the final between Italy and Brazil in a bar. Before Roberto Baggio's infamous penalty miss, she burst out crying, sensing what was to happen. 'Everyone was asking me whether we were Italian, and I had to tell them we weren't.' Like her dad, she simply had the passion to care, too much. 'She was introduced to football by despair,' he says, not needing to add that this was a natural precursor to a lifetime supporting City.

City take on Wrexham today and Stoke City at Maine Road on Monday. Cummins will embark on two 400-mile round trips from his home in south London. While a game against Stoke is attractive enough, he is affronted by the air of normality that awaits him at Maine Road for other games. 'I don't want to buy the match programme and read articles like 'Welcome to Gillingham'. I don't care who plays for Gillingham, we shouldn't be playing them. The programme should be edged in black.'

Saturday, 26 December 1998
Wrexham 0 Manchester City 1

City won for the first time in six matches thanks to an impressive display by Nicky Weaver at a windswept Racecourse Ground. Gerard Wiekens's headed goal secured the win and lifted them to seventh in the table.

Monday, 28 December 1998
Manchester City 2 Stoke City 1

A stirring performance ignited the 31,000 crowd who willed City to victory after they had fallen behind to a goal by Larus Sigurdsson. Paul Dickov scored City's first goal at Maine Road for almost two months and Gareth Taylor notched a late winner. 'You could feel the confidence flowing through the side once I had scored,' said Dickov, who had just celebrated the birth of a son, Sam.

Two successive league wins ended a wretched year on a relatively upbeat note.

Wednesday, 30 December 1998

Five young City players were nominated by Jim Cassell as potential future stars – Shaun Wright-Phillips, the son of West Ham United striker Ian Wright; Leon Mike; David Laycock; Steven Hodgson; and Shaun Holmes.

Six

The Return of the Native

TWIN TRIUMPH OFFERS GLIMMER OF HOPE
(*The Times*, Saturday, 2 January 1999)

The phone line was making and breaking. We could hear an intermittent blast of agitated chatter. Out there, on this cold, damp afternoon a group of Manchester City supporters were driving away from York. Their team had lost, the day was in ruins, so they rang their local radio station's phone-in. 'I don't know what more there is to say,' said the one with the mobile phone. There was a short silence, and then swearing and shouting, the sound of frustration foaming white-hot. York, beautiful city, great architecture. York 2, Manchester City 1. York, a long way from home.

Manchester City's defeat at York was just two weeks ago. It feels like a life time away. Two consecutive wins over Christmas have suddenly, wonderfully, transformed Maine Road. A fortuitous win at Wrexham was followed by a thrilling 2–1 victory against promotion favourites Stoke City.

'We've turned the corner, now. Just watch us go,' was the on-air message from the supporters at tea-time on Boxing Day. They were still buoyant, still drunk on the elixir of victory. During the second half against Stoke, Maine Road was no longer the mausoleum of moans and groans, but the epicentre of joy. They cheered relentlessly, believed in their team, and their generosity of spirit encouraged the players to hold the ball, enjoy its company, take on their opponents, shoot for goal – the simple tenets of a game of football that players renounce when they are bereft of confidence.

The relationship between City and their supporters has been

strained in the past few months. Where the fans expected a certain amount of style and flair, especially in the relatively impoverished surroundings of their division, the team has barely looked cohesive or, more importantly, particularly impassioned. Willie Donachie said a few weeks ago that no matter how disappointed the fans were, they should know that the players feel the pain of each defeat 'ten times as much'. Donachie, an ex-player and a marvellous club man, really has no right to quantify the hurt supporters feel. It is between them and their hearts.

In his programme notes for the Stoke game, Joe Royle complained of a section of support which was 'very vociferous and very negative'. There has undeniably been an air of disgruntled edginess about Maine Road for the past few seasons. The supporters are like the good child gone bad. They were loyal (through all those relegations), obedient (they bought the tickets when asked) and attentive (they have never diverted their eyes elsewhere, like Old Trafford, for example), but their efforts have gone without reward. So, 20 years later, a good number have grown up petulant, reckless, faithless and frustrated.

Inevitably, there has been a clamour for scapegoats. Various players have found the arrival of the ball at their feet accompanied by a cacophony of boos. Lee Bradbury became Lee Bad-Buy when he struggled to find form, while Richard Edghill, Tony Vaughan and Shaun Goater are currently under pressure to impress. The players should not fret too excessively, for the City faithful are famously forgiving. The deal is simple enough – they must wear the laser blue shirt with the same degree of pride as the fans would if given the chance themselves.

Until recently, Royle and David Bernstein have largely escaped criticism. Supporters have honoured what was effec-tively an agreement to remain patient while both implemented their changes. Royle has now been in tenure for ten months and Bernstein for nine. In the life of a football club, it is no time at all. During this period of transition, supporters steadied themselves for a level of inconsistency, but did not expect home defeats against the likes of Preston, Reading and Mansfield Town. So, throughout December in particular, they have started to question whether these are the men to restore City to greatness, or Division One of the Nationwide League at the very least.

The two Christmas victories have thrust City back into the promotion frame (most likely via the play-offs, to which a cluster of about 10 other clubs also have a claim), but they should not falsify what has been a woeful campaign. They were expected to storm through the division, treating the cloggers and battlers with contempt, but they have won just 9 of their 24 games and, in seventh place, they find themselves trailing the likes of Bournemouth and Gillingham.

All the same, they close the year on a rare note of optimism, and should be allowed, at last, to enjoy the satisfaction of a job well done. The current form might finally represent the 'turning of a corner' and not another harrowing trip around an Esher drawing, where 'corners' propagate themselves or lead to nowhere in particular. More goals and more wins will transform the passion within Maine Road into something positive and handsome, no longer negative and ugly.

Saturday, 2 January 1999
Wimbledon 1 Manchester City 0 (FA Cup Third Round)
City, FA Cup finalists on eight occasions and winners on four, had their stuttering cup run ended by Wimbledon in an ill-tempered match.

Jason Euell was sent off for two bookable offences. City's Andy Morrison and Wimbledon's Carl Cort were dismissed after a scuffle. 'The double sending-off was absolutely laughable. There was nothing in it,' said Joe Kinnear, the Wimbledon manager. It was City's seventh sending-off of the season.

Morrison, after watching a re-run of the incident on video, said: 'It's embarrassing, like watching a couple of kids in the playground.'

Carl Cort scored the only goal of the game which was watched by 6,312 City supporters among the crowd of 11,226.

Tuesday, 5 January 1999
Joe Royle gave further reassurance of his confidence in the team. 'Despite the cynics, the knockers and the strange beasts

who find themselves on radio phone-ins, promotion is still a very realistic target for us,' he snapped.

Wednesday, 6 January 1999

City revealed that they hoped to sign Manchester United winger Terry Cooke for a three-month loan period once he had completed a similar stint at Wrexham.

Cooke, 21, who had been with United since the age of 13, was resurrecting his career after a serious knee injury. He had impressed Joe Royle during City's recent trip to the Racecourse Ground.

NOBILITY REIGNS IN THE COURT OF KING COLIN
(*The Times*, Saturday, 9 January 1999)

Snorkel-jacket pockets were stuffed full of them, or else they were a blur in someone's hand as complex swaps were negotiated. Thin strips of pink chewing gum accompanied the cards and this gave them a fruity aroma, the sweet smell of youth.

Football cards were a schoolyard currency of their own. In Manchester, a City or United player was worth a bag of conkers; unless they were George Best or Colin Bell, then you were talking a Subbuteo team, three *Scorcher* annuals *and* a bag of conkers.

Best and Bell were the antithesis of each other. Best was young, gifted and reckless, Bell was young and gifted. Their personalities were disparate but, for different reasons, they personified a certain cool. On the field, Bell was both flamboyant and industrious, a natural athlete who was graceful on the ball, tenacious without it. Away from the pitch, he had a rare humility, a quiet dignity that is almost extinct in the modern game.

During his 13 years as a player at Maine Road, he helped win the First and Second Division Championships, the European Cup-Winners Cup, the FA Cup and two Football League Cups. He also collected 48 England caps after making his international début as a 22-year-old. He played his last game for City 20 years ago, yet the mention of his name still draws forth heartfelt eulogies from supporters. He reminds them, of course, of a classic era in the club's history, but he epitomises much more. He is without artifice, true to himself, devoid of ego and pretension. They call him King Colin in the blue parts of Manchester.

I usually travel light – a notebook and a pen – but, as I knock at the door of Bell's house, I have a bag over my shoulder containing numerous photos and football cards for him to autograph. Word has got around, and I'm suddenly an emissary for every football fan I have met in the preceding two days. 'Colin Bell? You're going to meet Colin Bell?' Soon, sun-stained and frayed posters from old *Shoot!* magazines are thrust before me: 'You've got to get him to sign this . . .'

The flowing, straw-coloured hair of his playing days has been replaced by a spiky cut that Ian Rush's barber might have supplied. His labrador pounds into the hall and Bell wrestles it into another room. Bell, 52, is still lithe, at just a few pounds over his playing weight. He rarely does interviews, so he converses like he would at a bus stop or on a train, without resorting to formula or overwrought anecdotes.

His father, John Bell, worked as a miner from the age of 12 in their home-town of Hesleden, Durham. Bell's mother, Elizabeth, died soon after he was born and he was brought up by her sister, Ella. He is indistinct about his mother's death. 'She went into hospital to have me, but didn't come out again,' he says.

As a boy, he was happy in his own company, and would spend hours playing football alone. 'I've never really needed close friends, I've always been a loner. I used to go on the Green and play football all day. I'd sometimes throw a tennis ball on to a sloping roof just to practise heading or chesting as it came down. I never walked anywhere, I would always run. I had to be where I was going in the shortest possible time.'

A clutch of clubs, including Arsenal, were interested in signing him but he chose Bury. 'I went there simply because they were the friendliest club. They had made me really welcome. I went for £12 a week, but if anyone else had offered me £50 a week I would still have gone to Bury.'

Bury were managed by Bob Stokoe, whose parents had moved to the town from the north-east to be near their son. 'A few of the players used to go round to their house on Sunday night and play cards with them. Bob's mum would bake a cake and biscuits. It used to be the highlight of the week.' He relates the story without acknowledging how downbeat and anachronistic it sounds.

He joined City in March 1966, when Joe Mercer and Malcolm Allison were building their classic City side. 'It was like a happy family. We couldn't wait to get into training in the morning, the ground was like a magnet. Joe did all the talking for the club and Malcolm did the graft with the players. He was a great motivator. You knew a lot of it was bull, but after he'd spoken to you, you felt you were the best player in the world.' Allison, recognising Bell's extraordinary stamina, nicknamed him Nijinsky after the famous racehorse.

Exceptional performances, especially during the championship-winning season of 1967–68, inevitably brought fame and Bell was uncomfortable with it. 'I hated all of it. They wanted me to make records and all kinds of things. I didn't even like opening school fêtes or signing autographs. I was okay with a ball at my feet, but I don't like microphones.'

His career effectively ended on a misty December evening in 1975 when he was just 29 years old. City were playing Manchester United in a League Cup Fourth-Round tie when Dennis Tueart pushed the ball into Bell's path. 'The ball kept bobbling and I couldn't get it to sit right at my feet. I was aware of a player coming across towards me.' He recalls contemplating – in a split second – several possible options but 'chose the wrong one of three'. He checked his run but was immediately 'clattered below the knee' by United's captain, Martin Buchan.

His knee was bent back the wrong way at great force, tearing ligaments and rupturing blood vessels. City won 4–0, but, according to legend, many of their supporters left the ground in tears, sensing the gravity of the injury. Bell did not play again for two years and among City fans there was a brooding resentment of Buchan. Bell, typically, has remained tactful about the incident. 'I *hope* it was an innocent challenge,' he says. Did Buchan ever contact him afterwards, to inquire about his well-being? He shakes his head. I ask Bell whether he would have done so if he had hurt another player to such a degree. 'If, in my own mind, I knew it was a complete accident I would have done, yes,' he says.

He returned to the side at Christmas 1977, coming on as a substitute at half-time against Newcastle United when the score was 0–0. 'As I waited in the tunnel, I could hear my name being mentioned all around the ground and everyone got to their feet when I appeared. I'm not an emotional person but I had a lump in my throat.' City went on to win 4–0.

Bell played 35 further games, though his knee injury restricted his movement. In the summer of 1979, he formally announced his retirement from the game. 'Malcolm came to me and said he thought it was time I called it a day. He could see that I was befuddling my brain to work around the limited movement I had. I would have gone on for forever and a day trying to get my leg right. But Malcolm was right; I'd given it long enough.'

For a while he worked with City's young players, passing on his vast experience, but he was laid off under Francis Lee's tenure as chairman. He would rather not discuss the issue, he feels the club has had enough bad publicity in recent years. Under David Bernstein's chairmanship, however, he was invited back and is now employed by the club in an 'ambassadorial role'. In practice, he attends supporters' functions and mixes on match days with the club's sponsors.

It is possible to detect a tinge of regret that his role does not run deeper. He still exudes a love and knowledge of the game. City are currently on a purge of their backroom staff, but there is – surely – a limit. Sign here, Mr Bell, nobility will never go out of fashion.

Saturday, 9 January 1999
Blackpool 0 Manchester City 0

A disappointing game saw City's winning run come to an end. The match kicked off at noon on police advice and 9,752 packed into a frost-bound Bloomfield Road, with City fans out-numbering the home supporters.

Their last league meeting at Bloomfield Road had been 28 years earlier in January 1971 when 30,000 watched a thrilling 3–3 draw.

City dropped to ninth in the table, 13 points behind an automatic promotion spot.

Tuesday, 12 January 1999

The FA confirmed that Andy Morrison would be suspended for three games after his dismissal at Wimbledon.

Joe Royle launched a scathing attack on the FA after Wimbledon's Carl Cort, also sent off in the game, had his red card reduced to a yellow. 'I find it incredible that their player gets off when he started the whole thing,' he said. 'It seems that there is one set of rules for Premiership players and another for those from the Nationwide League. It is the unfairness of the situation which really hurts.'

Wednesday, 13 January 1999

Terry Cooke arrived at Maine Road and completed his first training session with his new team-mates. 'He has great pace and is very skilful. He will give us another option in attack,' said Michael Brown, who had roomed with Cooke while they were both on England Under-21s duty.

OPULENT EXTERIOR HIDES GRIM REALITY
(*The Times*, Saturday, 16 January 1999)

Wheelie bins are left in alleyways. Children zip past on BMX bicycles. Grocers put boxes of vegetables and fruit outside their doorways and shoppers, well wrapped against the cold, select the best on offer. The houses are archetypal Manchester – red brick, terraced and arranged in neat rows.

Around the corner is the *City Chippy*, and then the streets – Beveridge, Wansford, Wykeham – stop abruptly. Standing incongruously in this slate-grey landscape is a football ground,

Maine Road, the home of Manchester City, something extra-ordinary among the ordinary.

Football grounds are places of pilgrimage. They are perceived as permanent, largely unchanging against the backdrop of a life that can be uncertain and fickle. Between this game and the next, there might be birth and death, new job or redundancy, marriage or divorce; but these lives, rich or fallow, will be played out against a fortnightly ritual – same place, same time, same faces.

The condition of the ground is irrelevant. Camaraderie and community are present at non-league grounds where broken terracing and a flimsy fence is the sum total. Maine Road, as it happens, is impressive, though wilfully asymmetrical. Perhaps it is apt that its four stands are so dissimilar, for City has been riven by disagreement and ego. When the wind blows and the pigeons huddle beneath them, the four mis-matched structures become symbolic of the men who have squabbled over this famous club – Peter Swales, Francis Lee, etc.

The heart of the club beats within the Main Stand which runs parallel to the road that lends its name to the stadium. There are two reception areas, the one on the first floor flanked by a circular trophy cabinet which, contrary to rumour, is laden with silverware and pennants. A marble bust of Joe Mercer stares out benignly as a steady stream of deliveries are made to the reception desk.

Down the years, there has been much criticism of City's financial extravagance, but there is little evidence of excessive spending on the club's interior. Both the Chairman's Lounge and the Boardroom are small and functional, similar to meeting rooms available for hire at a reasonable hotel. The various executive suites also have the same efficient, colour-coded neatness.

In the Boardroom is a colour photograph of Leighton Gobbett, a young Manchester City fan left broken-hearted after their relegation to Division Two of the Nationwide League. It is there as a reminder of the depth of feeling held for the club by its supporters.

The players and officials entrance is somewhat hidden away,

through a broom cupboard of a room and down a flight of stairs. Here, at the very core of the football club, there is again no concession to opulence. If supporters imagine their heroes change and shower in oak-panelled dressing-rooms with gilded taps, they would be mightily surprised. It is hearteningly basic – a small square room, a treatment table, a lay-out of a football pitch attached to the wall, a blackboard. Beyond is another room where there is a sauna in a ramshackle hut, three showers that are not screened from the rest of the room, an ordinary-sized bath and, finally, a huge communal bath covered in ceramic tiles. It feels like a place unchanged in the past 30 years, the bath plugs rusted dirty orange, the tiles fractured on the walls.

The away dressing-room is similar and the match officials' merely a scaled-down version of them both. Outside the officials' room is a bell-push which the referee presses when he is ready for the teams to assemble. The tunnel out to the pitch is about 30 metres long, an eerie concrete cave flushed by strip-lighting. Outside of match days it is closed off by two sets of metal gates and has a distinctly primitive feel.

Out on the pitch, the stands, by their sheer size, conspire to reinforce a sense of smallness on the individual. It is difficult not to be overwhelmed, drowned in the magnitude. A walk in an empty cathedral, or alongside a docked cruise-liner has the same effect of drawing air from the body, leaving it still and stranded.

The tallest stand is the Kippax, traditionally the home of City's most partisan and vociferous supporters. It was flattened in the close season of 1994 and a new, all-seater stand built in its place. Where it was once able to house 35,000 supporters when the ground was first built in 1923, and 18,300 when the old stand was demolished, its new capacity is 9,882.

The top tier would not be the ideal place to hold a convention of vertigo sufferers. The drop to the pitch is incredibly steep, but, if the game fails to absorb the visitor, the views across Manchester and beyond are magnificent. On a clear day, it is possible to see the Welsh hills while, in the foreground, Old Trafford is visible at just three miles away. 'You'll easily spot it, it's that thing that looks like a toast rack,' says a helpful member of the ground staff.

Maine Road has been the home of Manchester City for more than 70 years, but the club may soon be packing away the memorabilia and moving a few miles to the east of the city to a new purpose-built stadium. Since the club's formation, it has had six grounds and, though many supporters have a nostalgic affection for Maine Road, they are keen to put behind them the recent disastrous times. They want to re-invent the club, make it feel new and fresh again. They know that wherever they may play, it is they – the fans – that imbue it with a sense of the sacred.

● It would have been injudicious to say so at the time, but I thought the dressing-rooms were distinctly shabby. The washing area was open-plan, certainly no place for the bashful. None of the fittings seemed to match, as if they had been bought hurriedly in a closing-down sale.

There were few concessions to luxury. The area immediately beyond the dressing-rooms was pannelled in thin strips of hardboard. It felt like the waiting room in a taxi rank. Beyond this stretched the tunnel, a long, dark, concrete tube. Obviously, no one would want to see hanging baskets and Persian carpets in there, but this was like something out of *Rollerball.*

The proposed move to a new stadium obviously made it pointless to renovate the interior of Maine Road. All the same, these conditions had prevailed for many years. It was peculiar that the place set aside especially for the players – surely the most important sector of a club's community – had been left to fall into a state of dilapidation. No expense had been spared bringing footballers to Maine Road, and yet, while they undertook their job of work, they were housed in facilities barely a notch above those used by pub teams on local recreation grounds. Maybe it did fuel their hunger, hone their primal instinct, or perhaps it made them feel that they weren't particularly special in the general scheme of things.

Saturday, 16 January 1999
Manchester City 3 Fulham 0

Joe Royle promised that City would take a more direct route and their hurly-burly approach secured them a creditable win against league-leaders, Fulham. 'That's the best we have played all season. We were excellent and did not have a weakness,' said Royle.

First-half goals from Shaun Goater and Gareth Taylor were complemented by a third from Kevin Horlock who scored directly from a free-kick.

Terry Cooke enjoyed his first appearance in a City shirt, playing in front of 30,251 fans. 'It was totally different from the atmosphere at Old Trafford. The fans there just expect to win and sit back to enjoy the game. Here, the ground is full of fanatics and they can make such a difference,' he said.

The win lifted City to within two points of a promotion play-off spot.

Wednesday, 18 January 1999

Australians Danny Allsopp and Danny Tiatto were the star turns at the Junior Blues' annual pantomime. More than 500 attended Humpty Dumpty and representing Christmas-past were ex-City players Paul Power, Alex Williams and Roy Clarke.

ROYLE BEGINS TO PLAN LONG RETURN JOURNEY
(*The Times*, Saturday, 23 January 1999)

Alan Ball's already-shrill voice went a notch higher, his hair a shade more red. Frank Clark's skin turned pinky and he reportedly gave up strumming his beloved guitar. Steve Coppell, after a mere six matches, just blurted it out: 'Manchester City are making me ill.'

Conspicuously, Joe Royle has only lightly furnished his office but, by City's standards, he is practically a stalwart after nearly 11 months in the job. Time, perhaps, to put up a few pictures, invest in a coat-stand even, though best wait a little longer before depositing family photographs around the edge of the desk.

Back in 1989, a newspaper carried a cartoon drawing of this infamous office. A player poked his head around the door and exclaimed: 'I hear they've fitted an ejector seat in here.' Since then, City have had eight managers and numerous caretaker–managers. Clearly, the seat is well-oiled and efficient.

Royle, just three months short of his 50th birthday, has been involved in the professional game since signing for Everton on £7 a week at the age of 14. He is financially secure, respected within the game, and yet after being offered 14 other jobs, he elected to return to Maine Road where he had spent three seasons as a player in the 1970s. 'I always felt that City as a club had great warmth. I enjoyed my time here as a player and it had a feeling of familiarity for me.'

He has a surprisingly gentle handshake and eschews the routine bone-crunching wrench of most of his football contemporaries. He is a big man, as wide as a wardrobe, but with soft blue eyes. The smile is boyish. Sometimes he smiles for no particular reason. Perhaps he's thought of his next one-liner, for he excels in them. The twinkle in his eye will have got him out of a few scrapes.

Despite his physique, he was not a particularly aggressive footballer. When he first played for Everton, their manager, Harry Catterick, told the other players to kick him in training, to rouse his temper. He was sent off only once in nearly 500 games for hitting the Aston Villa centre-half, Allan Evans. 'It was retribution. He had been kicking me all afternoon. I didn't punch him, it was more of a forearm smash really, but I'm not proud of it.'

He was an only child, born to Joe and Irene Royle, from Norris Green, Liverpool. They lived with Royle's grandparents in a two-bedroom terrace house, and he often slept in the same room as his parents, on a camp-bed at the foot of their bed. 'I'd say there wasn't enough room to swing a cat, but it was such a small space I don't think you could fit a cat in there to swing in the first place!' His father was a steam engineer by day and a club pianist by night. 'In Liverpool, my dad is better known than me. As a musician, he's backed a lot of people who are now famous. Whenever I see Ken Dodd, he always asks me how my dad is.' Joe Royle Sr was born in Salford and supported Manchester United; so, as a boy, Royle had divided loyalties between United and Everton.

Although he excelled at football, he also represented his home city at swimming and high-jumping and played cricket to a good standard. He was approached by both his favourite clubs, but chose Everton rather than United. He spent eight years at Everton before joining City in 1974 and later moving to Bristol City and Norwich City.

As a manager he transformed Oldham Athletic into a superlative passing team, reaching the League Cup final and the semi-final of the FA Cup in 1990 and winning promotion to the top division in 1992. With a certain inevitability, he returned to Goodison Park as manager but after a run of poor results was sacked two years ago.

He replaced Frank Clark at City last February but was unable to avoid relegation to Division Two, with the team winning just two games from the last eight of the season. He inherited a huge squad of 53 professionals of whom only Georgi Kinkladze was really known outside Manchester. 'I thought the atmosphere around the place was too easy-going. Some of the players had an unprofessional attitude,' he says.

The club was heavily in debt – and still is – but Royle practically halved the wage bill by selling or releasing nearly 30 players. The sale of Kinkladze to Ajax upset many supporters for he had lit up many otherwise wretched Saturday afternoons with his quicksilver skills. 'Gio is blessed with sublime ability but it became a case of when we won it was all down to him, but when we lost it was everyone else's fault,' he says. Aside from any possible divisive effect on team spirit he might have had, the £5 million raised from Kinkladze's transfer was essential for the club's well-being.

Of the City team selected by Royle for his first game as manager, only three were included in the team that beat Fulham 3–0 last Saturday. 'We have tried to be fair and give everyone a chance but we have also had to make some tough decisions. I have asked my members of staff their opinions, but there has been no great dissension on who we should keep and let go.'

City have lost just six league games this season and though they feature in the promotion race, many supporters are disappointed. There has been little flair or artistry, and for a good while there was a shortage of endeavour and a willingness to trade tackles with the likes of Lincoln City and Bristol Rovers. 'It takes time to build a team,' says Royle. 'We are not going to turn round a tail-spin that has been in place for the last 23 years [their last trophy was the League Cup in 1976] in just 10 minutes. Alex Ferguson took four years to get it right at United, and that was with a great deal of money to spend and a team he inherited that already contained several inter-nationals.'

When Royle joined City as a player at Christmas 1974 he scored just one goal in his first 16 games. Many fans grumbled that their club had signed a centre-forward who couldn't score. The following season he scored in every round of their League Cup run except in the final against Newcastle United. He was also an integral member of the team that finished runners-up to the league champions Liverpool in the 1976–77 season. In short, he came good, even if it took some time.

● Royle was good company, attentive and witty. Unfortunately, he has been interviewed too many times and is over-familiar with the procedure. He is articulate and does not avoid questions, but returns constantly to formula. As he spoke, it felt like I was hearing a recording of an interview he had already given to GMR (Greater Manchester Radio) or Radio Five Live. I tried to make it flow like a normal conversation, but it always felt like a facsimile of a conversation. Like many football people, he was pre-occupied with delivering the quip, and sometimes forgot to listen or cut short his own train of thought to accommodate a one-liner.

At the end of the interview, he talked of his dislike of radio phone-ins and fanzines. He saw them as mediums for a small sector of the club's support to snipe. I argued that fanzines had been a powerful force of expression for the supporter. He was dismissive. I had the impression that he held an antipathy for the literate football fan, that they had nothing better to do than ponder the club's well-being and were too ready to criticise. He said he was most concerned about the feelings of the 'silent majority' who supported the club but kept their feelings largely to themselves, eschewing the blood-letting of the more ostentatious fans.

In the midst of City's poor run, many had begun to grow uneasy about Royle's position. They had shown him more patience than any manager in the club's history, yet they felt they were being mocked by the team's erratic form. Royle had made great play of the necessity to reduce the playing squad, but the performances undermined his claim that he had retained the best players. Nick Fenton and Gary Mason, the protégés of whom he had made, for him, substantial claims (and rewarded with long contracts), faded quickly. In fact, they made just one full appearance each after the turn of the year. Michael Brown, City's play-maker, was made to wait until half the season had elapsed before commanding a first-team place. Additionally, senior strikers Shaun Goater, Paul Dickov and Gareth Taylor had not distinguished themselves. They gave exemplary commitment, but they lacked the ability to hold the ball or turn and run for goal.

Obviously, Royle's judgement on players was more closely examined while the team struggled. In his defence, he could point to the successful signings of Andy Morrison and Terry Cooke. And for all City's failings, they did, at least, remain within sight of a promotion play-off place throughout the season.

Taking a broader view, Royle had proved himself as a manager of some calibre. His record at Oldham Athletic had been remarkable. He moulded a squad of ordinary players into a crafted, passing team, regularly beating sides with players of greater individual skill. His failure at Everton had significantly reduced his cache, but his time there coincided with board-room instability.

Royle was a man able to take decisive action and possessed a charisma that imbued teams with industry and doggedness.

David Bernstein said of him: 'His qualities were just what we needed. He adds experience, calmness and humour and brings resilience and pride to the side.' Bernstein had chosen his words carefully.

While City were in crisis – albeit a crisis under control – Royle resorted, as managers invariably did, to belligerence. Much of it, he claimed, was down to appalling luck, dreadful refereeing or their opponents playing above themselves. His prediction that City would embark upon a winning run was viewed as platitude. Eventually, he was proved right and they did hit upon this run.

Saturday, 23 January 1999
Walsall 1 Manchester City 1

A record crowd for the Bescot Stadium of 9,517 saw City extend their unbeaten run to five games. Andy Watson scored for Walsall before Jamie Pollock hit his first goal of the season. 'It's a disgrace that I've waited this long to get a goal but thank God it finally came,' said Pollock.

It was the first occasion when Royle had named an unchanged team for two consecutive matches.

Monday, 25 January 1999

Tony Vaughan, City's defender, postponed his wedding by a few weeks when he realised the original date in May could clash with City's involvement in the promotion play-offs.

City supporter Brian Channon gave his new-born son an immediate affiliation with the club, naming him Jack James Kippax Channon.

Friday, 29 January 1999
Stoke City 0 Manchester City 1

Gerard Wiekens secured City's first double of the season with a twentieth-minute goal which took them to the fringes of the play-off zone in eighth place.

Stoke's skipper, Phil Robinson, was sent off after a two-footed lunge at Michael Brown who was fortunate to escape injury.

VETERAN STILL ENJOYS SOMETHING IN THE CITY
(*The Times*, Saturday, 30 January 1999)

Rain lashes down on to the roof of the Main Stand. A slow rumble develops and the empty theatre becomes a huge echo chamber. Sidney Rose takes his seat in the directors' box. He is alone, but in the pitter-patter discord he will hear snippets of voices long gone.

Rose, aged 81, is, by Manchester City's standards, a war veteran. Now the club's life-president, he has survived where many others have fallen. Like a spectre in a smart club blazer, he has ghosted through the uprisings, the coups and the routine blood-letting of the club's infamous boardroom. He has given almost 60 years service to the sky blue cause. 'He's a different class,' says Chris Muir, a former City director. Muir should know, for he is one of the fallen. In fact, he once tried to oust Rose. 'He is a charmer, a brilliant schemer. He sees where the land lies and crawls towards it.'

He is a young 81; still dapper, still playing tennis, still charming. I'm told he will flatter me within seconds of first meeting. He does not disappoint, the silken tongue remains: 'I liked a phrase you used in an article the other week . . .' He has wonderfully plump vowels and the gentle but authoritative tone of the patrician.

At a reunion dinner of the 1967–68 League Championship-winning team, Joe Mercer prefaced his speech with the inquiry: 'Does Sidney Rose still pick the team around here?' The diners guffawed and turned to Rose. Was he upset to be portrayed as meddlesome or interfering? He was smiling broadly, obviously flattered.

Chris Muir remembers an occasion when they were together in Canada and wanted to play tennis. They did not have any rackets but found themselves in a prestigious sports shop. 'He picked out the most expensive racket in the shop and ever so cleverly convinced the assistant that we should try a couple out before buying them. We had a game and afterwards Sidney took them back, telling them they were just a little bit too heavy.'

When Rose first visited Maine Road, the streets around the ground thronged with bicycles and local residents rented out their backyards as bicycle parks. Spitting was not allowed on the pitch so players had handkerchiefs tucked in their shirt-sleeves. City won the first match he attended, a 2–1 victory against Sheffield United in 1929. 'The City crowd always appreciated fair play. They would even clap the opposition if they had done something exciting,' he says.

He is one of the few people able to authenticate the alleged curse that many blame for City's ill fortune down the years. While the pitch at Maine Road was being prepared for use in the early 1920s, a horse and cart fell into a deep pit close to the centre circle. The horse broke its leg and was shot where it lay and later covered with earth. 'Whatever way you look at it, there is a full skeleton of a horse under that pitch,' he says.

Rose trained as a surgeon and while he worked at Manchester Royal Infirmary he became increasingly involved with the club. He installed an X-ray machine at Maine Road and operated on several players at the hospital.

His most famous City patient was Bert Trautmann, the ex-prisoner-of-war who became their goalkeeper from 1949 to 1963. Famously, he injured his neck in the FA Cup final of 1956 when City beat Birmingham City 3–1. 'After the match we all went on to the Cafe Royal in London and Bert was continually rubbing his neck. I asked him how it was and he said it was a bit stiff but not too bad. On the Monday morning it was still bad so we took him to the hospital to have a look at it.'

Popular legend has it that Trautmann broke his neck, but the collision with Birmingham's Peter Murphy actually caused the bone to fall out of alignment, pinching and crushing several nerves. He was placed in traction and the bone eventually settled back into place. 'People say he had a broken neck, but he would have been paralysed if that had happened,' explains Rose.

He was regularly called from the stands to examine a player and in December 1970 he was given a police escort to the hospital to operate on City's full-back, Glyn Pardoe, who had suffered a fractured ankle in the derby match against United. 'Every time we put the fracture in place his foot went white. We scrubbed up around the fracture and saw an artery caught at the end. I held it out of the way with a little hook and we put the bone back together.'

His formal association with City began in 1964 when he joined the board. He resigned in 1983 after a disagreement with Peter Swales who, by way of compensation, invited him to become president. 'I served on the board during the club's most successful era,' he says immodestly, a smile across his face. 'Swales was a likeable man, but we didn't really agree on football matters.'

He supported the campaign that brought Francis Lee briefly to power at Maine Road. 'Francis is brusque and forceful and does not do anything by half. He might have made a few mistakes but he would not do any one down deliberately. He is a very kind-hearted person underneath.' Rose, it has been said, is highly adept at seeing the good in people. 'I'm like the manager who sees a bad foul done by one of his players. Afterwards, when he's asked about it, he says he was unsighted or looking the other way, doesn't he?'

City, such is its benevolence, has 10 'honorary presidents', but Rose is the only 'life-president' which means he is the club's most senior elder statesman. He still gives medical lectures and is a keen pianist and freemason, but his passion for City is undiminished. His charm might be old school, but he is resolutely up to date as he embarks on an informed critique of the merits or otherwise of City's two main fanzines, *King of the Kippax* and *Bert Trautmann's Helmet*.

After our meeting, he phones and invites me to be his guest at a forthcoming match. An act of kindness, the opening gesture of a developing friendship, or an insurance policy against a disagreeable portrayal in a national newspaper? City need more men of Sidney Rose's foresight.

Sunday, 31 January 1999

Tabloid reports linked City with a major cash injection from foreign backers, with American and Scandinavian investors placed in the frame.

Manchester financial consultant Peter Rickitt, father of

Coronation Street star Adam, was reportedly involved in negot-iations, brokering a deal that would see the sale of the late Stephen Boler's 26-per-cent share-holding.

Meanwhile, Paul McGuigan of Oasis, spoke of his love for the club in the *Sunday Express*. 'I didn't actually expect us to slip down this far. What we need is some people who know what they're doing in charge for once,' he said.

Seven

Far from the Madding Crowd

Wednesday, 3 February 1999
A report by leading accountants Deloitte & Touche revealed that City had the seventeenth best annual turnover of all English clubs.

Thursday, 4 February 1999
Two former City players passed away. Defender Arthur Mann, 51, who played a starring role in the 1970 League Cup-winning side, was killed in an accident involving a fork-lift truck. Joe Hayes, 63, a scorer of a first-minute goal in the 1956 FA Cup final, died after an illness.

WHERE MATCH-DAY WOES WASH AWAY
(*The Times*, Saturday, 6 February 1999)

Joyce and Janet know, and so does Elvis. The laundry room at Manchester City is a place where secrets must have been spilled, young souls left out to dry. So what do footballers, these men among men, confide when they walk into a warm room with warm hearts? Joyce smiles, says nothing. Janet fills the tumble dryer. Elvis keeps time and, tick tock, the secrets remain hidden among the suds.

Joyce Johnstone, a City fan, has given 25 years service to the club. In that time, the Elvis Presley clock on the wall has turned from white to ochre and a film of dust has fallen over his GI uniform. Along with general secretary, Bernard Halford, and the manager's secretary, Julia McCrindle, Joyce is a rare constant in the shifting sand that is Manchester City. Janet Kirby, meanwhile, is a relative newcomer with six years to her name. Between them they ensure that, win or lose, City look the part.

The laundry room is beneath the Main Stand, just a few yards from the dressing-room area. It provides a telling contrast, with its blast of parched soap-scented air and sprigs of domesticity – an ironing board, kettle, sewing machine, boxes of soap powder, children's drawings on the wall. It is also the only part of the football club that is exclusively female. There are no windows, just a small grille through which they can see strips of daylight. 'In summer we have to put our sunglasses on,' Janet laughs.

Joyce is a pragmatist, and Janet a trainee pragmatist. Ask her about the huge washing machines and she'll tell you: 'It's a big washing machine, isn't it?' And the players – who have been her favourites down the years? She smiles again, looks around the room. Janet pretends to be busy. Eventually, they volunteer a name. 'Kit Symons, he was lovely.' Symons, City's captain until he left for Fulham last summer, often eschewed the customary afternoon game of golf for a quiet half-hour with the ladies. 'He used to come in here with a packet of chocolate biscuits.' Did they learn his middle name? 'We knew his real name was Christopher, if that's what you mean' says Joyce. So you don't know that his other name is Jeremiah? 'Oooohh, you'd keep that quiet though, wouldn't you, love?'

Uwe Rosler, the German striker who played for City bet-ween 1993 and 1997, made the most memorable initial impact on them. He was living in a hotel and asked whether they would do his washing until he found somewhere to live. They agreed and when he called in he also asked them to clean the trousers he was wearing. His English was still poor and as he undid his belt he told them: 'Now, ladies, I am here to do a favour for you.'

Footballers are famously self-important, but not, it seems, at Manchester City. 'They pull your leg and give you a bit of cheek but we've never had a problem with any of them. I can't remember any nastiness or any of them being disrespectful,' says Joyce. The pair, both of them grandmothers, sometimes become surrogate mothers to young players arriving at Maine Road from across the UK. 'The worst part is when the YTS lads are released. They are heartbroken when they are not retained. You try to cheer them up and do your best for them, but they are so sad.'

Kit for washing is delivered to the laundry by the club's kit manager, Les Chapman, a former player who had a 20-year career with various northern clubs. It arrives in large metal skips and is separated into light and heavy items. Muddied kit is still washed by hand in a stone sink before it is put into the washing machine. 'Whenever it rains on a Saturday, I think, "Oh blimey, we're in for a hard day on Monday,"' Joyce laments.

The basic playing kit is supplemented by all manner of items, from manager's jackets to vests, and training tops to the towels from the various hospitality suites. The washing and drying machines do not stop turning from 8 a.m. on Monday morning until 4 p.m. on Friday afternoon.

After washing, the kit is ironed, folded and re-packed ready for collection. In 25 years, Joyce claims she has never burned a single item with the iron. 'We're good, that's why – aren't we, Janet?' Janet nods: 'Of course we are.' They also carry out repairs on ripped kits, replacing zips or collars damaged in the heat of battle. Every item is accounted for and wastage is minimal. Occasionally, old shirts are autographed by the players and sold off for charity. 'It's funny, the fans want the rips left in them. It's so they can say they were there when so-and-so had his shirt torn and then show everyone the rip.'

Finally, reluctantly, the pair let a secret or two slip out. Ian Brightwell (now at Coventry City) was the 'cheekiest' and Willie Donachie, the 'quietest'. And who was the nastiest, most arrogant monster in shin pads ever to darken their room? Joyce purses her lips, shakes her head. The lady's not for telling.

● I was surprised that Chris Bird attended the interview. His presence made it difficult to develop a rapport with the ladies. They continually looked to him, worried that they might have said something out of place. He joked along and remained fairly unintrusive, but it made the situation more awkward than it needed to be.

A few weeks later, while I was interviewing Marc Riley and Mark Radcliffe, Riley joked that Bird's zealousness was justified: 'Look, if the girls had let it slip that City used Lenor rather than Persil, God knows the consequences.'

Saturday, 6 February 1999
Manchester City 3 Millwall 0

Before the game, there were warnings of potential trouble following the stormy encounter back in September. Joe Royle's comment that City were lucky to escape the New Den 'alive' had been slammed as 'whinging' by the Millwall chairman, Theo Paphitis.

Police helicopters shadowed the trains carrying the Millwall fans from London. They managed to out-manoeuvre the police, however, when they disembarked at Stockport instead of the anticipated Piccadilly Station in Manchester city centre. They clashed with Manchester United fans on their way to United's game at Nottingham Forest.

Inside the ground, an uneasy peace reigned until Paul Dickov scored City's opening goal after an hour. Seats in the North Stand were ripped up and thrown at police and stewards. Nicky Weaver was pelted with coins. Police, many in riot gear, moved in on the mob and it took them several minutes to restore order.

Further disturbances followed the game as shops and property were damaged by supporters escorted to the railway station. Eleven arrests – eight of them Millwall fans and three of them City – were made for public order offences. 'I have been policing games for 22 years and this was a sad return to the dismal days of the past,' said Superintendent Clive Wolfendale, the officer-in-charge at the ground.

City's other goals were scored by Terry Cooke and Kevin Horlock.

Tuesday, 9 February 1999

The House of Commons played host to several famous City supporters as they celebrated the launch of a supporters' club branch at Westminster. Labour MPs and lifelong City fans Ivan Lewis (Bury South) and Paul Goggins (Wythenshawe and Sale East) were the forces behind the new branch.

Guest of honour David Bernstein revealed that 20 new supporters' branches have been opened in the previous month. 'It is always great to meet fellow City fans and it makes you doubly determined to get things right at the club,' he said. 'I honestly think we are on the brink of a dramatic recovery and that is what everyone is striving for.'

Among those attending the first meeting were Dennis Tueart, Eddie Large, author Colin Shindler, broadcaster James H. Reeve and the former deputy governor of the Bank of England, Howard Davies.

Wednesday, 10 February 1999

Tension reportedly increased between the club and the 'training ground mafia', a hardy bunch of supporters who spend their days watching the players in training.

Joe Royle had complained previously that the training ground was a cross between McDonalds and a zoo, such was its easy access to supporters. He insisted they were kept away from a practice match. The 'mafia' retaliated by refusing to return the ball every time it sailed over the fence behind which they were told to remain.

Thursday, 11 February 1999

A bizarre story appeared in the *Manchester Evening News* about Nicky Weaver. He was supposedly the victim of a female pick-pocket as he walked through Manchester city centre. His wallet, containing £40 and credit cards, went missing after a woman had 'thrown her arms around him' as he walked to his car.

DICKOV TICKLED BY TRICKLE OF SUCCESS
(*The Times*, Saturday, 13 February 1999)

Clearly, it will take some time to acclimatise to all this winning. No longer is it classic City of spectacular own goals, hilarious misses, last minute defeats and ex-players going nap. Far from it; Manchester City are currently on their best run of form for a decade.

In addition, the move to a new ground is viewed as a formality and there is talk of a substantial input of cash for new players. Further – and far more conclusive – proof of the new City came in the 61st minute of their game against Millwall last Saturday.

The ball was sent rolling towards the Millwall goal as if prodded by an 88-year-old in carpet slippers. This pitiable pea-roller hit a divot and Nigel Spink, their goalkeeper, kindly dived over it as it hobbled across the goal-line at precisely three miles per hour. Paul Dickov embarked on exactly the same extravagant routine of celebration had he whacked it from the half-way line and ripped the netting to shreds. And well he should, for he was commemorating something greater than a mere goal, it was a *lucky* goal.

City have won five and drawn two of their last seven league games, collecting a haul of consecutive points they have not bettered since early in 1989 when they won promotion to the old First Division. They are now in a promotion play-off position, and though they are nine points behind Preston North End in second place, there is real optimism that they can make up the ground.

The funds for additional players will be raised when a buyer is found for the 26 per cent of shares that belonged to the late Stephen Boler. David Bernstein is trying to broker a deal whereby investors would pay £7.5 million for the shares and supply an additional £20 million for team-building.

On the surface it would seem an optimistic notion, considering City's ignominious league position. Paradoxically, their woeful current status could make them prime for speculation. They are undeniably the most underachieving club in English football, and so the absolute logic is that they must also have the greatest unfulfilled potential. City are the ramshackle house overlooking the sea. Someone with imagination, ready cash and determination could build themselves a beautiful abode.

Deloitte & Touche has published a survey which shows City

have the seventeenth best annual turnover of any club in England with an income of nearly £13 million per year. By way of comparison, two of their league rivals, Colchester United and Wigan Athletic, accrue less than £1 million a year.

Their relative wealth is generated by an incredible fan base. The average home attendance this season has topped 28,000 per match, which is more than double the next best-supported club in their division, Stoke City. Fans are also highly supportive of City merchandise. The players may have let them down, but the City trademark, whether on replica shirts or writ large across a souvenir bedspread, is a badge of loyalty, representing passion in the face of adversity, a celebration of the supporters as much as the club itself.

Bernstein, typically, is conducting negotiations discreetly. He is wary of inflating the expectations of supporters. False promises have been left scattered like points lost and chances missed around Maine Road down the years. He is an experienced player in the wile and guile of corporate trading. Several finance companies have been linked with the club, but Bernstein is sworn to confidentiality, though he has declared that he wants to complete any deal before the transfer deadline in March which has heartened many supporters.

Peter Rickitt has been named as City's go-between in negotiations. Rickitt, a famously large man, has found himself pursued by several newspapers, most of them keen to make great play of his size, as much as his renowned financial wizardry. The basic subtext is that while his son boasts a much-vaunted six-pack tummy, his is more of a Party Seven. Either way, Rickitt, who has been a financial advisor to City for several years, has formed a vanguard behind Bernstein in the current dealings.

The move to a new stadium based in the Bradford district of Manchester is expected in 2002. It will be funded by the National Lottery and Manchester City Council at a cost of £90 million, with its first use for the Commonwealth Games to be held in the city in three years. The capacity will be 48,000, an extra 15,000 on the current full-house at Maine Road. Supporters and the club's hierarchy favour the move, though some retain an emotional attachment to Maine Road or are sceptical of an arrangement whereby the club is to inherit a showpiece stadium at a fraction of its true cost. Bernstein has no such doubts. 'It will be a wonderful facility and we will benefit greatly from the extra capacity. It is a positive step to take the club into the twenty-first century.'

Bernstein claims to detect a 'tremendous spirit of confidence flowing through the club'. He had an unlikely encounter last week to advance the view. He was spotted by a burly police officer while he queued to buy a newspaper at Manchester's Piccadilly Station. As he left the kiosk, the police officer beckoned him over. 'It's Mr Bernstein, isn't it, the City chairman?' he asked. 'That's right,' replied Bernstein. The officer gingerly opened his jacket to reveal a dark blue tie with 'MCFC' sewn into the cloth. 'We're doing a lot better, aren't we?' he chuckled. City are on the up; even the laughing policeman knows it.

Saturday, 13 February 1999
Bournemouth 0 Manchester City 0

Jamie Pollock was sent off for the third time this season after he lunged at Bournemouth's John Bailey. He had earlier been booked for dissent. Kevin Horlock was also dismissed for two bookable offences – a foul in the first half and for 'walking towards the referee in an aggressive manner' in injury time.

Pollock was furious. 'The referee was a shambles. We were playing against 12 today. If they outlaw tackling I'll get sent off every week.' Joe Royle made great play of the bizarre nature of Horlock's sending off. 'I've had a player sent off for aggressive walking! I think I must have missed a rule change somewhere.'

Monday, 15 February 1999

City were informed by the FA that four players – Kevin Horlock, Andy Morrison, Tony Vaughan and Jamie Pollock – would be suspended for their forthcoming visit to Chesterfield.

Tuesday, 16 February 1999

Jamie Pollock was stripped of the club captaincy and the armband handed to Andy Morrison, who had deputised on previous occasions. 'We are trying to help Jamie with his dissent problems, and now he has no reason to speak to the referee at all,' said Joe Royle. 'This is not a knee-jerk reaction – my motive is to keep Jamie on the pitch more. I believe it will be for his own good.'

David Bernstein announced that in the six months up until 30 November 1998, City had lost £400,000, a notable improvement on the near £6 million deficit for the same period the previous year.

CITY STILL NO.1 WITH LARDY BOY
(*The Times*, Saturday, 20 February 1999)

Surrounded. Mark on one side, Marc on the other. Surreal monologues all around. Radio 1's official, undisputed anarchy twins, Mark Radcliffe and Marc Riley (a.k.a. Lard or Lardy Boy or the Boy Lard) are on top form. Mark, according to Marc, spends his weekends propagating seeds in his garden shed; while Riley, poor soul, is burdened by an endless round of celebrity cheese-sniffing parties. Just occasionally, Manchester City get a mention too. All in a day's work, our kid.

Mark, in his sensible, roll-neck green sweater, looks dogmatically normal. Take note, as Nurse Ratched would warn, for those that appear most sane are invariably the most mad. Ha, ha. Marc sports a check shirt and jeans, attire last seen on your woodwork teacher, the malevolent one with a retractable tape-measure at the ready for a swift poke in the ribs.

Aside from 'Fat Harry White' and the 'Cheesily Cheerful Chart Challenge', a recurring theme on their Radio 1 afternoon programme, is a bulletin on the escapades of their favourite football club, Manchester City. Usually, as City are humbled by the likes of Mansfield Town, Mark articulates the gloom and disbelief while Lard provides the telling full stop: 'You're not wrong, our kid.'

Serious for a minute, Mark ponders the enigma in blue. 'It's just bewildering. How can so much money be spent to provide so little? It's a spectacular achievement to have so little tangible for all the cash that 30,000 fans must generate.'

He was first taken to Maine Road by his dad, Philip Radcliffe, who worked as a journalist for the *Bolton Evening News* and also reviewed classical records for *The Sunday Times.* 'We lived in Bolton, so we'd watch them one week and City the next. We'd go wherever he could get us into with his press pass!' Radcliffe defected full-time to City when he began his degree course at Manchester University in 1976.

Abruptly, Riley interjects. He can wait no longer. He must talk about John Burridge and he must do it now! Burridge, by way of explanation, was City's reserve goalkeeper for the 1994–95 season and was – metaphorically speaking – widely celebrated as one glove short of a full pair.

'I used to watch him warming up. He'd be rolling in puddles, jumping all over the place. He was always asking the crowd what time it was. The funny thing is, I don't think he ever got a game. He was mad, him. He used to watch *Match of the Day* in his full playing kit, didn't he? I mean, you do that when you're five-years-old, but not when you're a proper bloke.'

Radcliffe has a drumstick and begins tapping out a rhythm on a book in front of him. He looks around the BBC canteen, bored. Next question, please. He suddenly remembers an astoundingly bad idea they had. 'We were going to open a vodka and potato bar on Stretford Road. You know, near to Macari's Chippy, around the corner from Old Trafford. We'd call it 'Kinkladze's'. I don't know if the United fans would like that though.' 'Probably not,' says Lard. 'United fans don't have the same sense of humour as us lot, do they? Our humour comes from being beleaguered for so long.' A look of terror falls across Riley's face. He looks like a man who has just remembered that he was once a member of the non-pop group, The Fall. 'I might get set upon by United fans next time I'm at Tesco. No, just put this in: "Manchester United are great."'

Like 16,000 others, the pair renewed their season tickets despite relegation to Division Two. 'It's an act of faith, a kind of defiance. Sometimes it's like a blood sport: how low can City go?' says Radcliffe. 'It's like, you could be a fan of Bob Dylan and he might not make very good records any more, but you still go and see him.' Riley generously tramples on the analogy.

'Yeah, but Bob Dylan doesn't play every two weeks does he?'
'Oh aye, never thought of that.'

The debacle of Francis Lee's reign as City chairman inspired the pair to wondrous musical heights under the guise of their occasional band, The Shirehorses. 'The Ballad Of Franny Lee' was one of the stand-out tracks on their album, *The Worst Album In The World . . . Ever . . . Ever!* The alleged guest vocalist was Alan Bawl, apparently no relation to Alan Ball, the former City manager, though they share a similarly limited vocal range audible only to dogs and shire horses.

Their favourite City player at the moment is Terry Cooke, the winger on loan from Manchester United. Radcliffe and Riley have clandestine plans to purchase Cooke in a bizarre deal. 'We are going to organise a whipround among the fans. We'll own him then and we'll all meet up every Monday morning to gee him up for the week and make sure he's feeling OK,' says Riley. They refused to nominate their least favourite player. 'We might meet him at a celebrity cheese-sniffing party. We're in show business, you know,' says Riley.

They sometimes visit the club in an official capacity. At one game earlier this season, they made the half-time raffle draw, racing on to the pitch as if chased by a small man in a tracksuit and flat cap, quite possibly Alan Ball. They proceeded to jump around wantonly. 'Don't you know about rock 'n' roll?' asks Radcliffe. 'You've got to exaggerate your movements when you're playing a stadium gig.'

Unlike many celebrities, the pair make no claims to be football fanatics. 'We go to every other home game, something like that. Mark has to set aside time to propagate seeds in his garden shed, you see,' explains Riley. During his time with The Fall in the late 1970s, Riley was often away touring and lost touch with the club. 'And you lost touch with music then as well didn't you?' laughs Radcliffe.

Eventually they are summoned to the studio to spill forth the idiosyncratic madness that is perceived variously as infantile or inspired, or usually a bit of both. Riley escorts me back to the reception area. In the lift, he comes over all normal. 'We've both got kids now, that's why we can't get to City for every game,' he says. Warning: these men have children, loveable and cute now, but acerbic and askew in time and possibly staffing your nearest vodka and potato bar by 2015.

Saturday, 20 February 1999
Manchester City 2 Macclesfield Town 0

Former City idol Georgi Kinkladze was among the 31,086 crowd to see them defeat Macclesfield with goals from Shaun Goater and Gareth Taylor. City's unbeaten run of nine games lifted them into the play-off zone for the first time in three months.

Saturday, 27 February 1999
Chesterfield 1 Manchester City 1

City were missing six regular first-team players. David Reeves scored for Chesterfield before Lee Crooks equalised with his first goal of the season.

More than 3,500 City fans attended the match and, as the wind ripped through Saltergate, sang: 'We are not, we're not really here.'

Eight

The History Man

Thursday, 4 March 1999

West Ham's Australian winger Stan Lazaridis had a change of heart over a proposed loan move to Maine Road and opted to stay at Upton Park.

City sought advice from the FA in an attempt to recover the £750,000 still owed to them by Crystal Palace from the sale of Lee Bradbury.

MORRISON ADAPTS TO LEADING ROLE AS TOUGH MAN OF MAINE ROAD
(*The Times*, Saturday, 6 March 1999)

The three scamps in tracksuits giggle and jab each other in the ribs. They are footballers-to-be, full of life, full of themselves. Suddenly, Andy Morrison enters the canteen and sets about them, shadowboxing and jigging. They scatter; more laughter.

Manchester City, for once, is a happy place to be. The team is on a 10-match unbeaten league run and promotion (via the play-offs, at least) is within sight. No longer is their play effete and elegant. City are standing toe-to-toe with the journeymen of their division and slugging it out, sometimes with a little too much relish, as eight dismissals and nearly 70 bookings testify.

The epitome of their zero-tolerance approach is Andy Morrison who has just been made captain by Joe Royle. Morrison, since he has plied his trade outside the media glare of the FA Carling Premiership, is little known to football's passive audience, but the original Bovril boys of the

Nationwide League know him like a brother, a brother grim. Fittingly, he made his début for City last year on Halloween. He is your nightmare in football boots, six feet tall, nearly 14 stones in weight. The hair is short and spiky, the eyes cruel and narrow. He's the footballer they forgot (on purpose) to call when they cast *Lock, Stock and Two Smoking Barrels*; they would have needed wide-screen.

Already, after just 14 games in a City shirt, he is a cult hero. On the cover of the fanzine *City 'til I Cry!* he is in classic pose: fists clenched, arms outstretched, chest puffed out, a man running at the world. 'Raging Bull' reads the caption. This Bully Beef has been similarly adored at his previous clubs. Plymouth Argyle supporters drafted a petition to keep him at Home Park, while the Blackpool fans sang his name when he returned in his new colours a few weeks ago.

During the 90 minutes of a game of football he is an inspiration, a giant, the ultimate sporting caricature. The life either side of the next football match is a more enigmatic affair. Here Morrison is no icon, for there has been too much madness, too much sadness. Trouble has man-marked him for years. He is a big lad, punches his weight, and has a belly-full of pride. 'I should walk away, but I can't sometimes . . .'

His more recent outbursts have brought him face to face with a psychologist, and various magistrates. Two years ago he was involved in a fight with a nightclub doorman. He threw the doorman through a window and afterwards remembered little of the incident. 'I just lost it. I realised then that if I carried on like this I could end up killing either myself or someone else,' he said. In a less serious altercation, he was found guilty of threatening behaviour after a row with a bus driver. He has received counselling for the past 18 months and avoids pubs or clubs where he may find himself goaded into another fight.

Surprisingly, his voice is soft, sweetened further by a West Country burr. He lived in the remote Scottish village of Kinlochbervie until his family moved to Plymouth where his father, a trawlerman by trade, joined the Royal Marines. When he retired from the marines, he returned to fishing and Morrison, along with his three brothers, worked on the family boat, often sailing into strong gales when other boats were returning to harbour. 'My dad was used to the bad weather up in the north of Scotland. The other fishermen thought he was a bit mad. I'd have to weigh the catch, grade it and lay it out for sale,' he says.

He was barely a teenager, thrust into a world of harsh, rain-soaked graft. On shore, they lived in a high-rise flat in the notorious Plymouth district of Stonehouse. 'We were surrounded by prostitutes and drug dealers,' he rues. His father re-married twice, and Morrison rarely saw his natural mother. He is vague about her whereabouts and the last time they met.

His playing career began at Plymouth Argyle. Although just a decade ago, football was a very different game. 'I'd be marking the centre-forward and the manager would be screaming at me from the touchline to smack him. It was part and parcel of the game then. You were expected to smash their main striker. Not to break his legs or anything, but to keep him quiet for a bit.'

A £500,000 move to Blackburn Rovers during the Championship-winning season of 1994–95 foundered after he made just one full appearance. He was bought as a squad player and was in an ever-lengthening queue of defenders. Blackpool and Huddersfield Town made greater use of his combative services until City signed him for £80,000 after a successful loan period. 'Joe [Royle] said he's heard all about me, but wanted to see what I was like for himself. I knew it was a big chance for me.' The captaincy is a fine piece of brinkmanship by Royle. He has lifted Morrison to a new height, dared him not to fall from grace once more.

Within the game, Morrison is acknowledged as a good professional. He trains hard and long, perhaps with the vigour of a man who knows he must remain focused and too busy to accept the offer of a few pints after training with his team-mates or any number of hangers-on. 'I've been teetotal for a few months now,' he says, pleased with himself.

He regularly visits northern Scotland, disappearing for days into the wilderness. 'I'm happy on my own. I'll drive to a beach and gladly sit in the car for a couple of hours just staring out. It's another world up there. I'm learning to play the accordion and I'm always playing Scottish music on the CD in the car. The other lads take the piss a bit, but it's what I like.'

He talks about the scrapes he's been in, fights he's had. He does not glorify the violence, sequins are not painted on to the scars. He shakes his head sometimes, sighs at the memories. 'I've got to channel my aggression into my football,' he says.

He had a slight relapse recently during City's cup game with Wimbledon when he was sent off for a tussle with their striker, Carl Cort. 'It was absolute handbags,' he pleads. 'I said to the ref, "Don't be so bloody daft," when he sent me off.' If it had been any other way – something more foreboding – Morrison would say, for he is remarkably honest.

He stretches his long legs under the table. He faces a long drive from City's training ground to his home in Worksop. His wife, Paula, son Arron (five) and daughter Brooke (two) will be waiting for him. Arron will be wearing his goalkeeper's gloves, ready to face a few shots in the garden. 'I'm a big softie at home,' he confides. The raging bull might make him a good footballer; the rage-less bull is the better bloke. He knows it, too.

Saturday, 6 March 1999
Manchester City 0 Northampton Town 0
City missed numerous chances and were held to a draw by relegation candidates Northampton. They played for an hour with 10 men after Kevin Horlock was sent off for two bookable offences in a 90-second spell.

Monday, 8 March 1999
City learned that March contained a 'blue moon', following on from another just two months earlier. A blue moon is the name given to the second full moon to appear within the same calendar month. This was perceived as a good omen, and soon proved the case.

Tuesday, 9 March 1999
Burnley 0 Manchester City 6
A 15-minute hat-trick from Shaun Goater, together with goals from Kevin Horlock, Andy Morrison and substitute Danny

Allsopp steered City to a memorable victory at Turf Moor.

'We've been on top in other games just as much, but we scored the goals tonight,' said Joe Royle, adding a conciliatory word for Burnley's manager, Stan Ternent: 'I'm sad it's a mate like Stan who was on the receiving end, but we needed goals and that will do us a world of good.'

Wednesday, 10 March 1999

A league table of the FA Carling Premiership published in the *Bath Evening Chronicle* showed City at the top, four points clear of Chelsea. Mysteriously, there was no sight of Manchester United who were, at the time, league leaders, four points clear of Chelsea.

MADDOCKS'S KINGDOM A SHRINE OF INFORMATION
(*The Times*, Saturday, 13 March 1999)

The laughing statistician stands in the doorway, a City tracksuit zipped up to the top. The car next to him, the caravan on the drive, the windows of the house, they all – like him – sing their love of Manchester City with stickers, pennants and mini-kits hanging like oversized jewellery. 'You found us all right, then?' asks John Maddocks. Missing him would be an achievement since no other house on the estate sings the blues quite so triumphantly.

Maddocks is City's archivist. He has every home match programme since 1945, team line-ups (and we're talking first-team, reserves, youths and trial games) for the past 55 years and at least one press cutting for every game City have played since 1965. His house, on the outskirts of Manchester, is a shrine to the club. Two shelves of City videos are by the television, autographed footballs sit on top of the piano. Upstairs, in a spare bedroom, is the epicentre of Maddocks's kingdom. The room is swathed in books, programmes, files, scrapbooks, posters, photographs – all dedicated to City.

Centre stage in his blue-lined room is a computer, and within seconds John is *in situ.* 'Watch this,' he says. He stabs at the keyboard and information about the blues flashes on to the screen. All of it vital, of course. Uwe Rösler, for example, began his career at Traktor Starkenberg, while Andy Thackeray, a member of the FA Youth Cup-winning side of 1986, might not have made the first team, but he represented Huddersfield Boys on several occasions.

Career details of every player associated with City are logged and updated at the end of each season to include appearances and goals. 'I do most of the updating through the summer,' he says. So, while neighbours sunbathe in their back gardens, and the streets are alive with children on long sunny evenings, John prefers to close his curtains, pore over his statistics and input them into his computer. 'Too right,' he says, and chuckles.

In recent years, a new term has been invented for the likes of John, but he valiantly protests his innocence. 'I'm not an anorak,' he pleads. 'It is not an obsession, it is a hobby.' He has no need to worry. Anoraks are lonely, timorous souls, fussy and pedantic, while John is happily married to fellow City fan, Joyce; he's unfeasibly jolly, with a hearty chuckle borne from knowing he has more match programmes than you. Infinitely more. He also has an extensive collection of country and western records and mementoes from foreign holidays – ornaments of the leaning tower of Pisa, a gondola from Venice – could this man be any less of an anorak?

He first watched City in the 1945–46 season but is gravely embarrassed that he cannot recall his first game, which might explain why he has spent most of his life chronicling the rest. 'I was enthralled straight away, wrapped up in the whole thing,' he says. He worked as an English teacher in Stockport until he was forced to take early retirement five years ago. He suffered a heart attack and had six by-passes fitted. 'They took the veins from down here,' he says, lifting up his trouser leg to reveal a scar almost as long as the zip on his tracksuit top.

For many years he collected data on City with Bill Miles, a retired civil servant and father of a former City director. Not everyone at the club shared their devotion to chronicling the past. The club joiner, given his own room at Maine Road to use as a workshop, would light his fire every morning using old programmes. 'He eventually burnt the lot. Many of them were pre-war,' rues John.

Peter Swales was similarly dismissive. 'I got a call from the club saying that Swales had asked someone to clear out a load of files and put them in a skip. I got there as quickly as I could. There was all sorts in there, including handwritten ledgers of board meetings. They tell you things like how much a player really cost, right down to the last penny,' says John. After the death of Bill Miles, Maddocks was made the club's semi-official historian, contributing regular pieces to the programme and dealing with queries about the club's history.

He is one of a small band of City supporters who travel home and away to watch the reserves play. 'I enjoy the standard of football and it's nice to see the young lads progress from the junior teams through to the senior sides. The atmosphere isn't all that exciting, but I can't stand there leaping about anyway because I have to keep an eye on my stop-watch because I write the match reports for the programme,' he says.

While, like all City supporters, he is distraught to find the club at its lowest ever league status, it is not without some small compensation. In a month's time, for example, City will visit Gillingham's Priestfield Stadium. Already, Maddocks's mind is whirring. 'Now, City haven't played Gillingham before on their home ground, although this isn't strictly true. We were there once in the FA Cup but that was before 1913 when they were known as New Brompton . . . ' John, since he is so well-informed, will be aware that Kappa, the club's kit suppliers, do a nice line in anoraks after all.

● I interviewed Maddocks before travelling to City's training complex to see Andy Morrison. While I was waiting for Morrison, Maddocks walked into the canteen and queued up with the coaches and players, some of them first-teamers, but most of them youngsters from the various Academy teams. True to form, Maddocks had a clipboard clenched to his chest and quietly waited his turn while the young lads peered into the various vats of food, breaking off for a laugh and a joke with the kitchen staff.

I was struck once more by the wonderfully broad church of a football club. In just one room, there were people of various ages, colour, size, and each motivated by a different aspect of the game, but all of them wearing the same City badge.

Saturday, 13 March 1999
Manchester City 1 Oldham Athletic 2

A missed penalty by Gareth Taylor capped a miserable afternoon when wasted chances and defensive mistakes cost City dearly. Paul Reid's first-half goal for Oldham was followed by a penalty by skipper, Lee Duxbury. In a frantic finish, Gareth Taylor pulled one back but it was too late to preserve City's 12-match unbeaten run.

The game was interrupted briefly when a male streaker raced on to the pitch.

Sunday, 14 March 1999

Italian sportswear company Kappa said it wanted to sever its links with City, two years into a three-year deal. It was reportedly disappointed with the club's league status and announced that the pair's 'commercial objectives had grown apart'.

Tuesday, 16 March 1999
Manchester City 2 Notts County 1

First-half goals from Michael Brown and man-of-the-match Terry Cooke were enough to beat a much improved County who twice hit the woodwork.

Friday, 19 March 1999

Andy Morrison was told he would be called before an FA disciplinary commission after receiving his eleventh yellow card of the season against Notts County. The booking, his fourth in six games, brought a warning from Joe Royle: 'I've spoken to Andy and told him that these bookings for dissent have got to stop. There really is no need to talk back to referees.'

CITY REMAIN A GIFT TO COMEDY
(*The Times*, Saturday, 20 March 1999)

A lady in shell-suit bottoms answers the door, presumably his cleaner. 'He's in there,' she says, pointing to a room across from the hall. I hear him before I see him. 'Look what he's done now. What a pillock!' Bernard Manning is shouting at the television, and cackling that famous Woodbine cackle. He empties another swear word from the packet, and suddenly he's in front of me, except I don't see him at first.

'Hello, son.' I follow the sound. 'I'm here,' he says. And boy is he here, behind the door, which is the last place you'd expect to find Bernard Manning. He is reclined in a luxurious leather chair wearing nothing but a white vest, white underpants and black ankle socks, his hair neatly combed and parted. He looks like a schoolboy waiting to see the district nurse. 'Right, lad, you want to talk about City do you? We're jinxed, we can't get anything right. If Dolly Parton had triplets, Joe Royle would be the one on the bottle.' Boom-boom.

By his side is life's essentials – several television remote controls, a copy of *The Sun*, a cup of tea and a tube of insulin. He was mugged a few years ago outside his nightclub and has been diabetic ever since. 'They were tooled up and everything,' he sighs. The house is crammed with trinkets and pictures. It looks like the final resting place for all the unsold items from a gigantic car boot sale. The mantelpiece, which runs along the length of the room, contains scores of framed photographs. 'That's my life story along there,' he says. 'Have a look if you want.'

Clearly his state of undress leaves him unabashed. As we begin to talk, he lightens the load even further, slipping out his top set of teeth every time he takes a sip of tea. 'I'm blue all the way through, me. Blue on stage, blue with my football team. It's always been City for me. I never dreamed of going to Old Trafford.'

He was first taken to Maine Road by his father, John Manning, in the 1930s. 'I'd do all my chores in the morning, black-leading the grate and things like that, and my dad would take me in the afternoon. There was always a good atmosphere at City,' he says. Whenever a joke comes to mind, his eyes dance. 'There were five kids in our family and we all slept together. The other four used to wet the bed. I learned to swim before I learned to walk.' Boom-boom, again.

While he has not been coy with his wealth (there's a stretch limousine outside his house), he has never been tempted to invest in City, though his son, another Bernard, is chairman of non-league Radcliffe Borough. 'I'm too much involved in show business. Give me a microphone and a spotlight and I can give non-stop entertainment for a couple of hours. It's my forte. I wouldn't know where to start buying and selling players, though. If I did spend any of my money on football, I'd buy Old Trafford to build houses on it.'

He is proud of his friendship with footballers. 'That's me and Mike Summerbee there, and me and Georgie Best,' he says, pointing to photographs. 'Bestie went to launch a ship in Newcastle, but he wouldn't let go of the bottle.' I ask about his relationship with black players. His alleged racial intolerance must make them wary. 'I have a go at everybody when I'm on stage. A joke's a joke, nothing more. They go on about me being racist, but so is every comedian, they just single me out. I get on well with Alex Williams [City's black former goalkeeper] and I like Shaun Goater, he's a good player. He knows what he's doing.'

He is a whole-hearted supporter of the new regime at City, though he claims also to have been a friend of previous chairmen, Peter Swales and Francis Lee. 'I've always got on with the people down at City. David Bernstein is a thorough gentleman and he knows his football. Joe Royle knows the game inside out. They're slowly getting it right.'

Inevitably, City are included in his stage act. The eyes dance, time for another joke of an uncertifiable age. 'Snow White's house got burned down. She went inside and heard a voice from under the floorboards saying, "City will win the cup, City will win the league." Snow White said, "Thank God – Dopey's OK!"'

After the interview, Manning faces a long drive to Peterborough where he is due to appear on stage. 'I'm 68 years old and I'm working harder than ever,' he says, proudly. He plans to live out the remainder of his days in 'Shalom' – the name he has given his detached house in north Manchester – among his photographs and prints of the *Hay Wain*. 'Aye, they'll be carrying me out of the front door here,' he says. And what of his ashes, will they be scattered over his beloved Maine Road? 'Ashes? There'll be six tons of lard left when they've done with me. They should pile me up by the goal post, I might be a help to the goalkeeper!'

Manning announces that he's 'got to take a pee' and slowly levers himself out of the chair. He shuffles from the room, black socks padding across thick carpet. Close up, close enough to see the white of his eyes and the off-white of his vest, Manning is surprisingly guileless company, your kindly, trusting grandad. On stage, of course, he is crude and cruel, bombastic and barbaric. All are welcome at Manchester City – the insanely loyal, the insanely optimistic and, even, the insanely undressed.

● A good way to gauge a celebrity's opinion of himself is by their reaction to a 'cold' call from a journalist. The vainglorious invariably start to whine and demand from where their number was attained. Your manner can remain polite and low-key, but they will become flustered and rude. Manning was immediately friendly, albeit in his gruff, non-committal way. Within seconds he had given me directions to his home. Incidentally, he didn't really say, 'What a pillock!'; he said: 'What a wanker!'

Saturday, 20 March 1999
Colchester United 0 Manchester City 1

A poor performance still earned City maximum points. 'How often have I said in the past that City have played well and not got what they deserved?' asked Royle. 'We haven't played well today, but I thought we just about shaded it. Half the side never got out of the starting blocks, but we're going home with three points.'

In an experimental broadcast by Sky TV, Shaun Goater's 54th-minute goal made football history, becoming the first scored live on pay-per-view television.

Monday, 22 March 1999

Promotion rivals Reading, Wigan Athletic and Preston North End were City's next three opponents. 'This is now crunch time. We have raised ourselves for the big games this season, and we need to do the same again,' said Royle.

Thursday, 25 March 1999

Former Manchester United striker Mark Robins was signed on loan until the end of the season from Greek side Panionios.

FAVOURITE UNCLE STILL A CITY GENT
(*The Times*, Saturday, 27 March 1999)

Within the portal of every football club – no matter its size – is a community of people, a village where the measure of morality is in its hospitality to strangers. Is there a smile at the reception desk? Has someone offered to make a cup of tea?

Manchester City has long been perceived as a 'friendly' club. Cynics argue this is primarily because they are the counterpoint to Manchester's other famous football club. In stereotypical terms, United is your out-of-town hypermarket, faceless, homogenised and shamelessly avaricious, while City is your friendly corner shop, all how-are-you? and nice-to-see-you, love.

While City have undoubtedly picked up passive support by virtue of not being United, their historical legacy – the people that have inhabited the village – have generally stood for fair play, integrity and a good heart. Their supporters also play a critical role. They are romantic fools, damned for ever for falling in love with the wrong team. They are dreamers, sentimentalists, optimists and fatalists, and we both pity and envy them. All that pain, but such a sense of allegiance and purpose. In the past decade, City's appeal has been further heightened by a liberal dose of bathos; they are the sport's unofficial Slapstick FC though, it has to be said, concerted efforts are being made to curtail the metaphorical banana skins.

The first welcome to Maine Road is in a Glaswegian accent,

the sandpaper rasp of Mike Corbett, who staffs the reception desk. A former bombardier, Corbett's greeting is hardly the fawning, Americanised simper beloved of many companies with ideas above their station. He has the efficient, to-the-point manner of the bloke in a fawn coat running your local hardware store. Try, just try, telling him about rawl plugs or even the merits of a course for public-corporate interface personnel. He'll give you a quizzical smile. 'What could they teach me?' he'll ask, astounded. 'I say "hello" to people and ask them what they want.'

Most clubs have an avuncular figure felt to epitomise its authentic historical spirit. These are invariably men who have conducted themselves with dignity and selflessness, unpolluted by ego or greed. In other words, they are great *club* men. At Maine Road the undisputed Uncle City is Roy Clarke, an ex-player who has given more than 50 years service to the cause.

He joined them in May 1947 from Cardiff City and in 11 years played 369 games, scoring 79 goals. He also played 22 times for Wales. After his playing career ended, he helped raise funds for City and managed its famously successful social club for nearly 25 years. Now, aged 73, he takes match sponsors on tours of the ground and is secretary of the club's former players' association.

On the cigarette cards of the time, Clarke was pictured all floppy hair and soft brown eyes, his skin without a line or blemish. He was 21 with a 14-year-old's complexion when he left Wales for the first time and travelled to Manchester in a Harris tweed suit. It was a hot day in early summer, but he had been warned it was 10 degrees colder in the north. His wage was £10 a week plus a £2 bonus for a win and £1 for a draw – '. . . and a good hiding if we were beaten,' he adds.

City's manager at the time was Sam Cowan and Clarke had eagerly anticipated his first pre-match team-talk. 'I imagined it would be quite tactical and I would learn a lot from it. He came in five minutes before the kick-off, bounced a ball a few times on the dressing-room floor, and said, "Get bloody stuck in today," and then he left.' Cowan, like many other managers, had precious time for the views of players. 'He would pin up the team-sheet and sneak off again before anyone could stop him and ask why they weren't in the side,' says Clarke.

Players were hardly the precious commodities of the modern game. When Clarke contracted a skin disease he was dispatched to Manchester Skin Hospital to spend time on a public ward. 'It was an old Victorian hospital, they used to call it Scratcher's Castle. At night, I could tell every bed by its own particular scratch,' he says.

For a short while he ran a sports shop in Manchester, but answered the call from City to run their new social club when it was launched in 1966. 'The sports shop did OK, but I was too soft, which has always been my trouble,' he says. The social club flourished and became an integral part of the touring circuit for pop groups and cabaret acts. Clarke lived above the club, before leaving for a house supplied by City in Salford. 'They've always been good to me, though I'm not one to ask for much,' he says.

During his playing career he never earned more than £20 per week and he concedes to 'a little bit of jealousy' when he hears of modern salaries. 'I don't associate with them, so it's not too bad. I don't know any of the current City team.'

It is hard to reconcile the slight but athletic man of whom one football reporter wrote 'a player built for speed' with the white-haired elderly gentleman sitting in the small conservatory of a home supplied at someone else's benevolence. These tin-bath, hob-nail footballers who played in front of thousands to great acclaim but paltry earnings should each own their own castle. Especially when, like Clarke, they served their club when personal glory had long expired.

Clarke was mugged a few years ago close to Maine Road and he blames the incident for a failing memory. 'I can remember things that happened years ago, but yesterday not so well. It gets me down.' He embarks on another story but forgets the name of the protagonist, scratching the air for inspiration. It doesn't come. He sighs, shakes his head.

Finally, there is the obvious question about the current City side – the worst (according to league position) to wear the blue shirts. 'I still find it hard to criticise City,' he says. 'You know, I still can't eat before a game, I get that nervous. This is a hard one to answer. How can I say it? I think they go about the job too gingerly. In my opinion, he who is first, always wins.'

Saturday, 27 March 1999
Reading 1 Manchester City 3

A bumper crowd of 20,055 for City's first visit to the Madejski Stadium delayed the kick-off for 30 minutes.

Two superb goals from free kicks by Terry Cooke were complemented by Shaun Goater's eighteenth goal of the season. Reading's goal was scored by Keith Scott in the 92nd minute.

Monday, 29 March 1999

City announced a kit sponsorship deal with French sportswear company Le Coq Sportif. The contract was thought to be worth £1 million over the next three seasons.

Andy Morrison was fined £400 by an FA disciplinary hearing. 'Some referees have found it difficult to cope with the pressure when they handle a City game,' said Joe Royle. 'I think the FA are sympathetic to our case, and I was pleased that Andy's punishment was not harsher.'

Tuesday, 30 March 1999

Bernard Halford, club secretary, revealed that 7,500 season tickets had been sold for the forthcoming season. 'I expect the ground to be more that 50 per cent full of season-ticket holders for next season's campaign,' he said.

Nine

Seize the Day

Thursday, 1 April 1999

Alex Ferguson, the Manchester United manager, said he wanted Terry Cooke to return to Old Trafford after completing his loan period. 'Terry is a United player and we want him to stay a United player,' he said. 'He's got a terrific future in front of him. There have been one or two enquiries for him, but we have turned them down.'

CITY DIARIST HOPES TO WRITE A HAPPY ENDING
(*The Times*, Saturday, 3 April 1999)

Hot news. Rodney Marsh has been on the phone. A Paraguayan player – pretty handy, apparently – is looking for a club. There's a civil war in his home country. Cover his board and lodgings, and he'll cover every blade of grass for you. Yvonne Donachie has scribbled down the details. She passes the note to her husband. Willie Donachie smiles. We'll see.

The familiarity or otherwise of the current Manchester City team-sheet is commensurate with their league position. Allsopp, Mason, Wiekens, Crooks, *et al*, are little known outside the fanaticism that drives the club. The men in the wings, however, those on the non-playing side of the white line, are much more familiar: Joe Royle, Asa Hartford, Paul Power, Dennis Tueart, Tony Book, Willie Donachie – recognisable names, recognisably City. And on the phone, another old boy, Rodney Marsh, pushing his Paraguayan.

Royle and Donachie are the two former City players

entrusted to inspire the club's renaissance. It is a double act that has already toured Oldham Athletic and Everton to varying success. Royle is your original Uncle Joe, knockabout, instinctive, pragmatic, a touch of the burlesque, and with enough one-liners to service a sitcom or two. Donachie is Cousin Willie, thoughtful, shrewd, speaks when he's spoken to.

Surprisingly, Royle, who celebrates his 50th birthday this week, is only three years the elder. From up in the stands, this burly silhouette skirting the edge of the pitch can appear older than his years. He has been slowed down by arthritis and the recent hip-replacement operation. Close up, when the day's work is done and a win secured, he is smiling and laughing, 16 again, fresh as you like. Donachie, meanwhile, looks good from any angle. Thin, full head of hair, he still has the incandescence of a professional sportsman. He feels his current fitness level would be enough for him to play the odd game for City reserves. He is being modest.

Royle and Donachie are contrary personalities, but they share a cultural background from which much of British football is still forged. Donachie was brought up in the Gorbals district of Glasgow, one of five children living in a house without a bath where several families shared the same outside toilet. Royle lived in inner-city Liverpool, forced to sleep on a camp-bed in his parent's bedroom because of a shortage of space. Football was their ticket to somewhere better.

Time has not lent enchantment to Donachie's view of his home city of the '50s and early '60s. 'The shipyards were closing down and it was a hard place to grow up in. There were gangs on the streets and it was a very aggressive environment. If you showed any interest in your school work you were seen as a swot,' he says. His mother died when he was 12 and he did not get on particularly well with his lorry-driver father. 'He was a hard Glasgow man who would never show his feelings or emotions. He didn't really give me much encouragement, except to say I was crap! He gave me one good piece of advice though; he told me to try and find a club in England.'

He signed for Manchester City in December 1968, just months after they had won the League Championship. He made his first-team début two years later and went on to play more than 400 games for the club in a ten-year period. 'I found everyone at City so friendly. I loved it straight away. The club was staffed by unbelievably strong men. They kept you down to earth. They shouted at you sometimes, but you always knew it was because they loved you and wanted the best for you.'

He finished his playing career at Oldham Athletic and became their coach until he moved with Royle to Everton in 1994. After three seasons at Goodison Park, he left for Sheffield United and finally returned to Maine Road last year. 'I thought the club was being badly run when we first arrived. We had a squad of 54 players, which meant straight away, you've got 43 players who are not in the team. We needed about 10 coaches just keeping them all busy. There wasn't enough hunger about the place.'

Quietly, but ruthlessly, Royle and Donachie rationalised the club's playing staff but during this unsettled period just before Christmas, the team's league form was infuriatingly inconsistent. The supporters were restless, anxiety turning to panic. Donachie, for the first time in his long career in football, left the shadows and broke his silence. It was worth the wait. 'Our supporters are beginning to wallow in City's misfortune,' he wrote in his regular column in the *Manchester Evening News*. It got stronger: 'There is a growing tide of negativity around this club. It is creeping into every area – the media, the board, supporters, and even the players.'

The broadside was heartfelt and powerful. It was also the truth. City supporters are famously loyal and considered the aristocracy of football support, but this has bred a certain conceit, an imperiousness where moaning and tetchiness is now part of their mindset. Donachie had confronted the sacred cow of City's phenomenal support and although some were offended by his remarks, many realised that their anti-support was worsening their plight.

Donachie has returned to the shadows and left the media to Royle once more. He continues with his weekly column – now back to less controversial fare – only because Dennis Tueart, a City director, persuaded him that he needed a higher profile.

Donachie, when he is away from the training pitch, studies the science of sports coaching so that City, for example, have a US-trained fitness specialist and a sports psychologist on call.

Ultimately, and by whatever means, his aim is to instil into the current team the devotion and flair of the successful City side both he and Royle played in during the 1970s. When they lost a recent home game, club captain Andy Morrison stormed off the pitch, hoisted a huge four-wheeled stretcher over his head and hurled it down the tunnel. Donachie was heartened to see defeat cause so much hurt, for glory invariably follows passion.

Saturday, 3 April 1999
Manchester City 1 Wigan Athletic 0
An even contest was settled after a mistake by Wigan goal-keeper Roy Carroll. He went to gather a hopeful punt from Jamie Pollock, but realised his momentum would carry him outside the penalty area. He released the ball and Terry Cooke scored from a tight angle.

The win moved City up into fourth place, their highest League position since the start of the season.

Monday, 5 April 1999
Preston North End 1 Manchester City 1
The noon kick-off caught City cold when they fell behind to a Steve Basham header after just 52 seconds.

Spurred on by the 20,857 crowd – Preston's biggest for 26 years – City created and missed several chances before Michael Brown equalised. 'We need to win our last six games and see where it takes us,' said Joe Royle, 'I have never said never. We can still finish in the top two, that is our aim.'

Friday, 9 April 1999
Five first-team regulars were just one booking away from suspension – Kevin Horlock, Michael Brown, Shaun Goater, Jamie Pollock and Gerard Wiekens. During the season City had already collected 78 yellow cards (13 for Morrison alone) and had had nine players sent off.

(*The Times*, Saturday, 10 April 1999)

The paint has faded down the years, but still visible on many walls in and around Manchester is the legend: '5–1'. It refers to City's triumphant victory against Manchester United on Saturday, 23 September 1989. The newspaper headlines seem outlandish now, make-believe even: 'City Leave Sad United Behind', 'Fans Turn On Fergie' and 'United, This Was Simply A Disgrace!' The most striking photograph from the match shows David Oldfield tapping home City's fourth. Behind him, Gary Pallister, the ex-United defender, is on his hands and knees: tired, exasperated, crushed.

A decade later, and City still wear blue and United are in red. Otherwise, the two clubs have been completely reinvented. In crude terms, United are success, money, glamour and a 1–1 draw with Juventus in the semi-final of the European Champions League, while City are failure, debt, calamity, and a 2–1 home defeat to Mansfield Town in the Auto Windscreens Shield.

Sensibly, staff at Maine Road seldom mention Manchester's other team these days. Their hearts might skip a beat when they recall 'the 5–1' – as it has become known – but they know it is old news. Both literally and metaphorically, they accept that United are now in a different league. Besides, they are busy rebuilding the club and have recognised the futility of concentrating their minds and energy on anyone but themselves.

Due to their divergent league status, the two clubs no longer play each other on a regular basis at first-team or reserves level. On Tuesday, however, City finally came within touching distance of their old rivals. They met in the Manchester Senior Cup, a competition designed to give match practice to the reserves of various north-west clubs. These ties are invariably watched by a handful of supporters, but since this was the closest to a *bona fide* Manchester derby for several years, 3,457 fans decided to stir the memory of derbies past.

The match, staged at Ewen Fields, the home of UniBond Premier League-side Hyde United was all-ticket. Hearsay had it that City might play their first team in an attempt to bloody the nose of their haughty neighbours, while there were fears that the game would become an excuse to detonate hostility among supporters. Mounted police were in attendance and scores of stewards but, thankfully, the atmosphere was akin to a testimonial game. City made the dignified decision of fielding their usual reserves team and David May was the only United player with any real first-team pedigree.

The attendance was 10 times greater than Hyde United's average for a home match. 'What's going on out there?' asked the lady in the corner shop just a few hundred yards away. 'I've just sold my last cheese and tomato butty. I would have made more if I'd known.'

Amateur footballers arrived to play on a pitch adjacent to Ewen Fields. They changed in their cars and endured the jibes of passing fans. 'You're probably good enough to get a game for City,' shouted someone in a blue and white scarf. Before the main event, many dallied to watch Moss Tavern defending valiantly on a field comprised of mud, water, sand and traces of grass.

Hyde United's pitch, just a car park away, was remarkably verdant. Laid just four years ago, it is recognised as one of the best in the north-west, which is why City pay for the privilege of using it for their reserves. The press facilities are not quite as prestigious, with room for just two reporters who have to sit either side of Dave Gresty, a man of many jobs including receptionist, club historian, press assistant and match announcer. If you ask nicely, he might also order you a taxi.

'Aren't Hyde famous for once losing heavily in the FA Cup?' asks the man from *The Times*, referring obliquely to the famous match of 1887 when Preston North End beat Hyde 26–0. Gresty sighs. He's heard this one before. 'Actually, that was a different Hyde. We were formed as Hyde United in 1919.' Point taken.

The match kicks off and the phone starts to ring. 'Hello, Hyde United,' says Gresty. 'Yes, tickets are still available. You'll have to ask for them in the social club, but you'd better get a move on, they've just kicked off.' He repeats the same information to several callers, but the next query is more complex. 'So, have I got this straight?' he asks. 'You want me to put out an announcement to tell your grandparents that there'll be a taxi waiting for them on the car park? Hang on, have you already rung for the taxi?' A police officer, a City fan, barges in: 'Any United fans in here?' He hears a faint shout of assent from down the corridor. 'Who said that? Right, you're arrested.'

City are soon losing. Rain lashes down. A sycamore tree, still without leaves, shivers in the wind at the perimeter fence. Umbrellas and anoraks appear. The ground is on the flightpath of Manchester Airport. People look upwards and dream of aeroplanes and holidays, somewhere that is not wet, windy, dark and, in truth, an anti-climax. Two brothers, both aged under 10, huddle inside a union flag. This was supposed to be fun, City and United in the flesh, but it is flesh turning from white to purple, with goose-pimples thrown in.

The phone rings again. Is it always so busy? 'We have one fan, Norman, he's getting on a bit now and can't make it to the games. He phones to check on the score. His record is 17 times during one match – we counted them,' says Gresty. Our police officer hears on the radio that the first arrest of the night has been made. 'It was one of the lads banned from all City's matches for his previous behaviour,' says the burly sergeant. 'I hope you nabbed him *after* he'd paid to get in,' jokes Gresty.

City fans stream out long before the end. Another defeat, another night when their optimism and loyalty is mocked. At least the first team are mounting a sustained promotion challenge. It's Lincoln City at home next, three points for sure. Probably, hopefully, maybe. This was always a nothing match, a bit of a kick-about. No one's bothered about a reserves game anyway. And the score-line? 5–1 to United. Irony and Manchester City remain inseparable.

Saturday, 10 April 1999
Manchester City 4 Lincoln City 0

A hat-trick from Paul Dickov, his first in senior football, brought his goal tally to eleven for the season as City stretched their unbeaten run to six games. The other goal was scored by Kevin Horlock.

Promotion rivals Walsall, Preston North End and Wigan Athletic all suffered defeats. 'A marvellous set of results,' said Joe Royle. 'We're closing up on all quarters now, points and goals.' City remained in fourth place, eight points adrift of leaders Fulham, but just two behind second-placed Walsall.

Monday, 12 April 1999

City supporter Alison Anderson of Havant claimed the club's future success depended on a lamp she had bought for her boyfriend's fish tank. The lamp, called 'Blue Moon', had to be switched on before each City game if they were to stand a chance of winning. On the occasions they had forgotten to put it on, City lost.

Wednesday, 14 April 1999
Manchester City 2 Luton Town 0

Two goals in the first nine minutes from Paul Dickov and Tony Vaughan looked to have set City up for another comprehensive win, but they were the only goals of the game.

The win moved City above Preston North End into third place, still trailing Walsall by two points.

Thursday, 15 April 1999

Chip-shop owner Mike Turner promised to supply free fish and chips to all members of the Reddish branch of the City supporters' club if they won promotion. The offer would stand for just one day – Monday, 31 May, the day after the promotion play-off final at Wembley.

Friday, 16 April 1999

Terry Cooke completed his move to City, signing a three-year contract after the club agreed a £1 million deal with Manchester United. The fee was an initial £600,000 with a further £400,000 payable in stages.

In an eventful 24 hours, Cooke also became a father for the first time after his fiancée Nadine gave birth to a son, Charlie.

WHEN SUPPORT BECOMES DIVORCED FROM REALITY
(*The Times*, Saturday, 17 April 1999)

Love Hearts are all over the house. Shame not to eat one or two. The first out of the packet reads: 'Ever Yours'. Tom Ritchie holds it to the camera. He's a clever man, the irony has not passed him by. It's only a sweet, like Manchester City is only a football club. Best not to go any further, any deeper.

Unfortunately, Ritchie has been deeper, to a place where fanaticism meets obsession, frustration runs to illness, and your wife files for a divorce. He and Manchester City are joined at the hip, the blues brothers. City are on his mind constantly, on his lips, on his word processor. He's at the meetings, the matches, and if he can wangle a day off work he's at the perimeter fence watching them train.

There is a famous song about addiction to football, a jaunty ditty from the early 1960s called 'Football Crazy'. It unwittingly forged the fanatic as the hare-brained fool, Norman Wisdom in a football scarf. So, your team lost and someone swiped your bobble cap. It's all a laugh, isn't it? *Isn't it?*

Football, for many, is a solemn business, no laughing matter at all. It made Tom Ritchie ill. 'City had taken over all my waking hours. Work suffered, my wife and three kids were all sidelined and the pleasure I obtained supporting them was rapidly replaced by mounting anger and frustration,' he says. 'This was not the normal emotional highs and lows routinely experienced by a football fan. This bordered on the unhealthy obsessive. I started acting like the nutter on the bus.'

At the end of last season, with City in relegation quicksand, Ritchie stopped going to matches for the sake of his own health. He was suffering from severe headaches, and had been prescribed tranquillisers for depression. 'It was physically hurting me. It felt like they were killing me. I put all my City shirts and anything that reminded me of them in bin bags in the garage. It helped relieve the pressure for a short period of time.'

Thirteen years earlier, his first wife had cited his passion for the club in the divorce proceedings. Lynne, his second wife and with whom he has three children, is, he says, understanding. Noticeably, he does not say that she is supportive. He stands his ground, as he will many times during our meeting. 'There's nothing wrong with an obsession. I admire people who have interests, whether it be trainspotting, steam engines or whatever. It's better than staying in every night watching telly isn't it?' he says. He is sheepish for a moment. 'I only watch them training every few months now anyway.'

He has doleful eyes and the lugubrious demeanour of a First World War soldier, two weeks in mud, three days without sleep, nearly 35 years a City fan. 'I define myself through my support of City,' he says. 'It's like a badge of honour. City fans are of a similar mind. They tend to be humanitarian, left-of-centre, individualistic.' He feels these characteristics have been formed through adversity. 'The football is appalling. We've currently got the worst team I've ever seen up there, but we keep on going, it's like an act-of-war effect. We are the most loyal fans bar none.'

His last claim is widely accepted within the football fraternity. City's average home attendance this season is more than 28,000 per game. They have sold 10,000 season tickets for next season already. In contrast, when Newcastle United and Leeds United dropped into the old Second Division (and City are now a division below that) their attendances were below 17,000.

Ritchie is a principal personnel officer at Lancashire County Council. He is literate and erudite and one of many similar City supporters banished to an extraordinary kind of purgatory. This coterie of support is more intelligent than the people that have run the club, more passionate, yet they have been excluded because they speak in too many tongues and are too unwieldy to mobilise. They are left excluded, frustrated and, in some cases, ill, their only form of expression reduced to a jeer or shout when they are people of great eloquence. Their predicament is not exclusive to City, supporters of other under-achieving clubs will empathise. City just happen to be the champions of under-achievement.

Ritchie has found succour in producing a fanzine, *City 'til I*

Cry! Today, at the game against Gillingham, he will hand out Love Hearts to everyone who buys a copy. He has published a special 'love issue' and – as City close in on promotion – he has called a truce on cynicism and negativity. He is, of course, delighted to witness City's valiant promotion run-in, though even this is tempered with biting realism. 'We shouldn't even be in this division,' he mutters. A win against the likes of Lincoln City or Luton Town provides little cheer. City fans feel their club is like a company director asked to sweep the canteen. Tell him he has done a good job, and he'll tell you he should be doing something else, somewhere else; something that matters.

Meanwhile, Ritchie has spent a few hours pondering his life and City's part in it. He phones me a few hours after the interview. 'I thought you'd like to know, I took the family out for something to eat this afternoon and bought the kids some new shoes.' Manchester City 0, Tom Ritchie 1.

● I was a little apprehensive about my portrayal of Ritchie. He had been extremely trusting with personal information. His writing in the fanzine had often been candid and confessional; in fact, the self-discussive tone gave it the intrigue of a personal diary. I gathered, then, that he would not take offence. Thankfully, he was happy with it and said afterwards that he had been approached by several supporters who said they empathised with his suffering.

Saturday, 17 April 1999
Gillingham 0 Manchester City 2

Terry Cooke's sixth goal of the season invigorated City after Gillingham made the better start. Kevin Horlock added a second with a 64th-minute free-kick.

Nicky Weaver kept his 21st clean sheet of the season, equalling Alex Williams's record of 21 shut-outs in 42 league games during the promotion season of 1984–85.

A correspondent of the Manchester United fanzine, *United We Stand*, secreted himself among the City fans and lambasted them in his article. He said some of them failed to observe the minute's silence to mark the Hillsborough disaster and one supporter threw a coin which hit an elderly Gillingham fan, cutting his head. 'The sight of him mopping the blood from his forehead as his grandson stood by his side crying was sickening . . . They're nobodies, social zeros united by their loathing of Manchester United and their bitter camaraderie in the face of deserved adversity,' he wrote.

Tuesday, 20 April 1999

Michael Lally, thought to be City's oldest supporter at 104, died. He was a veteran of the First World War.

LOOK ON MY WORDS AND DESPAIR
(*The Times*, Saturday, 24 April 1999)

Gold watch, gold buttons, gold skin. The voice drips gold too, a molten flow of sing-song syntax. The R's roll rrrrichly, the C's are clipped curtly and we are told of rutting stags, yaks, snowflakes, slate-grey roofs and – of course – Ozymandias, king of kings. The match ended as a draw, incidentally. As if we still cared.

Stuart Hall is in town, and everyone knows it. 'Joe, Joe Royle,' he shouts as the City manager gets out of his car. The waiting press corps want a quote about City's new signing, Terry Cooke. Stuart Hall wants Joe Royle. Stuart Hall gets Joe Royle. 'You're late,' he admonishes, and issues the famous hee-hee, ho-ho chuckle. Royle, this large, pallid man in a washed-out tracksuit, is led to his office by the small man in a smart suit.

Hall is about to interview Royle for a radio station. 'Right, Joe, the first thing I'm going to say will be along the lines, "City were off the pace and crap for a while, but now you're charging towards promotion. What's happened?" Something like that, anyway. Okay?' 'Fine,' replies Royle. Hall claps his hands, then rubs them together. He is kindling an invisible flame with happiness, sheer bloody-minded happiness; has Moss Side ever seen a sunnier morning?

During the interview, Hall draws in close. His nimble fingers tug at Royle's clothing. He wants him to get the joke, share the joy. Royle, since he is a football man, cut from granite and turf, does not reciprocate but the smile reveals everything. He is thinking, 'This man is mad, but I like him.' Hall will later say as much himself: 'I live in fantasyland, I have a following of fellow nutcases.'

Manchester City is Hall's football team. 'It's in my blood,' he says. 'I used to stand on the terraces as a boy with my father. I call Maine Road the theatre of base comedy.' A few years ago, his tennis partner Martin Edwards, the Manchester United chairman, encouraged him to buy shares in United. 'I said, Martin, I'm a City supporter, what are you talking about?'

After his interview with Royle, Hall wants a cup of tea. He strides into the canteen at City's training ground. There is no one to be seen. Onwards to the kitchen. Through the swing doors. 'Helloooo,' he sings, 'Helloooo.' His father told him never to miss an opportunity, and this has become a doctrine. Television, radio, corporate parties, business schemes – he doesn't so much run at life as knock it over, pin it to the ground and pose for the victory photograph afterwards. 'Everything I do I am enthusiastic about. If I'm bored with something I don't do it,' he says.

Hall is 68-years-old and looking good, not that he would agree. The dashes of gold, the Perma-tan and the beatific smile are probably man-made diversions. He has said before that he is not happy in his skin. 'I hate my body. I am runty, ill-formed, 5ft 8ins, and desperately wish I was 6ft-plus.' Later, he will joke with our photographer and ask him to super-impose some 'thick black hair' onto his head. Healthwise, a recent hospital check-up revealed that he had 'the heart of a 10-year-old and arteries like Bentley exhaust pipes'.

Every Saturday, he brings a touch of Las Vegas to wet and windy football grounds in the north of England, from where he is asked by Radio 5 Live to file a match report. The station and its listeners, know that 'match report' is a loose term. Extremely loose. His contemporaries tell us who passed to whom, who suffered a thigh strain, who scored the goal. Hall, in a voice as rich as crumbling fruit cake, mixes the profound with the absurd. His surreal monologues have become part of the nation's sporting fabric. The sentences are short and resonant, the pitch dramatic and tense. 'Snowflakes. Floated like a gauze. Through the floodlights. Ice, cold, vinegar. Hitting red hot steak and kidney pies. And fresh chips . . . I just self-indulge. I make noises in my head. I like to entertain myself.'

His father was a self-made millionaire in baking and confectionery. His Irish-born mother cluttered the home with books. He was encouraged to read the likes of George Bernard Shaw, Oscar Wilde and Brian Friel, writers of great eloquence and wit. They have remained with him, they have become him. 'We always bandied words around. My mother had a great gift for English,' he says. His expressive voice, more Gielgud than Motson, was nurtured at Glossop Grammar School where he played the piano and was taught to infuse his speaking voice with the same rhythm and melody.

He joined BBC Radio in 1959 and became a television presenter six years later on the magazine programme *Northwest Tonight*. He wore cardigans and sat in an easy chair, 'to reflect the lives of the people and not talk down to them'. He came to national prominence in 1966 with *It's a Knockout* which ran for 16 years. His irresistible, out-to-lunch laughter was the delightful accompaniment to 15ft-high styrofoam chickens toppling from rope-bridges into oversized paddling pools. It was Stuart Hall's inner world come to life. Millions visited this world on a weekly basis, but in a moment of unforgivable sniffiness the BBC axed the programme. Hall did not sulk. He bought the rights and £500,000 of props. It is now a successful touring event; MicroSoft has just booked it for a staff party. The chicken is still crossing the rope-bridge.

Hall's life has not been without tragedy. His first son, Nicholas, died in his arms in a hospital waiting room when he was just three years old. He had suffered a heart seizure. 'It was as if a black hole had opened up in my life,' he says. In 1989 he came close to bankruptcy as a Lloyd's 'name' when the financial crisis hit the insurance syndicates. 'I was frightened every time I heard the postman walking down the path. I didn't know what the next letter would say. I nearly lost everything.' Two years later, he was charged with shoplifting from his local Safeway. He was acquitted of stealing a jar of coffee and a packet of sausages. There have also been several failed businesses.

'I've had my dog days,' he says. 'You've just got to give 110 per cent, haven't you? I've never been brilliant in business. If you have an artistic bent you're never going to be good at the logistics of business. I've no time for all that. I'm the man who ran Shit Travel, what a great venture that was!' He is referring to Stuart Hall International Travel, the acronym from hell.

During his shoplifting court case, a procession of Safeway staff – who might have been expected to follow the company line – spoke of their fondness for Hall. He had a smile and a word for everyone, he brightened up their day. 'The girls were lovely for speaking up for me,' he told reporters afterwards. Hall has maintained the common touch. When he visits Bolton Wanderers, for instance, he cherishes his reunion with the club's octogenarian tea ladies. 'They always say to me, "Oh, you look lovely today." I say, "I know." "Who got you ready?" they ask. "Me mam," I tell them.' He laughs, and laughs some more.

He is still giggling when we hit the street. A City fan passes him by on crutches. 'Alright, lad?' shouts Hall. 'Not bad,' he replies. 'Yes you are, you're on crutches!' They both laugh. It feels momentarily like a politician's walk-about, except there are no votes to be had: our protagonist is doing it just for fun. 'Why are you so popular, Stuart?' I ask. 'I don't know, I really don't know.'

Saturday, 24 April 1999
Manchester City 1 Wycombe Wanderers 2

A crowd of almost 30,000 were left in disbelief as the struggling visitors raced to a 2–0 lead inside the opening 30 minutes with goals from Andrew Baird and Sean Devine.

Shaun Goater's nineteenth goal of the season brought City back into the game just before half-time. After the break, City laid siege to the Wycombe goal without finding an equaliser. 'We started sloppily and from then on it was one-way traffic, but it just wouldn't come,' said Joe Royle. 'I can't be too critical of the lads. After all, it's only our second defeat in 22 games. I'm almost conceding that we can't now go up automatically but football is a strange game and we now have to go to Bristol Rovers and lift ourselves again.'

Sunday, 25 April 1999
David Ginola was named the PFA's player-of-the-year. There was consternation at City when they learned that none of their players had made the divisional team.

Ten

The Road to Wigan Pier

STEPNEY NOW A CITY MAN FOR KEEPS
(*The Times*, Saturday, 1 May 1999)

The sigh is just about audible. It turns into words. Alex Stepney has said them before, many times. 'I finished at United in 1979 and I've never worked for them since.' But, Alex, you played 433 times for Manchester United over a 12-year period. You were the solid, dependable goalkeeper behind the expansive out-field flair of Best, Charlton, Law and others. You were a member of the European Cup-winning team of 1968. That great save at the feet of Eusebio. Admit it, you're a red. He shakes his head, exasperated.

Alex Stepney, and don't even question this, is now in the blue corner of Manchester. He has been City's specialist goalkeeping coach for almost four years. He is not the only goalkeeper around these parts to swap colours. Tony Coton (162 games for City) is now the coach at United, while Joe Corrigan (476 games for City) is at Liverpool. The trend appears to be: gather lots of experience and know-how with one club, and pass it on to a local rival.

Stepney takes issue with the word 'rival'. 'I like to see both Manchester clubs doing well. I want to see City back in the Premiership with United. It is where this club belongs.' I tell him that two of my City-supporting friends, both of them equitable and intelligent, are uneasy about his defection. They noted his terminology when he visited a recent supporters' club meeting. He was, everyone agreed, likeable enough but, oh dear, whenever he referred to City it was 'they' and not 'we'. Stepney, though he does not say so, clearly believes that their level of partisanship is small-minded and peevish. Likewise, at its most crude, they – and other City fans – counter that Stepney, and the others who have crossed the blue–red divide, are mercenaries; the wage packet will govern the shirt.

Among the staff at Maine Road there is no such cynicism. Alex Stepney is one of them. They have seen the hours and effort he has put in for the blue cause. The football community of City, like that of all clubs, lives for the moment: are you good at your job? Do you talk sense? Can you take a joke? Are you someone to be respected? They don't ask about former clubs, or cup finals from 31 years ago. The past is for supporters and journalists.

Stepney is glad to be among a football community once more. He spent many years out of the game. After a period coaching in the United States he worked as a transport manager and then became a pub landlord. In the early 1980s, two regular visitors to the Navigation Inn in Stockport were Alex Williams and Gary Bailey, goalkeepers who were then in the first teams of Manchester City and Manchester United respectively. Stepney would take them to a nearby field where they practised the art of goalkeeping. 'I don't know what people would have thought, seeing the two goalkeepers from City and United diving around on a rugby pitch,' says Stepney.

Back then there was little emphasis on goalkeeping and Stepney believes the legacy of this indifference has been a shortage of home-grown talent and a necessity to bring in foreign players between the posts. 'We always had the attitude that foreign keepers were poor at coming for crosses, a bit eccentric and everything, but they worked at their game while we stood still. It is only in recent years that clubs have seen the importance of specialised coaching. It will be a few years yet before we really see the English lads coming through.'

His own protégé is Nicky Weaver, City's 20-year-old goalkeeper. Weaver played for Mansfield Town against City in a reserves match two years ago. Stepney was impressed by his natural ability and set about researching his background. 'It is important to go into a lad's temperament and attitude. He's not got to be someone who lets mistakes worry him. An out-field

171

player is allowed them, but a goalkeeper gets crucified.'

Although he cost the comparatively low fee of £100,000, Weaver was still something of a gamble. He had played just one first-team match for Mansfield and the reserves had lost 23 of their previous 24 games. In his final appearance for them, they lost 9–0. 'I saw that he had confidence and a good command of his area. I said to Nicky that in two years' time he could be in the first team if he worked hard at his game.' In fact, he made the first-team after just one season when Joe Royle elevated him from third choice to first. He has since been put on stand-by for the England Under-21s squad.

City, not slow to recognise a player of cult status, have issued special Nicky Weaver T-shirts which are selling well, especially to his female admirers. The club's claim that he is 'City's David Beckham' is a bit rich, but Weaver, shaggy hair and cherubic features, does have the look of a pin-up-to-be.

Stepney goes looking for him at City's training complex so they can be photographed together. 'Weaver, are you in there, Weaver?' he shouts into the gym. Weaver untangles himself from a weights machine and lolls towards Stepney. Loose-limbed and cheerful, he is like an escapee from *Home and Away*. At 6ft 3ins, he towers over Stepney. The two keepers make a good contrast; young and old, blond and dark, large and small, pupil and teacher, two goalies united. United, who mentioned United?

Saturday, 1 May 1999
Bristol Rovers 2 Manchester City 2

The game was put back to 6 p.m. to accommodate Sky TV's pay-per-view coverage and this made the encounter largely meaningless. Walsall had beaten Oldham Athletic earlier in the day to clinch the second automatic promotion place behind Fulham.

City were 2–0 in front by half-time with goals from Shaun Goater and Terry Cooke. A late rally by Bristol Rovers salvaged a draw for the home side. The point at least guaranteed City a play-off spot.

Monday, 3 May 1999

Andy Morrison, who had picked up his fourteenth booking of the season against Bristol Rovers, was told he would once more have to appear before an FA disciplinary commission.

Wednesday, 5 May 1999

City's shirt sponsor, Brother, announced that it did not plan to renew its contract with City for the 1999–2000 season.

CITY PREPARE TO UNDERGO TORMENT OF PLAY-OFFS
(*The Times*, Saturday, 8 May 1999)

Moss Side in the early-morning May sunshine has its own kind of sullen beauty. The sun flushes away the dread and unease of the inner-city night before and bathes the streets in light. Students from the nearby university campus amble by, milk bottles in hand. The old-boy walks his dog on an overgrown football pitch, stretching and yawning. A small queue develops at the bus stop.

In a few hours Moss Side will change again. Mike Corbett, Manchester City's commissionaire, will bid farewell to the night security staff and hunt out his first cup of tea of the day. 'That's better,' he'll sigh, and push open the metal gates that separate Manchester City from the world. Thereafter, Maine Road will become a magnet for an itinerant population. The ground staff will arrive, the kitchen staff, stewards, police, players and, finally, the fans.

Despite City's current league status, Maine Road is still a special place on a Saturday afternoon. It will be even more so today, the last day of the regular Nationwide League season when York City are the visitors. A sell-out crowd of more than 32,000 is expected, which will mirror the attendance of the opening game of the season against Blackpool.

August to May, Blackpool to York City, has been a long nine months in the history of the club. While they have qualified for the promotion play-offs, it has largely been a season of phlegmatic endeavour rather than joyous rejuvenation. Rarely have they looked anything greater than the solid but inconsistent outfit that – Fulham aside – typifies the division in which they play.

During the first half of the season, City were more than disappointing. Their nadir came just before Christmas when a defeat at York City left them in twelfth position. They were collecting more sendings off than points and Joe Royle's habitual after-match utterance of lambasting the referee or whining that it was 'their cup final' was beginning to grate.

After the York defeat, City embarked upon a run which Royle had forecast for some time, though fans had started to question this assertion. They lost just once in 21 games and propelled themselves defiantly into the promotion play-offs. Supporters were pleased to witness this recovery, though a play-off place is more an appeasement than a cause for celebration.

The arrival of two players of contrasting talents are widely seen as the galvanising force behind a team that hitherto held a neurosis about its own ability. Andy Morrison is your man in a crisis. He looks like something assembled from debris left on a construction site – thighs like oil drums, chest built from breeze-blocks, neck as wide as an industrial drain. A stalwart of the lower divisions, he has supplied the studs-and-thuds ruthlessness essential for any defence in lower league football.

Terry Cooke, a signing from Manchester United, is Joe Royle's compromise to class. He has that celebrated air of confidence that almost a decade spent at Old Trafford bestows upon a player. He holds the ball when all around him is hurly-burly and will tease a defender into a heedless lunge. He is impish, exciting and plays the game with a chuckle in his boots.

Many observers believe City's progress through the play-offs is a formality. They feel the sheer weight of support from the stands will propel them to victory in these death-or-glory matches. History would suggest otherwise, for City are not good under pressure. Their supporters invariably out-number and out-sing their counterparts but this has often served only to make players edgy and afraid. They have lost the same number of times at home as they have away this season, so who does their fanatical support inspire most – themselves or their opponents?

Preston North End have already secured their play-off spot while the other two places are between Gillingham, Bournemouth and Wigan Athletic. Of these, only Bournemouth, like City, are new to the breathless madness that is play-off football. In basic terms, then, City have only a one-in-four chance of securing the promotion spot.

Of course, City supporters, with their enigmatic mixture of optimism and fatalism, will argue that theirs is the team currently in best form. They have lost just twice in the league in nearly five months but, worry-worry, their last three games have been a win, a defeat and a draw. No fear, at least the current issue of the City fanzine, *King of the Kippax* provides solace. It contains a spoof advert marketing City as a cure for low blood pressure: 'as proven over the last 30 years' is the claim.

Saturday, 8 May 1999
Manchester City 4 York City 0

Without hitting top form, City brushed aside York City who were relegated because of the defeat and results elsewhere. The City scorers were Paul Dickov, Jeff Whitley, Kevin Horlock and Danny Allsopp. The win meant City finished the regular season in third place, six points ahead of Wigan in seventh spot.

Before the game, City players unfurled a banner on the pitch carrying the message: 'You're the Best and You Know You Are! Thanks for Your Support.' A rainbow also appeared behind the Platt Lane Stand. At the final whistle, City learned they would meet Wigan Athletic in the semi-final of the promotion play-offs.

The attendance was 32,471, the highest at Maine Road for five years. City's average league home attendance for the season was 28,261. This was more than double the next best average for the division, Stoke City. Only one team surpassed the average in Division One, Sunderland, and it was greater than nine clubs in the FA Carling Premiership.

In keeping a clean-sheet, Nicky Weaver surpassed Alex Williams's record of 21 during a season, though Weaver had played in four extra matches.

Monday, 11 May 1999

Gerard Wiekens was voted the club's player-of-the-season, with Nicky Weaver runner-up and Andy Morrison in third place. Shaun Wright-Phillips, although still to make his first-team début, won the young-player-of-the-year prize.

Wednesday, 13 May 1999

Tickets went on sale for the away leg at Springfield Park, Wigan. Only 1,400 were available to City supporters and they were allocated to season-ticket holders who could produce ticket stubs from at least five away matches.

Fans began queuing at 4 a.m., even though tickets did not go on sale until 5.30 p.m. The queue stretched half way along Maine Road and there was consternation when many missed out. Their anger was intensified when they were given raffle tickets as proof of their position in the queue – they wrongly believed that these guaranteed them a match ticket.

City announced they would install a huge screen at Maine Road and beam the match live.

PSYCHOLOGIST GETS EMOTIONAL ABOUT CITY'S MIND GAMES
(*The Times*, Saturday, 15 May 1999)

Suddenly, my first name trebles in length. 'Maaark, nice to meet ya.' The smile complements the rainbow sweater. It dazzles, it glows, it sings happiness and a sunny morning to the world. 'Hey, you know what, when I'm on TV they sometimes call me the sweater psychologist. It's kinda my image I suppose,' says the Mancunian from California.

Professor Cary Cooper, the man with stretch-limo vowels, is a leading expert in the study of stress. Tense, nervous headache? A two-minute spot at the end of the news that needs filling with some animated, user-friendly psycho-babble? Cooper's your man, a Technicolor, made-for-TV psychologist. Jeeez, he was even named after Cary Grant, and has the look of a wiry, up-for-it Richard Dreyfuss.

Lamentably, this savant of stress holds a dark, dark secret. A great deal of his own life has been lived out against a backdrop of unremitting anxiety. He is, and always will be, a supporter of Manchester City. 'Hey! I'm a psychologist. I'm allowed to have at least one obsession, aren't I?' Perhaps he has plotted a rationale to counter City-induced tension, for Cooper is 59, with the skin of a 40-year-old, and the incandescence of a teenager.

He fidgets in his chair, asks too many questions. In his attempt to draw closer, to communicate, he bangs his chair against the table. 'That's another reason why I like football, people show their emotions and open up. As a psychologist, I'm always trying to make them do that,' he says.

He is already known to the club and has offered his counsel in their hour of need – their first encounter with the promotion play-offs. They play at Wigan Athletic today in the first-leg of the semi-final. 'I think it is important that whatever they do over the next few days, they do it as a team. It really is team stuff now,' he says. 'They should spend time together, play a game of golf, maybe go for a walk in the countryside. The players should know that, whatever happens, the fans are going to be there for them. City fans will back them, win or lose, as long as they give it their best goddam effort.'

Cooper is the pro-vice-chancellor of the University of Manchester Institute of Science and Technology. It was his idea for the university to bestow an honorary degree on Mick Hucknall of Simply Red. Showbiz and academia, round-rimmed glasses and multi-coloured sweaters, Cooper makes them a comfortable fit.

Unsurprisingly, he is a good friend of the television presenter and fellow City supporter, Stuart Hall. He even spoke up for him during the court case when Hall was acquitted of a shoplifting charge. They are both sunshine on legs, people so in love with life they make others sceptical, resentful even.

'You know, I can't understand that. It's one of the few British characteristics that I don't really like,' he says. Otherwise, Cooper is the ultimate Anglophile. 'My best friend in the States had lived for a long while in England. He told me about things like 'The Goons' and the 'Carry On' series. It all seemed so off-the-wall and eccentric.'

In 1964 he left the University of California to continue his studies in England, at Leeds University. Within weeks he had attended his first football match, watching Leeds United at Elland Road. 'I liked it straight away. It was fast and constant. I was used to all the razzmatazz of American sport. With soccer it was, "what you see is what you get", without any of that cheer-leaders garbage. It wasn't about peanuts or hot dogs, they just got right down to it.'

He lectured for several years in Southampton, where he sometimes attended The Dell, but it was only when he came to Manchester that he found a true affinity with a football club. 'I went to see United, but when I got to my car after the match a tyre on my car had been slashed. I don't know what it was, but the atmosphere back in the 1970s wasn't all that pleasant at United.' His eyes sparkle when he talks of City. 'My heart and soul is with City. I like to see United do well because I'm a Mancunian now, but City is my club. I've always seen them as more of a family club, a place where there is a sense of community.'

Like many others, he is fascinated by the phenomenon of City's fiercely loyal support. He feels they are an anachronism, a snapshot of better days gone by. 'You do not have loyalty any more in life. Everyone is on short-term contracts or part-time work. No one is willing to show commitment. City supporters go against this trend. They have a great camaraderie among each other. They are holding on to values that few people believe in any more, but which are so important.' Isn't this all a tad sentimental for a social scientist? 'Look, mate, this is the birthplace of the industrial revolution, this is where it all started, this is Manchester grit, a poke in the eye to everyone else.' He is leaning across the table, touching my arm, repeating my first name constantly. Perhaps we should chorus *Blue Moon* or *The Red Flag*; either way, this man makes me want to sing. Take note, Joe Royle.

Saturday, 15 May 1999
Wigan Athletic 1 Manchester City 1
(Nationwide League Division Two Semi-Final Play-off First Leg)
City conceded a goal after just 19 seconds when Stuart Barlow capitalised on a misunderstanding between Nicky Weaver and Gerard Wiekens. Paul Dickov scored an equaliser to set up a thrilling second leg at Maine Road.

CITY AND WIGAN KEEN TO LINGER NO LONGER
(match report, *The Times*, Monday, 17 May 1999)

Noticeably, Joe Royle had left his car parked in close proximity to the main entrance. Springfield Park, Wigan, rather like Nationwide League Division Two, is not a place where it pays to linger. Indeed, Wigan themselves will depart for Robin Park this summer, leaving behind the weeds, the graffiti, the patched-up stands and the cloying aura of a small patch of Britain that has remained for ever 1973 or thereabouts.

Demolition is due to begin in a few weeks, but City supporters, benevolent to a fault, have already set work in progress. Seconds before kick-off, a section of corrugated fencing wobbled behind the visitors' end. It was abruptly flattened and about a dozen skipped through a small meadow to reach the terracing.

Their ingenuity and zeal was rewarded in typical City style. Wigan kicked off and booted the ball resolutely but aimlessly upfield. Richard Edghill took the resultant throw-in and, as the ball rolled between Wiekens and Weaver, both fell into a state of soft-focus apoplexy. Barlow, firmly of the real world, danced between them and tapped it into an empty net. The game had been under way for just 19 seconds.

City were in deep shock, their defence wandering around randomly like car crash victims on the hard shoulder. Passes were over-hit, the ball constantly kicked high and long, and the mere glimpse of a Wigan striker provoked abject terror. Wigan, sensing the trepidation, were direct and purposeful, though they could not increase their lead.

179

Royle has built a team high on endeavour and heart, if lacking in guile. They scamper through a game of football like eager puppies, snapping at ankles, everything hurry-hurry and breathless. Michael Brown, their best player, finally resolved to keep the ball and struck the bar after a fine solo run. At last, something considered, some air to breathe. The equaliser came 14 minutes before the end when Dickov slammed home a cross from Brown.

Earlier, Wigan's Liddell chose to shoot when a pass to Jones might have brought more reward and they were denied a penalty when Wiekens appeared to handle inside the area. They played chiefly on the counter-attack and their subtlety and craft formed an intriguing contrast to their visitors' exuberance.

Before the end, about 100 police officers and stewards formed a cordon in front of the City supporters. They were standing at first but then kneeled down. 'Sit down, if you love City,' was the response from the crowd.

Unfortunately, Wigan supporters invaded the playing area at the final whistle and, again true to the spirit of 1973, tried to revive hooliganism by goading the City fans. Thwarted by a police vanguard, they decided instead to break up sections of the ground to take away as souvenirs. The sight of a teenager, his face painted blue and white, a curly wig on his head, haring off with the seats from the dug-out will remain in the memory for some time.

'We'll see you all back at our place on Wednesday,' said Royle afterwards. Get set for high drama at Maine Road, for these are two well-matched teams, one seeking a renaissance, the other a re-invention.

Wednesday, 19 May 1999
Manchester City 1 Wigan Athletic 0
(Nationwide League Division Two Semi-final Play-off Second Leg)
A goal in the first half by Shaun Goater settled a tight, nervous game. The final whistle signalled a pitch invasion and scenes of unbridled euphoria.

CITY'S STOCK STILL RISES THANKS TO GOATER
(match report, *The Times*, Thursday, 20 May 1999)

Dignity has finally been restored to the part of Manchester that remains forever blue. Pitched against the festival of triumph on the other side of town, qualification to a Division Two promotion play-off final seems particularly trifling. No matter. Raise the blue flag, book the ticket to Wembley: City and success – of the qualified variety – are allies once more.

In a scrappy, tense match last night they eased nervously past a Wigan side of some assurance. Though playing the more considered football, Wigan barely escaped their own half as City took the game to their visitors relentlessly from the kick-off. City were spirited rather than crafted and finally knocked a hole through Wigan's defence.

Terry Cooke, who had been by-passed in the frenzy, broke on the right and sent a deep cross to the far post. Shaun Goater threw himself at the ball and forced it over the line with his chest. It was the clumsy, scrambled goal the game deserved. Wigan players claimed he had used his hand.

On the counter-attack Wigan were far more precise, with both Barlow and Bradshaw finding their team-mates while City preferred to play the ball long and chase it to ground. After the interval, Wigan were forced on the offensive and the game became a much better spectacle. Dickov twice fired wide, while Jones, for Wigan, headed a good chance on to the bar.

Long before the end, City's passionate crowd bayed for the final whistle. Gareth Taylor came close to sealing victory minutes before the end but shot tamely at Carroll from close range. The victory was slim, the nerves frayed, but, at last, the streets of Manchester will be painted blue instead of red. Wembley awaits; Bayern who?

● Manchester United were due to play Bayern Munich in the final of the European Cup a week later.

Friday, 21 May 1999
City officials were furious to learn they would receive just

37,000 tickets for the promotion play-off final. Gillingham, with an average league attendance of 6,339, were to get 34,000.

Ray Mathias, the Wigan Athletic manager, was dismissed. 'We said we wanted to be out of the Second Division by the millennium. We gave Ray a job to do. The stark reality is that we are still in the Second Division,' said Dave Whelan, the club's chairman. 'This has hit me with a massive jolt. I'm devastated,' said Mathias.

Eleven

Goodbye to All That

REJOICING MASKS THE WEAKNESSES
(The Times, Saturday, 22 May 1999)

'Wembley, Wembley,' muttered Joe Royle, as if he believed saying the word constantly would make it easier to believe. A shake of the head, a swig of beer, a huge smile: 'Wembley!'

Indeed, next Sunday, Manchester City will visit Wembley Stadium to take on Gillingham in the Division Two promotion play-off final. It has been a long, fraught season for City but victory against Wigan Athletic on Wednesday in the play-off semi-final set them dancing on the pitch. 'The fans deserve a day out,' said Royle, 'The love they have for this club is unbelievable, they are on a crusade.'

Royle has been in the professional game for more than 35 years. He has seen it all, done it all. Football has enabled him to live a life to the full – happiness, sadness, league titles, England caps, cup finals, friends, humour, ignominy, not to mention the inevitable war-wounds, in his case osteoarthritis and a plastic hip. Before City he managed Everton and in his final days at Goodison Park he had the pallor of a ghost. He became invisible in his suit. The gags evaporated and he could barely lift up his head at the after-match press conferences.

Heartening, then, to see the smiles and the bonhomie on Wednesday, the flesh put back on the bones. It was more of a love-in than a press conference. 'Hello Weasel,' he said as he entered. 'Mr Weasel, to you,' countered the journalist. Royle had a can of cider in his hand, but wanted lager. 'I've saved you one, Joe,' said the hospitality lady. 'Good girl.' Wouldn't champagne be more appropriate, someone asked. 'I hate champagne, it makes me fart!'

Back on the pitch and in the streets, the celebrations among the fans were wanton. They drank in this rare success lustily, as if they had simultaneously learned that the world would never again be at war and – more importantly – the council had planned to build a housing estate on Old Trafford. It was ridiculously overdone. A quiet glass of sherry would have been more apt, a chink-chink rather than a crash, bang, wallop! The ferocity of their joy served only to emphasise the barrenness of their recent history. It is 23 years since they last visited Wembley in a meaningful competition.

City finished third in the league, so feel they already have a moral claim on a promotion place. It has not, however, been a season of mellifluous, rarefied football that habitually sweeps teams towards the top of the league. Much of their play has been fractured and hopeful, their victories earned by virtue of having a bigger heart than their opponents. They are like the hurdler who has won a medal, but turns to see the hurdles upturned behind him, his legs covered in bruises. Promoted or not, Royle must spend the summer searching for ball-players to complement the grafters.

Unfortunately, City will not be able to count on the support of their club chaplain, Tony Porter, next Sunday. 'I hope all the supporters have a good day out, but it is not for me. Sunday is the day we celebrate the resurrection and I would rather keep it that way. I'm not a killjoy or anything, it is just my personal decision.'

Porter is the minister at Holy Trinity Platt, a church based a few hundred yards from Maine Road. 'There was a lot of noise outside the church after Wednesday's game, car horns being hooted and people singing. It was all out of tune mind, but sung in a good spirit. I am absolutely delighted for the supporters. They've not had a lot to shout about, especially the younger ones.'

In recent years, City, like many progressive clubs, has fostered a sense of community both within themselves and in the surrounding neighbourhood. Porter was invited by a previous manager, Alan Ball, to provide some spiritual succour to this football village. 'City are part of my parish. Everyone immediately thinks of the first team, but I spend a lot of time with the young lads at the club, and also the ground staff,' he said. 'I'm not a social worker, though, I talk things through from a Christian perspective.'

At Christmas he organised a carol service which was well-attended by the club's staff. 'Joe [Royle] was incredibly supportive. He wrote to everyone at the club and invited them to come along. He didn't need to do that.' Although he did not play football, Porter was a keen hockey player, and represented England Schoolboys on six occasions. 'I am used to the atmosphere around dressing-rooms. It doesn't bother me that people might take the mick when they see my collar. I've been a vicar for 20 years, I've heard all the jokes. They're OK at City, a good set of people.'

He will not be praying that City beat Gillingham, preferring instead to address – in prayer – a problem that he feels has undermined the club for years. 'I pray for stability, that the club has finally abandoned it's "hello, goodbye" policy. I think the younger players have really suffered because of it. They were so dispirited by it all.'

Monday, 24 May 1999
Police were called to Maine Road to deal with angry scenes among supporters queuing for Wembley tickets. Some fans had waited for up to 15 hours and there were real fears that there would not be enough tickets to meet the demand. Wembley tickets on sale via London agencies were reportedly fetching up to £150 each.

POWER PLUGGED INTO CITY FOR LIFE
(*The Times*, Saturday 29 May 1999)

Old footballers don't die, they go to Mottram Hall. There, among the tree-lined walks and undulating pastures, they can lose themselves to nostalgia, laugh at their first ever curly perm, rummage in their kit-bags to find shorts one size larger than a pair of swimming trunks and exclaim: 'We used to wear *these!*'

Amazingly, the players from your old football cards of the 1970s and 1980s still walk the earth. They might be grey at the temples, thicker around the middle but, look, there's Dave Watson, the Everton stalwart, trying to find the 'off' button on his mobile phone. Gordon Hill, the ex-Manchester United winger, is still playing the cheeky Cockney, except with his teenage son in tow. Danny Wilson, Sheffield Wednesday manager and ex-just-about-every-team-in-the-League, is talking conspiratorially with two men in the bar.

The FA has hired the historic hall in Cheshire for one of its more prestigious coaching courses. Howard Wilkinson and Don Howe are among the speakers, so it's clearly not a quick shimmy around a few traffic cones. 'Howard gave one of the lectures this morning,' Paul Power, the former Manchester City captain, explains. 'He was teaching us how to work the ball out in little triangles.' Cue the subtitles: 'He was teaching us how to use short, intricate passes to move forward when we are closely marked.'

Paul Power, now a senior member of City's coaching staff, has not wallowed in opulence for some time. When he was a City player (1975 to 1986), however, the posh country hotel was often part of the pre-match itinerary. Back then, City played in enough momentous games to justify stop-overs at ivy-clad mansions in quaint rural villages. Besides, tracksuits among the colonnades always made for great TV on cup final morning.

Power was the last player to captain City at Wembley, where he played for them on three occasions. He was a goalscorer in the San Siro when City drew a UEFA Cup tie with AC Milan in November 1978. He played more than 400 times for City, and kept the faith even when he left for Everton. On their march to the 1986–87 League Championship, he scored against City in a 3–1 win. A Mancunian and a City fan from boyhood, he refused to celebrate the goal. He looks much the same as he did then – thin and rangy, wiry moustache, thick eyebrows and that famously peculiar blink, as if he has kindly offered to break in a pair of contact lenses for a mate. He made the offer in 1973, and hasn't seen him since.

City are back at Wembley tomorrow, though a Division Two

promotion play-off final against Gillingham seems small-time measured against the 1981 FA Cup final against Tottenham Hotspur, or even the game against Chelsea in the Full Members Cup final of 1986. 'I don't know, it's a trip to Wembley and there's a lot at stake,' says Power diplomatically. 'I'm not one for nostalgia. I won't be thinking about when I was last there, but going there as a fan and as someone still working at the club and hoping they win.'

Football clubs routinely pronounce that a particular game is the most important in their history. Usually this is hyperbole, but tomorrow's is the authentic article for Manchester City. A defeat will inflict a massive financial cost. The club is burdened by a lingering debt and another season in this division will lead to more cutbacks and further down-sizing. The walls leading to escape will become steeper still. One season in the third tier of English football is an aberration, an away-day through football's backwater. Two seasons – or more – is a lifetime. It will change the image of Manchester City for ever, spoil its good name.

The demoralisation of defeat will seep like mustard gas over the staff and supporters. There are a lot of hearts to break, for City have an average home attendance of 28,261, a figure that nine clubs in the FA Carling Premiership cannot match. It has been said to the point of cliché: City supporters deserve better. This season they have stood on open terraces in the pouring rain, suffered the jeers of every small-town Johnny, and the football has been only fleetingly entertaining. They have pulled themselves through it, with a crate of ale and a yard of good humour.

Paul Power will travel to Wembley with a party of young players from City's Academy. He spends his time mainly coaching the 9 to 13-year-olds. 'Whether we win or not, the Academy will remain in place,' he says. 'The structure of the club is so much better than it was before. When I came to City as a kid, there'd be 30 of us and just five footballs. We'd do a bit of running, finish with a game and go home. I was small for my age and never got to touch the ball.'

He is confident City will leave Wembley as victors. 'I'm not worried about Sunday. We have always done well in the important games this season. We've performed badly against the likes of Lincoln City and teams like that.' Of course, an additional burden this season for City supporters has been the great success of United. City's lowest point ever has, inevitably, corresponded with United's highest. 'I don't really care about United,' says Power. 'They've done the treble, and good luck to them, but it's City I'm bothered about. Historically, it runs in parallel that we tend to do well when they do, so it might be a good omen.'

Sunday, 30 May 1999

The News Of The World warned of impending violence in and around Wembley in their story, 'Police Fear Wembley Carnage'. It was rumoured that Millwall fans had bought up to 4,000 tickets from Gillingham's allocation and planned to attack the City contingent.

Sunday, 30 May 1999

Gillingham 2 Manchester City 2 (City win 3–1 on penalties)
Nationwide League Division Two Promotion Play-off Final
Promotion was secured in dramatic fashion after City staged a late, late comeback. Trailing by two goals from Carl Asaba and Robert Taylor, they pulled one back through Kevin Horlock with a minute remaining. Paul Dickov scored the equaliser in injury time. There were no more goals in extra-time, but City went on to win after Nicky Weaver saved two Gillingham penalties. 'As always, we had to do it the hard way but I hope this has gone some way towards curing one of our old traditions of losing on big occasions,' said Royle.

NOW THAT OLD BLUE MOON REALLY IS RISING
(match report, *The Times*, Monday, 31 May 1999)

Heads bowed, they streamed down the aisles. Trailing by two goals, just one minute left – time for home. City, you see, don't do comebacks; magic and Manchester City parted company long ago. Suddenly, Horlock whacks a loose ball into the net. A consolation, surely. Tick-tock, more time gone. Another frenzied attack and Dickov strikes the ball home. City are everywhere, there's magic in the air.

Time for penalties and City can field their most consistent performer of the season – their magnificent support. Forced to take their kicks in front of the City fans, Gillingham faced a cacophony of noise, not to mention a goalkeeper called Nicky Weaver. All lank hair and gangling legs, Weaver has the laid-back, shoulder-shrugging demeanour of a fifth-former asked to join a kickabout with a few urchins on the park. Two penalty saves later, he is skipping, jumping, hopping across the Wembley turf. City are up and the road maps to Colchester, and Wycombe are redundant.

Fittingly, City had brought Manchester weather with them and, if it felt like October for the most of the game, both teams played as if they were wearing duffle coats and wellingtons. Ominously, as the rain came down, stewards donned white raincoats with pointed hoods. They hunched in front of the supporters like grim reapers waiting for their quarry.

Back in December, Royle had already given up on discretion when he blurted: 'I hate this division.' As a player and manager, his previous visit to football's hinterland had been for the occasional spat in the cup. Then opponents would roll out the barrel-chested defenders and, after some thud in the mud, Royle and Co. were back on the team coach, 3–0 to the good and a hearty sing-song all the way home.

It has been a tortuous season for City. In their smart club blazers, they have disembarked from luxury coaches on to weed-strewn car parks. They have picked their way through puddles and pot holes, to run out on pitches surrounded by broken stands. Facing them at *every* game has been a set of players passionate to beat Manchester City, the very Manchester City who used to be on television, used to be famous. You know, Colin Bell, Franny Lee, Rodney Marsh. It felt like great fun, the equivalent of a date with Claudia Schiffer at the scruffiest pub in town.

A good percentage of the players could be said to deserve the dishonour, since nine of those on duty at Wembley were in the squad that was relegated last season. The supporters, meanwhile, merit no part in this arbitrary punishment. If 'Blue Moon' is the club theme song, 'You're not famous any more' has become the scornful anti-theme. It has hurt, but the same fans who once waved inflatable bananas at their rivals have gamely put their arms around one another, or a bottle of beer. Why else, for example, would they depart for an away game at Macclesfield Town, just 15 miles away, at 9 a.m., if it wasn't as much about indulgence and camaraderie as it was football? At some games, the pungent aroma of non-High Street tobacco has wafted across the terraces. The players are clearly not the only ones on grass; sometimes it's whatever gets you through.

The clamour for Wembley tickets in Manchester was relentless. City, the thirteenth best-supported club in the country, were given practically the same allocation as Gillingham, whose average home attendance made them England's 52nd most 'popular' club. The Football League is evidently a friend of the passive day-tripper with a vague interest in football, and a foe of the fanatic. 'The allocation was a joke,' said Willie Donachie. No one was laughing in Manchester, where some fans – season ticket holders at that – had to queue for up to 12 hours or haggle outside Wembley with gleeful touts. One City supporter trudged around the outside of the stadium with a placard reading: 'City fan from New York – and I can prove it! Ticket wanted.'

The enigma of City fans will go on. They are every character Shakespeare created, but all in the same person: foolish, loyal, proud, dogged, sentimental and headstrong. They are the type of people who still cry at re-runs of *The Incredible Journey*. Happy or sad, they howl, 'Blue Moon, you saw me standing alone', to the night sky, or the pub landlady. It is a beautiful song. When they sing it, they are the sailor drifting down the Ship Canal after too many years at sea. They didn't get the girl, but what the hell, City beat Gillingham – Division One here we come!

So, United did the treble. Big deal. Very big, actually, but that's another story from another part of town. Wembley is Wembley and a promotion play-off final is more important to a club's well-being than a cup final. The latter is a pleasant day out, a celebration regardless of the result. The former is the future of your club condensed into 90 minutes. A dodgy back-pass, a goalkeeping fluff and you remain in Nowheresville for another season, at least.

The Grim Reaper left Wembley with Gillingham under his arm. The other lot were singing their hearts out. How does that song go again?

● Football writing is littered with hyperbole, but this was truly breathtaking. At the full-time whistle, the stadium buzzed with a sense of disbelief. They had seen City's goals, but they had not registered. Their supporters had abandoned hope, resigned themselves to heartbreak. Suddenly, hope was re-born. At moments like this, football was regenerative, celestial, delirious, more than mere sport. It lifted the soul, made the head swim in joy. The City fans cried, hugged one another, pulled on each other's arm for confirmation: 'Has this really happened?' 'Thank you, God, thank you.'

Earlier in the day, it had been fascinating to note the marked difference between the two sets of supporters. Gillingham fans arriving on coaches looked like families heading to the coast, all packed-lunches and best clothes. They were all ages, with home-made flags and specially-knitted jumpers carrying messages like 'Good Luck You Gills'. The mood on the City coaches was noticeably more reckless. They were at the windows, gesturing and clapping, clutching beer cans. Some were halfway out of the coach roofs, waving flags and shouting. On the street, many City fans were already drunk, welcoming their fellow supporters by banging on the side of their vehicles. Gillingham fans passed by without any opposition and the jibes were good humoured. In a sidestreet, a couple climbed out of a car wearing bridal wear, as if they had dashed to the ground from the church. 'You're not single any more,' came the chant from a group of City fans.

Inside Wembley, most of the Gillingham supporters were in their seats by 1.45 p.m., while City filed in much closer to kick-off time. Once the game was under way, the Gillingham supporters matched City for passion and many who had earlier criticised the Football League's ticket policy, conceded that

Gillingham had contributed significantly to the atmosphere.

The press enclosure at Wembley gave a superb vantage point. At the end, when City had secured promotion, I became aware of a cameo being played out directly beneath the press area. While the vast majority of City fans were clapping and cheering, a young boy of about eight was goading the Gillingham supporters across the other side of the Royal Box. He held up the middle finger of his right hand, while slipping over it a circle made from the thumb and forefinger of his left hand. I scanned the row to see if his father was about to rebuke him. His dad, however, was rapt, running on the spot and, looking over to the Gillingham fans, began simulating oral sex. Like father, like son.

Many City fans, estimated as high as 5,000, streamed out of the stadium when Gillingham scored their second goal. Noel Gallagher of Oasis was among them. They were made aware of the team's comeback by police officers, coach drivers or fans carrying portable radios. Hundreds raced back to the ground. Wembley had a policy of no re-admission, but waived the rule in the circumstances. Some over-officious stewards valiantly tried to stop the flow but they were pushed aside by the exuberant fans. One City supporter was on a train heading away from the stadium when he heard news of the equaliser. He pulled the emergency cord and ran down the tracks back towards Wembley. Police were waiting for him, but charged him in double-quick time and allowed him to return to the ground.

Unexpectedly, David Bernstein and Chris Bird appeared on the pitch for a rather apologetic lap of honour. Many commented afterwards that it was peculiar that a chairman should spend all season forging his image as a man without ego or ostentation, to suddenly thrust himself into the limelight. The distance between the VIP area and the pitch was considerable, and the pair had to negotiate several obstacles; they had plenty of time to deliberate over their actions. Admittedly, once on the pitch, Bernstein shuffled around shyly as if he had realised immediately his mistake. Later, he was abashed: 'It will be a one-off. I won't be making a habit of it, you can be sure of that,' he said.

The celebrations ran for some time out on the pitch. 'Roll

with It' by Oasis was played several times and later became the theme tune of the day for many supporters. At several points the City players bowed before the fans as a mark of respect. Once the Gillingham contingent had left the stadium, a number of City fans became visible in their section. About 100 huddled together and joined in the singing and dancing. The players noticed and broke off to salute these supporters, many of whom – out of desperation – had bought their tickets from touts and suffered the unpleasant experience of sitting among rival supporters. It mattered not at the end; they were there, and being there was everything.

Nicky Weaver's victory dance was the most memorable image of the day. He charged towards the Tunnel End, cleared the advertising hoardings, then doubled back halfway along the Wembley touch-line with the entire team in crazed pursuit. On the official team photo afterwards, he dived headlong across the frame, his smile as wide as Piccadilly Gardens. He was 20, he had made the penalty saves that had secured promotion for his team. For a few seconds we were all 20 again, and running headlong at life, happy as hell.

Tuesday, 1 June 1999

City announced that they would not emulate Manchester United and parade through the city on an open-top bus. 'We should not be celebrating promotion from the old third division. This is only the first stage of a long road back to respectability. We can celebrate when we are in the Premiership,' said Royle.

Wednesday, 2 June 1999

The price-freeze on season tickets was extended by a further week. Victory at Wembley had helped push sales through the 14,000 barrier.

Thursday, 3 June 1999

Chris Bird and the club's financial consultant, Alistair Mackintosh, were invited to join City's board of directors. 'It's unbelievable. When I was a kid I always dreamed of playing for

City,' said Bird. 'Becoming a director is something I never really thought about. I know it sounds cheesy, but this is a real honour.' As well as the directorship, Bird was appointed Chief Operating Officer, with responsibilities ranging from stadium management to merchandising.

Friday, 4 June 1999

David Bernstein made a formal apology to supporters who had queued hours for Wembley tickets. 'I am sorry for our fans' disappointment,' said Bernstein. 'I hold my hands up. We should have done better.'

ROYLE ASCENT ENDS SEASON OF SUSPENSE
(*The Times*, Saturday, 5 June 1999)

So quiet. Just the odd twitter of birds, otherwise a sleepy, sprawling silence. A church steeple rises in the distance above a cluster of trees. Potato crops are fanned by a cool breeze. There's not a soul around. This is the place football managers come home to when all the kicking and screaming and stressing is finished.

Joe Royle carries stress well. Win or lose, he'll have a laugh with the press lads. We're all 'lads', even the girls; they don't seem to mind. Look closely, though, when City have lost, and note the tilt of his head or the way he holds his body as he leaves the room. Not quite slumped, but bowed, as if two of the four strings holding him upright have snapped. Only now, as he dances across his driveway, a smile like car headlights in the darkness, does it become clear the stress he has been under. Job done, City promoted, he is a different man.

He had spent the previous night at the home of Willie Donachie after the staff promotion party. They are great friends and it's easy to imagine the scenario after lights-out, both of them giddy: 'We did it, Willie. We bloody did it.' 'Och, Joe, will ye get tae sleep.' It goes quiet for a minute. Suddenly, two voices in unison: 'Blue moon, I saw you standing alone . . . '

Seldom does football transcend the prosaic. It is routinely

banal, predictable and monochrome: pass, tackle, pass, punt upfield, miscontrol, tackle, pass, throw-in, corner, pass, stay awake at the back. City's Division Two play-off final against Gillingham last Sunday was thus, until one minute before the end of normal time. Then, for no good reason, football became your favourite record played at the youth club disco; the night you first realised you were in love; the afternoon when – elbows in the breeze – you drove your first car; the birth of your first child. All these things. At once.

'It still feels surreal,' concedes Royle. 'I don't think anyone can believe we came back like that. We went through such a gamut of emotions. Someone clearly decreed that if we were to get promotion it would have to be the hard way.' To recap, City, through Horlock and Dickov, made it 2–2 with goals in the 90th and 94th minute, and then won 3–1 after a penalty shoot-out. Nicky Weaver saved two penalties and was so pleased with himself that his profuse and erratic celebrations drew concerned glances from members of the St John's Ambulance Service.

As Royle has emphasised since, it shouldn't have seemed such a big deal. It wasn't a cup final, it was merely City completing a job that had caused them unnecessary labour in the first place. 'I think I seriously underestimated how much it would mean to the fans. It was as if we had to exorcise a lot of ghosts,' he says. Much has been made of the delirium at Wembley, but when Dickov's equaliser hit the roof of the net, there was briefly an extraordinary silence. Supporters were apoplectic, unable to believe their eyes. Shirt-sleeves were tugged, affirmation was required. 'Did I just see what I think I saw just then?' 'Well, I saw it too.' Strangers hugged like brothers, children were lifted off their feet; a blue moon had risen.

The season has been long and arduous for City. At Christmas they were twelfth, the stroll had become a six-mile hike, uphill. 'It was as if all the other teams were out to ambush us,' says Royle. 'They played so much above themselves it was unbelievable. We'd have them watched the week before we were due to play them and the report I'd get back would be worth-less. Likewise, we noticed their results for their next match and they would invariably lose. I had a few low moments, but I never doubted that we had the players who could do the job.'

The run of form Royle had defiantly forecast duly arrived and they lost just twice in their final 24 matches of the normal season. He was dreading the play-offs and did everything possible to maintain an air of normality. The squad stayed in their usual London hotel for the match at Wembley, arriving just the day before, and leaving for the ground as late as possible. 'I remember when I played in the FA Cup final of 1968 for Everton. I was only 18 at the time, and I became really nervous as we travelled to the ground past all the fans. I didn't say anything to anyone, but I was continually bringing up bile, and swallowing it because I didn't want anyone to see how bad I felt.'

He kept his pre-match pep-talk to just three or four minutes on Sunday; all the preparation had already been done. 'I always try and keep a cool head during the game, but I must say that was the most dramatic match I have ever been involved in.' When City conceded the first goal, Royle's 28-year-old son, Lee, was too distressed to remain in the stadium. Distraught, he headed back to the hotel, a walk breaking into a dash for the television as various cabbies relayed the sequence of goals. Back on the pitch, Royle gathered his players around him just before extra-time. 'I just told them, "We've got them here, we've got them."' Indeed they had.

Within seconds of Weaver's match-winning save, Royle was approached by a Wembley official. He wondered if City minded prolonging their on-pitch celebrations while they cleared the stadium of Gillingham fans. 'I told him I didn't think that would be a problem!' says Royle. In the midst of the noise and madness, Royle slipped away quietly to the dressing-room with Donachie for a can of beer and a few moments of reflection.

Over the next few weeks, there will be more time for reflection. Royle will walk his three labradors through the country lanes around his home. He plans a holiday in Sardinia. Donachie is also going away, for three weeks. When he returns, the two pals will soon be on the phone to one another: 'We did it, Willie. We bloody did it.'

● I spoke with Royle on the telephone early on Thursday

morning while he was at Platt Lane. He was dealing with the final paperwork before the summer recess. I imagined I would get about 20 minutes with him for my end-of-season piece. I was surprised, then, when he invited me to his home later that afternoon. I was impressed that after a long, stamina-sapping week and, indeed, a long season, he was willing to put time aside to talk once more about City in depth.

Although a large house, the furnishings were similar to any other – 20 or so CDs in a rack; family portraits on the wall; a book (a biography of Queen Elizabeth I) on the coffee table, alongside a plastic wallet containing scores of snapshots; a left-handed Rickenbacker guitar propped up against the wall. Royle said it was his son's: 'He's really good, but he won't do anything with it. I keep telling him to.'

We sat in the conservatory, overlooking a large, well-tended garden. It was bright and humid, the kind of day when it was easy to forget that winter had ever existed, and with it defeats at Lincoln or York. I had arrived before him, and he asked me to wait a few minutes while he had a shower. Just four days earlier, he had been on the pitch at Wembley, fêted by thousands, projected to icon status by television. Yet here he was, freshly showered in baggy tracksuit bottoms. His wife returned from shopping and admonished him mildly for not clearing up the mess one of the dogs had left on the kitchen floor.

At several junctures during the season, there had been – certainly among supporters – scepticism about Royle's capability. Promotion, albeit due to Gillingham's ineptitude from the penalty spot, had at least served to postpone this particular debate. The exhilarating victory at Wembley had suddenly put the season into a new perspective, one which was largely specious. It had been a pretty undignified slog, at least until the closing weeks. City, with their greater wealth, support and overall strength in depth, *should* have strolled through the division. If every game was a cup final, they should have passed the ball beyond, through and around these demons, made their enthusiasm look rash and infantile; didn't United (at another level) do so every week?

Instead, they settled for attrition and aggression, only

sporadically revealing their greater skill. This was not to say Royle and his boot-room team did not deserve their accolades. They had delivered. They had built a team and set upon a game-plan which, over the course of the season, had succeeded. Royle had taken the criticism, the complaints, the snide remarks, the misgivings about his choice of players or tactics, and refused to budge, to compromise. He had maintained that infuriating, belligerent self-belief from which great managers are cut. It didn't matter that promotion was achieved by virtue of the play-offs and then penalties; success was habitually achieved via a convoluted, troublesome process. By whatever means, he had delivered.

On that quiet afternoon he was not boastful or conceited about the team's success. In fact, he insisted repeatedly that it was merely the starting point. We talked for about an hour. He made no attempt to hurry along the interview, but I felt obliged to keep it relatively short because I realised it was his final piece of business for the season. He was ready, finally, to open a bottle of wine, stroll across the garden and enjoy the silence.

Saturday, 5 June 1999

Gillingham's chairman Paul Scally called for the play-off final to be replayed when he learned that match referee Mark Halsey had been seen celebrating with City supporters just a few hours after the match. Halsey had stayed at the Wembley Hilton Hotel where many City supporters were also booked. 'The whole idea that the match should be replayed just because the referee found himself in the company of City fans on Sunday night is completely ridiculous,' said Chris Bird.

Sunday, 6 June 1999

The Football League announced that City would not have to replay their play-off final, but reprimanded match referee Mark Halsey. 'There is a time and a place for everything and we shall remind him that it is unwise to mix with supporters so soon after an important match,' said a spokesman.

Monday, 7 June 1999

Supporters were offered the chance to buy a piece of the Maine

Road turf for just £10. The pitch had been cut up into 1,000 pieces ready to be re-laid over the summer. The sell-off was to raise money for the Youth Academy.

UP, UP AND BLACKBURN AWAY
(*City Life*, Tuesday, 9 June 1999)

A yellow blur passes by at great speed. It's Nicky Weaver, Manchester City's 20-year-old goalkeeper. He has just saved a penalty at Wembley and ensured his team's promotion to Division One of the Nationwide League. It's some celebration, half-running, half-twitching, halfway round Wembley in under 12 seconds.

Soon afterwards, David Bernstein, City's chairman, is on the pitch. Clearly, his low-profile administration has worked well. Too well. The faithful are mystified. Eventually they realise the toff in the suit is their man and applaud generously. Bernstein demurely raises his hand. Already he is regretting that he didn't stay in the posh seats and make use of the tartan blanket kindly supplied by Wembley. He could have mopped his brow with it because, phew, that was close.

Another season in Division Two would have been disastrous for Manchester City. The club, although the thirteenth best-supported in England, is more than £12 million in debt. The interest on the deficit is £21,000 per week. Imagine that: the equivalent of buying a brand new, top-of-the-range family car every week, just to push it into the River Irwell.

When Bernstein took over from Francis Lee in March 1998, City were like a credit card that had been passed around a few reckless mates; a new stand here, an east European full-back there, a couple of hundred executive boxes. Anyone for another drink? Put it on the tab. City's tab that is. Bernstein's season-long entreaty was for stability, prudence, patience and an end to the policy of indiscriminate speculation. It didn't make for great headlines, but the quiet rationalisation, like reducing a first-team squad from 53 to 24, looked like a terminal outbreak of common sense. Many City fans were taking nervous glances at Lancashire outposts like Burnley, Blackpool and Preston North End, former football giants, and wondering whether another season in Division Two would draw them into the same quicksand of perpetual mediocrity. They need not have worried. More than 12,000 season tickets were sold before the play-off final, so City's greatest asset – their support – would have remained regardless. As long as the support is constant, City will have the 'foundations' (another of the chairman's buzz words) on which to build.

Obviously, promotion should now accelerate City's return to the big-time. Gate receipts will improve only nominally, however, since Maine Road can hold just a few thousand more in addition to last season's average of 28,261. The revenue leg-up of around £3 million will come via Sky TV and the corporate beano that spills over from the Premiership into Division One. Clubs like Blackburn Rovers, Fulham, Nottingham Forest, Birmingham City, Wolverhampton Wanderers and, indeed, City themselves, will give the division a certain cache next season.

An immediate tangible benefit of promotion will be the improvement in City's negotiating power with a new club sponsor. The 12-year deal with Brother has now ended and City's new status should push up the stakes considerably. Harsh but true, few blue-chip companies would even open talks with a club set to take their brand-name to places like Scunthorpe United and Wycombe Wanderers. On a wider issue, Bernstein now runs a club primed for takeover. This has always been the aim – to pass the club over to new owners with the financial acumen and the good of City at heart. This, potentially at least, could fast-track City to glory, though negotiations would be long and complex; there are still plenty of egos to accommodate within the City hierarchy.

So, Division One, here we come. Just watch out for a spot of bother come mid-September. City are already out of the promotion frame, and the fans are screaming for new players. Get your cheque book out, Mr Chairman. 'Sorry, chaps, we've been down that road before . . . ' At this point, City's future will once more fall into the balance.

● *City Life*, the listings magazine covering Greater Manchester, had asked me to contribute an article on City for their cover story about the success of both Manchester clubs.

Wednesday, 9 June 1999

Speculation grew that City were about to benefit from a major cash injection. David Bernstein said he was in talks with a 'major institution' who had 'very deep pockets'. He said any deal would not amount to a takeover but would involve people who could 'work with us and continue the continuity and stability we have started'. It was rumoured that the company was the Manchester brewers, Boddingtons.

Friday, 11 June 1999

In early betting, City were quoted by Tote at 16–1 to win the Division One title. Blackburn Rovers were clear favourites at 13–8, ahead of Bolton and Fulham, who were each rated at 9–1. City were tenth favourites.

Saturday, 12 June 1999

Lee Sharpe, the former Manchester United winger, said he wanted to join City from Leeds United now they had been promoted to Division One. In March he had turned down Joe Royle, preferring instead to sign on loan to Bradford City. 'I've got to be honest and say that I hated being in Division Two, so I can hardly blame Lee for feeling the same way,' said Royle.

Sunday, 13 June 1999

Computer game company Eidos were announced as City's new club sponsor for the next three seasons. 'We see Manchester City as a unique property in domestic football with enormous potential for the future. Eidos is impressed with the board's vision for the future and felt it should be part of the new era,' said Ian Livingstone, executive chairman of Eidos.

The company was most famous for its games, *Tomb Raider*, *UEFA Champions League* and *Championship Manager*.

Twelve

Fiesta the Sun Also Rises

The Manchester City Internet noticeboard, MCIVTA, was inundated with supporters anxious to share their Wembley joy. Their testimonies made for emotional reading . . .

Ashley Birch: The match simply has to be the most memorable I've experienced as a City fan, and will most probably never be bettered as long as I live. I was driving along today and it still seems vaguely surreal. How could any team – let alone City – recover from 2–0 down with only seconds of normal time remaining? My memories are diverse: the sheer ecstasy of the equaliser; the emotion of Weaver's last save and the victory it bestowed; the guy in the row in front who hugged me like his own mother, and the guy and his girlfriend/wife behind me with tears in their eyes.

Colin Jonas: Unbelievable. Never have Man City produced such an amazing comeback as this in all the years I've been following them. To do it in such an important game as this is pure fantasy. After all the recent years of misery that have been heaped on us City fans, this Sunday's amazing performance has finally rewarded our blind loyalty. Thanks to the City fan who returned my camera and match programme that fell out while I went mad. Never have I seen City come back in such a fashion, let alone such an important game as this. Unbelievable. City are back!

Geoff Donkin: I guess this will be one of those occasions we'll tell our grandchildren about. I had a suspicion City might make it hard for us; I'd also felt for some time that we were going to do it, but at 2–0 down with only injury time remaining I have to admit I'd given up hope. Who hadn't? We've invested a lot of emotional energy in earning this the hard way and we've had to live with the increasing hype and media obsession with 'that lot next door'. To have lost this game after they'd done the treble would have been a nightmare too horrible to contemplate. So, goodbye Div. 2, we hope you've enjoyed our brief stay but we're on our way back to where we belong. One small step for men, one giant leap for Man City.

Toh Hsien Min: When City win the European Cup in twenty years time, I'm going to tell my children I was there at Wembley when they won promotion to the First Division in the most dramatic of matches. When Nicky Weaver saved their first and then their fourth penalty to give City victory . . . man, it was something just to have been there.

Peter Brophy: In almost a quarter of a century following the club, I thought I'd experienced more or less everything they could throw at me – from smashing the British transfer record to signing mediocre journeymen, to playing keep-ball in the corner with an eye on preserving a result which would seal relegation. On Sunday they surpassed themselves. Even if it was just the Third (in real terms) Division play-off trophy, we've seen a City captain go up the Wembley steps to lift a trophy for the first time since Harold Wilson was Prime Minister. And most importantly, even though making further advances will be far from easy, we've taken the first step on the way back. Hopefully the worst is now behind us and in my book, that's a thought to savour.

Salt?: We were on Wembley Way when a copper said City had pulled one back. Still, we thought, no way will they get another. Next thing, we are in the car park, and the coach drivers were shouting like mad, that City had equalised, and then it was a mad dash back to the ground. Got to our block, only to find a steward there blocking our path. There were angry exchanges and a lot of verbal, then he relented and let us in.

Paul Rawling: When it went to penalties, the words of my father came back to haunt me. A blue for 55 years and ever the pessimist, he said at the start of the season – when things looked good for an instant return to Div. 1 – 'I bet we'll get to Wembley in the play-offs and lose to someone like Gillingham on penalties.' At the time, I thought the gods were just prolonging the agony of defeat which made the victory all the more incredible. Even sitting watching it on TV round at my father's and not being at Wembley itself did not take anything away from a magnificent occasion and City's best performance for years.

Tom Ritchie: As I made my way out, a roar. Horlock had pulled one back. Big deal. As I reached the top of Wembley Way, another roar. Gillingham were victorious. But no, hundreds of people started leaping about, charging out of coaches and from the tube station, heading back to celebrate Dickov's incredible equaliser. I stood and thought. For 87 minutes I had watched us go 2–0 down. Within three minutes of my leaving we had drawn level. So it was obvious what I had to do. Don't go back! I found a pub and walked in to be confronted by City fans all standing silent. Shit! We'd lost in extra-time. I then glanced up at the television to see Nicky Weaver facing a penalty. I had no idea what the situation was. Seconds later, the pub erupts. 'What's happened?' I stupidly asked of the hairy, bouncing Blue hanging around my neck. 'We're up, we're fucking up,' he bellowed. I let go and leaped deliriously around the room with all the other zealots. Having watched City at just about every nondescript ground in the division, I was seemingly fated to watch the last act away from the main event. It was a surreal feeling, but one I would not have changed. Someone had to make the ultimate sacrifice to ensure City got promoted, and it was just good fortune it was down to me!

John Shearer: We couldn't get a ticket, so we went back to the Wembley Hilton. At 3 p.m., along with another 98 City fans, and none from Gillingham, we start to console ourselves. We've saved a lot of money. We've got a good, comfortable view of the television. There's a bar, a toilet. There's a chap next to us who flew over from Jersey just for the game. Another guy paid £80 for his City-end ticket only to find it was a forgery. Atmosphere – absolutely superbly, breathtakingly, mindblowingly, brilliant. I know I'd rather have been inside the ground, but as an alternative it was pretty damn good. Roll on Grimsby.

Derel McGarry: It is probably the most exciting City game I've ever heard on the radio and I love listening to Radio Five Live. Even if the tension was almost unbearable, I can't help feeling that this game and this season have pulled the team and supporters together in a way that no other could have. Hopefully, it is onward and upward for all of us. With a very badly needed cash injection, maybe we could continue to improve our squad and get back to the big-time sooner rather than later. Well done everyone!

Stephen Hewitt: When Paul Dickov equalised you knew that you were witnessing something special, something that will be talked about for many years to come. The fans went into overdrive. With support like that there was no way City were going to lose. The Gillingham fans just couldn't compete. The jeers and whistles that greeted each of their penalty takers were deafening. When Nicky Weaver's save won us the match, the place went beserk. Fans stood on their seats, strangers – their shirts and scarves the only things they had in common – hugged and kissed like long-lost relatives. At one stage I swear I saw a man get out of his wheel-chair and dance!

Peter Astbury: It's Sunday morning and I've just woken up after having an unbelievable dream. No, it's Monday morning and it's true. All together now, Wem-ber-lee, Wem-ber-lee, we're the famous Man City and we won at Wem-ber-lee (repeat several times).

Noel Bayley: A slow-burner of a match suddenly came alight in the closing minutes as Gillingham scored two goals in quick succession to silence the Northern hordes. I was ready to leave as all around me tears of sorrow flowed, but Leanne thought otherwise, protesting that she wanted to stay. I thought I knew better as I had never seen City triumph at Wembley, but with the benefit of hindsight she was right and for that I shall be eternally grateful to her. For once, the gods smiled kindly on Manchester's only team as Paul Dickov hammered the ball into the roof of the Gillingham net in the 94th minute. This goal was greeted with the loudest roar I have ever heard in my life as those of us who stayed went wild with sheer delight. Extra-time was a mere formality. It came and went in a blink and it appeared that Gillingham were playing for penalties. I feared City were delaying the inevitable, but when it came, our players were more than equal to the penalty shoot-out, as was our goalkeeper, Nicky Weaver. Kevin Horlock, Terry Cooke and Richard Edghill all scored while Dickov somehow contrived to hit both posts without scoring. Weaver managed to save two of theirs, one went high and wide and the other hit the back of the net. Weaver's final save was the cue for possibly the longest celebration in Wembley's long and illustrious history as City's team and fans came together in an unprecedented display of mutual admiration.

Mark Braude: What elation, what a feeling, what an emotional rollercoaster. And how incredible to see Captain Morrison leading the blues up the steps, the famous steps, and lifting our first piece of silverware for 23 years. This only half an hour after seemingly losing. I'll never forget yesterday.

Paul Fegan: There's eight minutes left at Wembley. The first Gills goal goes in. My eight-year-old son is in tears. I'm wondering why I ever brought him to Maine Road. Most Irish kids follow the rags or Liverpool; why put him through this? The second goal goes in; the poor kid is devastated. Surely there can be no way back. The rest is history. I have been a City fan for nearly 30 years and I cannot remember the blues having that kind of luck before; but we deserved that luck. God, I wish I was at Wembley today but like so many blues I had to settle for the television. I don't think I will ever forget 30 May 1999.

Ian Ferguson: What more can you say? Being at Wembley on Sunday was up there with the birth of my children! The elation of the Dickov goal was the most amazing moment I've *ever* experienced, when he struck the ball you could here a pin drop. The ball moved in slow motion . . . you had to be there. Fantastic.

Jon Reese: Stone the flipping crows – what a fantastic day! I still cannot believe how we made it through when we were looking down the barrel at another season in the backwaters of Division Two. What courage, what guts, what joy!

Sharon Hargreaves: I have never, ever experienced a match like that before and I never want to again. The incredible lows then highs of emotion as City continued to live up to all our expectations and try to ruin our day were just indescribable (so I'll try anyway . . .). I started screaming until I thought my vocal chords would burst. The scenes on the pitch and in the stands will stay with me for the rest of my life. This time the tears were of joy. We'd won a cup and who cares that it was only the Second Division play-off final? This was *our* day, it belonged to the fans, and the players fell to their knees and worshipped *us*.

Tony Burns: Quite simply, Wembley exploded. I have never, and doubt I ever will again, experience anything like it. Bodies tumbled into each other as we crashed around in the craziest of celebrations. Those that didn't scream and cheer were numbed by the enormity of what we had witnessed. Rivers of tears cascaded across the Wembley concrete as we were swept along in an unending tide of emotion, elation and thanksgiving. This was indeed a modern footballing miracle. We stood on our seats for 30 minutes or so, as we sang, cheered, screamed and released the years of frustration, barbed comments, cheap jokes, snide lines from rags, press and just about anyone who will never ever understand that we are not an ordinary club. I loved Sunday; my wife cried, my daughter danced, my son said it was the best day of his life, my brother, nephew and I danced and screamed. This was blue heaven.

Peter Llewellyn: We go completely, ballistically, bananas. Hugging, cheering, punching the air, 'City 'til I die'-ing, Blue moon-ing and making some outrageous noise. Gills players are distraught. A bloke in a City shirt is carried past us on a stretcher with a saline drip attached. Heart attack, someone says. No one is surprised. The crowd definitely made the penalty competition one-sided. I should feel sorry for Gillingham but I don't. City fans have put up with so much. It was our turn and it was the most fantastic day.

Averil Capes: It's Tuesday, 1 June, I've been to Wembley, I've watched the video twice (4 hours) and I've even watched the highlights, and yet I still can't bloody believe it. I still can't believe that we came back from a two goal deficit with less than five minutes left on the clock, plus what injury time the referee decided to add on. I still can't believe that we scored two goals and went on to win the penalty shoot-out. My everlasting memories of Sunday, 30 May 1999 will be the noise the City fans made, Nicky's sheer delight after he'd saved the second penalty and the sight of the players paying homage to the fans. Do you know what? I still don't bloody believe it.

Nigel Edney: Forty thousand fans in laser blue and yellow leapt into the air in unison, the despair of the last few minutes matched and then beaten to a pulp by the relief and ecstasy we now felt. People around me had tears in their eyes, and grown men were openly hugging at a footy game.

Mark Bell: I smiled from start to finish, proud to be with my dad, proud of my club and most proud of it's unique supporters. I turned to dad in the 88th minute and said something along the lines of, 'What a great day out for us – it can't end like this.' He looked at me tearfully and said, 'Yes, a great day son – but that's City for you.' Over the next eight minutes, we seemed to just stand with arms aloft or around each other or some similar soul. As the penalties came, we helped dad up to stand on the bench, held him tight, and I whispered, 'Now see a bit of history' – he looked and laughed

– me the eternal optimist, him the reverse. Ten minutes later we were all crying with joy. I couldn't help feeling that this was what we all deserved after the disappointment of the last decades. As we moved back to King's Cross, we sang and danced and chanted with our fellow blues so much that we never wanted the journey to end. We arrived at King's Cross with 10 minutes to spare. Dad got on the train and I ran along the platform with a bottle of gin in my hand, waving goodbye and mouthing, 'I love you.' He just waved back, smiling and shaking his head as he explained to the people opposite that this was his mad City-fan son from South Africa. I cried. My mate Allan was also crying. He said I looked like a 10-year-old again. Ironic, that was exactly how I felt, like the days when we would leave the ground and walk down the pink passage together after City had won. My dad was the best in the world and me and him were City fans.

David Scally: Then the two most amazing goals I have ever seen! Thank you referee! It was at this point I thought I was going to die. I have never been so excited in all my life, and I doubt I ever will. The tension was unbearable in the stands for extra-time, everyone was looking around giving those looks which say, 'Oh my God, you look as bad as I feel!' Then the penalties. When Weaver saved that last penalty, I was over the 'Blue Moon'. I was cheering so much that I couldn't breathe properly. In the car, trying to get on to the M1 again, I heard a load of beeping and cheering, looked out, and saw the entire team walking down the road into the Wembley Hilton. I'd taken my trainers off, but ran out on to the wet streets of Wembley holding an inflatable banana! Most of the team had gone in, but I managed to hit Gerard Wiekins on the head with my banana, to which he went 'Ow, what ya doing?' and grinned. I also shook Andy Morrison's hand. He's a bloody big fella he is. That was almost it, apart from the fact that every service station that we stopped off at on the way home was packed full of Blues. It was a really amazing sight. Got home at 11 p.m. Watched the match again until 1 p.m. and went to bed, completely knackered!

John Riley: I thought my brain was going to leak, poor Gillingham didn't stand a chance. If we went ballistic when we equalised, we went bloody medieval when Nicky Weaver won it for us. Oh, and who scored the winning goal? The bloke who hasn't scored in nine years – obviously! I finally got back to Hong Kong yesterday evening, several pounds lighter (sterling, that is) with a larynx that was shot to fuck.

Mark Braude: The greatest game in the history of the world. Quite simply, in terms of elation, football and City will never get any better than this. How us fans deserved that day. And how I can't get that game out of my mind!

Neil Towse: What I will remember most about Sunday is 'Blue Moon' ringing around Wembley before, during and after the game. I truly never thought that would ever happen. A City fan summed it all up on the train home from King's Cross, when he said that this just doesn't happen to City. On Sunday, 30 May 1999, it did. I saw my team win at Wembley.

Sharon Marsland: I cheered Horlock's goal, although few around me did; but then when that ball took off from Dickov's foot and 20 minutes later (or so it seemed) hit the back of the net, I had a moment of hysteria and screamed and screamed (typical girlie!). I have to say that I have never thanked my husband for introducing me to the blues eight years ago – let's face it, we've not had any reason to. But I wouldn't have missed that day at Wembley for anything. I know it's only a promotion to the First Division but we are travelling in the right direction at last and I really enjoyed that day. So thanks, John, for making me a blue!

Elaine Clegg: The next day I couldn't move – everything hurt and ached, so I used it as an excuse to spend the whole day lying on the settee watching the game over and over and over . . .

Jim Simmons: One of the happiest days of my life. I wanted to scream and dance about but it would hardly have been appropriate. I opted for a smug, self-satisfied grin which I still have, and no doubt will have until I'm stood in the away end at Port Vale next season, when it's raining and we're three nil down or similar. No, wait! I must have dreamt it. Maybe I'm still asleep, maybe you're still asleep and you only think you're reading this e-mail. Maybe Alan Ball is still in charge. You see what this club does to you . . .

Geoff Collins: Weaver, you beauty. The screaming in the bedroom reached Boeing 747 proportions. Edghill – great penalty taken with great confidence. Then the crowning moment: Weaver makes himself look even bigger than he is by stretching his arms wide and pulls off the greatest of saves. Oh what joy. I almost came through the bloody ceiling. Memorable moments of the day: Dicky's face after he scored the equaliser – pure joy. Nick Weaver encouraging the team to chase him after his final save . . . brilliant. I watch that bit on tape time and time again and I fill up with tears, it is such a brilliant moment. The whole team doing the 'We are not worthy' salute to the amazing blue horde. Joe Royle alone in the dressing-room at the end, quietly contemplating the day with a can of Carlsberg in his hand. Fantastic day, fantastic team, fantastic support.

Martin Price: Having flown in for the day (from New Jersey) the emotional extremes of the match were particularly acute for me. When the second Gillingham goal went in I just felt sick, and sat in my seat close to tears thinking that this was the lowest point in all my years of supporting City – worse even than the Luton relegation defeat because I'd gone to such extremes to get to this match. I wondered how long it would be before I could forgive them for putting me through this.

Roger Sharp: Well, quite frankly, I don't know where to begin. That game was one of the most amazing experiences I have ever had. I laughed, I cried (literally) and I certainly almost died from the stress of it all. But, oh, we're up and promoted in a way which only Manchester City could achieve. In the central London pubs after the game, the word on everyone's lips seemed to be 'unbelievable' and the feeling was more of shock and amazement than sheer elation. For myself, even though I was there, I had to go out and buy all the major newspapers the next day just to prove we had done it in quite such a fairy-tale fashion.

Kevin Duckworth: And then it happened. I have not seen that much hysteria since Little Jimmy Osmond came to Manchester. This could not happen to City. In fact, I look at my watch, 30 seconds to go. I know what it is; God is taking the piss. Gillingham will now go to the other end, Wiekens will pass the ball back to Nicky Weaver and it will be an own goal. The celebrations went on and on, the fans singing away to the *Dambusters* theme, 'Rocking All over the World', the *Match of the Day* theme tune. Another thing that stayed in my mind was Dennis Tueart pushing Nick Weaver back to the City fans as if to say – make the most of this lad.

Benjamin Bloom: Never, ever have I witnessed scenes of pure ecstasy like the ones at Wembley in the 93rd minute of our last ever game in the Second Division. I reacted by bursting into tears. Within two seconds I was being embraced by around five City fans. I remember a young married couple behind me hugging and crying. When we finally won it, the joy on the boys' faces made everything worth it. We had done the impossible. When the boys came over and got on their knees and worshipped us, it just summed it up perfectly. These boys did their best. We, the fans did our best. As a team, we and they got the job done. I must have cried more on Sunday than I have in 15 years. Hugging every blue in sight, last Sunday will be a game which will be looked back on as I look back on the 10–1 and the 5–1. A game never to be forgotten. We're on the up!

Paul Howe: I recorded the game last Sunday and every evening since I have to play the last 15 minutes of the 90 with the four goals. I just can't stop thinking about it. Will I be like this all summer? Is there a cure? (I hope not.) Maybe it's because I (we) have waited so long, but success (even if it's only the Second

Division play-off final) seems so sweet. If Andy Morrison hadn't caught Nicky Weaver and pulled him to the ground would he still be running now? Brilliant. What a perfect day.

Nigel Timperley: I know everyone has different memories of it, and I wish I too had been there instead of leaping around like a total loony with my mum in a half-deserted, and slightly bemused, Sheffield pub, but I'll never forget Weaver's run at the end, playing catch-me-if-you-can with the rest of the team on the most crazy, exultant victory lap that I bet Wembley has *ever* seen. We did it. Keep the faith.

Steve Cooper: My dad was an avid City nut for more than 40 years – he said he remembered the 1956 Cup final against the mighty Huddersfield. He was at St James's Park when City won the League in '68 and all the other finals over the next 13 years. He was blue mad. He passed away on 26 March this year after losing the one battle not one of us escapes, but he always maintained that City would win the play-offs; a sure thing, he said. I was very fortunate to be at Wembley on Sunday to see the greatest day of my football life (if not my whole life – why, a friend said it was a better day than the day he lost his virginity). I, along with all you fans, have special, magic, unbelievable memories of that day that will never, ever go away and I want to dedicate all my memories of Sunday, 30 May 1999 to my best mate, my dad.

Tony Kerr: Sat in a bar at five o'clock on a hot Sunday in Zante, surrounded by City and Gills fans in their own emotional turmoil. Our teams are at Wembley (hooray!) and we're not there with them (boo!). Eighty-eight minutes later and an Oldham fan, who has been celebrating with the Gills, decides to leave before the larger City contingent take him round the back and force feed him moussaka. Six minutes later and we're all hopping about, but cautiously. Extra-time, penalties, and City are oil and water in their ability to mix. When Weaver makes his second save, I am stunned. The one-eyed City fan across the table from me grabs me by the shoulders, screaming,

'We've done it, yeeeeeeeeesss!' An unbelievable, great, unforgettable day, and the best one I've had as a City fan since 1974.

Andrew Phang: Tired and jet-lagged, and without access to the Internet, I tried the BBC World Service, thinking there would be some sort of limited commentary. I was wrong. Past midnight, I was on the verge of going to bed but somehow lingered on. My heart sank at news of the two Gillingham goals. But this was a night of 'lingering'. A goal for City: alas, too little too late. But, no, a fleeting second later, the commentary was almost hysterical and I knew that the impossible had happened as Dickov equalized. The commentary had lagged behind the match and it was actually almost the end of extra-time. Then, an almost casual (and again fleeting) observation that City had won on penalties! After decades in the wilderness, perhaps this match might mark a turning-point.

Mark Jones: As the game was not broadcast on TV or radio in Australia, I phoned my brother up in Manchester and got him to put his phone next to the radio and listened to the game on Radio Five Live. Three hours later I put the phone down exhausted from both the tension of the game and the fact that it was now 3 a.m. Jesus, they don't do things easy do they?

Samuel Green: When Weaver made his final save, I just jumped and jumped and sang and sang. It was the weirdest feeling to actually be at the most famous ground in the world and be celebrating a meaningful victory. The irony of the whole evening was that I was walking with my head down, almost suicidal (well, not quite); and one minute and an hour later, I was stuck in a queue to get out, which I did not want to do, with happy City fans (for once) cheering about a memorable victory that none of us will ever forget.

Stephen Wallwork: As I, and many fans, got to the tube line a policeman took his hand away from his ear-piece and said, 'I hate to tell you this guys, but it's 2–2.' 'Rubbish,' I thought, City do *not* come back from 2–0 down with only two minutes to go. But it was confirmed and hoards of blues turned and ran back to the ground. Being on the portly side, I decided not to. Anyway, I'd only get there to see Gillingham take the lead again. So I decided to get on the tube to Uxbridge and drive home from there. In the future, when people ask, 'Were you there when City finally turned the corner?' I'll say, yes . . . and no.

John Bradley: When Paul Dickov scored, the emotion built up inside me over countless years exploded in a massive sense of relief and exuberance (my mate – I won't reveal his name – even let his excitement boil over by wetting himself!). Did we really do what the rags have become so adept at doing countless times over the years?

Gary Pritchard: Having failed miserably to get Wembley tickets, my pal and myself found a South Wales pub showing the game. Surrounded by Sunday diners, the surreal atmosphere was enhanced considerably by a cabaret band striking up cheesy '60s songs in the second half. 1–0! Shit! 2–0! We look at each other, stand up and leave. Speechless, we tune in to Radio Five Live to hear the inevitable final humiliation. 'City have pulled one back through Horlock!' I turn the car around and head back for the pub. Pal can't cope so he stays in the car. Within one minute I'm running out to the car screaming '2–2!' He's scrambling out of the door to get into the pub – we're both drunk with disbelief. We settle in for extra-time – regular glances to each other of sheer euphoria. Penalties, and we're strangely confident. Weaver running away from his players in one of the most memorable scenes I think I'll ever witness. We both weep.

Charles Augarde: The White Hart in Wolvercote, Oxford, was where I saw the match, largely on my own. A Coventry fan dragged himself away from the pool match to watch as the amazing finale took shape, and by the end of penalties a big group were jumping about shouting, 'Yes . . . ' This is what it's about.

Hugh Doyle: My thirteen-year-old son was sobbing uncontrollably and I was trying to hold back my tears (unsuccessfully) as we watched the match in the Dover Castle pub in Cheetham Hill. This is one of the unique pubs whose landlady is red and landlord is blue with the walls adorned with photos of both teams. The red contingent were in the bar playing pool and mocking the boys in the lounge glued to the big screen. It was unbearable for the blues until Nicky Weaver pulled off that penalty save and made me feel 10 feet tall with my heart pounding, tears of joy streaming down my face and my son spilling my beer as he jumped around like a Tasmanian devil, knocking into tables left, right and Chelsea. I truly believe that this will act as the catalyst to enable the phoenix to rise and once again soar with the eagles. Oh! I forgot to say, I just love, love, love our club with all my heart.

Phil Heally: What a result. I wanted to leave the pub after that Gills goal, then even more so after the second, but thanks to my stubborn southern girlfriend who wouldn't drink up for some unknown reason, we were still there to witness that miracle. So I'd just like to say that Joe should be given a big thanks as he called the club 'We' from the very first press conference announcing his arrival with true pride and a definite show of love for the club.

John Howes: I was on holiday in Cornwall – booked 12 months before. I could not get it on TV, but I heard it on radio – sort of. Anyone who has been to the Cornwall coast knows how undulating it is. At the top of the cliffs, radio reception is great. At the bottom of the valley, there is no reception. At the top of the valley, it was 0–0 with 15 minutes to play. Down in the valley – no reception. At the top of the next valley we were 2–0 down. By the next valley it was full-time. I was in a foul mood. I would not watch TV or buy a paper. The following day was my birthday. That evening, it was only a chance remark from someone across the room that indicated that we had won on the day. Of course I didn't believe it and it was not until someone showed me a paper with the match report that I would accept it. I must have read the report about 30 times.

Tony Hulme: For all those who were not there, for all those who left early – don't feel bad. I was there, I did not leave, but I did not see one of our goals. When we were 2–0 down, I buried my head into my hands, held my crucifix and prayed. I prayed to God, I prayed to my mother (she had died several months earlier). I prayed so hard that my hands had the imprint of my cross. I did not see any of the goals until later that night (thanks, Paul, aka ChinnorBLU for tapping it). My mum came through again! She must have sneaked onto the pitch and turned off the ref's watch (so *that's* where the five minutes came from). The letters from people telling how they had gone to the game with their father/mother/brothers/sisters all touched me, because I was there with the two people I love more than anyone, my girlfriend and my mum. What more can a blue boy want!

Ian Pilkington: These things stick vividly in my mind . . . the eruption of noise at Dickov's goal, the applause given to Edghill as he strode forward to take a penalty (the only City player to receive such a clap), the noise (absolutely deafening) as Gillingham players approached for penalties, the rendition of 'Blue Moon' at the end. To the pub afterwards, more singing and dancing around restaurants and bars in West Hampstead, a conga in Trafalgar Square at 3 a.m. and back to the hotel for the first editions of Monday's newspapers. Best achievement of the weekend has to be the confirmation that my nephew will be the fourth generation of Blues in the family. Still reeling from the shock of it all . . . bring on Blackburn, Stockport and all. I know I am, I'm sure I am, I'm City till I die.

David Gordon: All I can add is that I will never, ever forget that moment when we equalised. If I live to be 90, I'm sure I'll be shouting, 'Paul Dickov' at the wall in my nursing home. What I can say is that City fans deserved the victory. The supporters

I met at Wembley were among the nicest people I have ever come across. I know it sounds strange, but I feel we earned that day and that it somehow made the last few years worthwhile. This is what football is all about. There is no comparison with what United fans went through with the Bayern match. They only needed one goal to get back into it and they also had the small matter of a domestic double as consolation. We were dead and buried and we had absolutely nothing to fall back on – and we still came back. You have to experience real lows to reach the heights we did at Wembley. No one but City fans will ever know what it felt like.

Steve Nolan: I was one of those City fans who watched the wonder of Wembley from the Gillingham end. Apart from the obvious disadvantages of not being able to muster much of a chorus for 'Blue Moon', it was not as bad as I thought it would be. Most of the Gillingham fans had never been to a match before so the atmosphere was fairly light-hearted among the grannies, very young kids with colouring books on their laps and French exchange students based in Kent. I actually knew more of the Gills players than most of the people around me. Many thanks to the players for spotting us at the wrong end of the ground and coming up there to show off the trophy on the lap of honour.

Malcolm Plaiter: As an old campaigner, with three minutes remaining, I left. Years of experience taught me to ignore the consolation goal which was scored as I was on my way out of the door. Successive disappointments failed to convince me to return to the ground when I knew we had equalised. I draw consolation from knowing that I was the jinx and City triumphed because of my absence, so you can all thank me.

John Stewart: Being a City fan is all about tradition, birthright, tears of torment and joy. A feeling of belonging to something you can't just join because they've won something. Total commitment through thick and thin.

Carol Darvill: The emotion was definitely getting to me. Up came Butters – I think it was – and Nick saved again. I burst into tears, I am not ashamed to say I sobbed my heart out on Maggie's shoulder. I know I vowed after Halifax in '79 I would never cry at a football match again, but sod it! Sunday was a one-off roller-coaster ride of emotions and I don't think for one moment that I was the only one in tears at the end. More hugging and kissing took place, although the looks of disbelief on people's faces will stick with me for years to come. My husband picked me up from Maine Road at the end of the night and we drove home. It was my birthday on the 25th and he'd put a bottle of champagne in the fridge which we didn't get round to drinking, but the bottle was opened at midnight and we celebrated in style! Thanks for the birthday present boys! Monday I wore my laser blue shirt whilst driving around (the citrus was finally in the wash!!) and more horns were honked and people waved at me!

Pat Poynton: Things I will never forget about Wembley 30 May 1999 – the little boy two rows behind us sobbing uncontrollably; grown men sitting staring into space with tears in their eyes; my poor 15-year-old daughter Allegra, saying bitterly and tearfully, 'Why did you make me support such a horrible football team?' – within a few minutes, she had her answer; the muted cheer which accompanied Horlock's goal; then, unbelievably, the roar from inside; Weaver's celebrations (surely one of the maddest, craziest in Wembley history – at one point a steward tried to rugby tackle him, perhaps thinking he was a supporter); the tannoy shutting up for once to allow an unaccompanied, spine-tingling chorus of 'Blue Moon'; the tiny bands of brave City fans left exposed in the Gills end, getting their own visit from the players; the strange, unfamiliar feeling of having seen perhaps a new Manchester City, a team that doesn't keel over and die when someone scores against them, a team that other teams might actually be afraid of, a team that actually wants to live up to its supporters hopes and expectations instead of being intimidated by them, and perhaps, as Churchill once said in a different context, the end of the beginning.

David Kilroy: The last week has driven home to me the reason why I'll always be blue. Only people who have truly lived through such awful times can actually share more *true* emotion at finishing third in Division Two than was shown by those winning the treble.

David Buxton: Horlock's well-struck shot raised a wan smile, but Dickov's excellent equaliser had me leaping at least two feet into the air, arms outstretched and a yell echoing round New Moston. Behaviour that was repeated seven times during the penalty shoot-out (eight times, if I'm honest, as I thought Dickov's penalty was in!). I'm sure I caught my mother-in-law giving me some strange looks during the rest of our stay, and suspect that things will never be quite the same again. On the other hand, I might well go there to watch next season's play-offs . . .

Jim Parson: I was on a plane the whole bloody time. I'd asked Emma (my wife) to leave a message on the mobile for when I landed in Beirut. As soon as I got a signal, there was the message icon. I got through and rather than hearing her voice telling me the score all I could hear was Radio Five Live saying it had gone to penalties. For the next ten minutes the whole of the baggage hall and customs at Beirut airport was able to witness a stange Englishman with a mobile clutched to his head going through the agony and the ecstasy of the whole thing via the commentary! Suprisingly I wasn't strip searched or even stopped by customs despite the peculiar behaviour.

Elaine Clegg: Having spent three days away from home, the first thing I did when I got back (even before I unloaded the car) was to put on the video of the game and revel in the sheer blissfulness that overwhelms me when I watch it – this is surely better than taking drugs and I'm truly addicted!

Jo Lakeland: All I can say, Joe Royle, is get your bleeding act together and win these games earlier in the season, then my life can be smoother and I can come off the Valium.

Ken Corfield: Around 2 p.m. on Sunday at the top of Wembley Way you might have noticed a big white sign that said 'Came from New York – Tickets Needed' with the 'needed' replaced by 'GOT!' Hope it made you smile. It made a lot of Gillingham fans laugh. Daft sods aren't laughing now!

Andrea Hanlon: We met Gerard Wiekens's father-in-law and his fellow travellers on the tube after the match. He couldn't speak a word of English but got his City bobble-hat out of his pocket when we got on our laser blue and smiled and smiled – hilarious.

Martin Farmer: Forget United, this was the real thing. Grit, determination and a will to succeed. The players could see how much we as fans needed that victory, and I only see things getting better and better. We should not worry about many teams in Division One if we never say die like that.

Chris Cobb: Why do women hate footballers? They do nothing for 90 minutes, put it in twice and think they're the best in the world.

Sue Wallace: Nine months, and then off to Wembley to deliver our new 'baby' – promotion. Our neighbour had just had triplets (the treble), with every assistance that money could bribe, er, buy. The bitch paraded her offspring like no one's ever had one before! Well I have, but they're grown up now, and I've been down on my luck.

A difficult pregnancy – I almost lost it around Christmas time – followed by a long labour, making little progress. Then Gillingham scored. 'Your baby's distressed – you must push harder,' implored the midwife. Gillingham scored again. Such agony, but I could hear my husband calling, 'Come on City!' One more big push, I didn't care if it killed me – Horlock's goal! Gulping the gas and air I rode the pain for another desperate effort. Dickov's goal! 'I can see the head!' cried the midwife and, through my tears, the sound of my old man's voice gave me the strength to continue, 'Come on City!'

The penalty shoot-out. Push. Push. HEAVE! WE'VE DONE IT!!!! Baby's first cry (the roar of the City faithful); everyone hugging each other; and Manchester City, smiling, the pain forgotten. We left Wembley in joyful silence.

John Wallace: I have watched City, man and boy, at Wembley, in Europe, in relegation and promotion battles, but I have never experienced such tension at a football match as I did against Gillingham. The magnitude of the game was lost on no one. At 2–0 down, the tension finally got to me. My 25 years of following the Blues suddenly seemed to make no sense and for the first time ever I began to question my unconditional love for the club. Despite the sheer unadulterated joy of what followed in injury time and penalties, something inside me changed that day. Maybe it was the football equivalent of 'coming of age', who can say. All I know is that as a result, football, and Manchester City, seem just that little bit less important than they used to.

NATIONWIDE LEAGUE DIVISION TWO (FINAL TABLE, 1998–99)

Home Away

	P	W	D	L	F	A	W	D	L	F	A	Pts	GS
Fulham	46	19	3	1	50	12	12	5	6	29	20	101	79
Walsall	46	13	7	3	37	23	13	2	8	26	24	87	63
MANCHESTER CITY	46	13	6	4	38	14	9	10	4	31	19	82	69
Gillingham	46	15	5	3	45	17	7	9	7	30	27	80	75
Preston North End	46	12	6	5	46	23	10	7	6	32	27	79	78
Wigan Athletic	46	14	5	4	44	17	8	5	10	31	31	76	75
Bournemouth	46	14	7	2	37	11	7	6	10	26	30	76	63
Stoke City	46	10	4	9	32	32	11	2	10	27	31	69	59
Chesterfield	46	14	5	4	34	16	3	8	12	12	28	64	46
Millwall	46	9	8	6	33	24	8	3	12	19	35	62	52
Reading	46	10	6	7	29	26	6	7	10	25	37	61	54
Luton Town	46	10	4	9	25	26	6	6	11	26	34	58	51
Bristol Rovers	46	8	9	6	35	28	5	8	10	30	28	56	65
Blackpool	46	7	8	8	24	24	7	6	10	20	30	56	44
Burnley	46	8	7	8	23	33	5	9	9	31	40	55	54
Notts County	46	8	6	9	29	27	6	6	11	23	34	54	52
Wrexham	46	8	6	9	21	28	5	8	10	22	34	53	43
Colchester United	46	9	7	7	25	30	3	9	11	27	40	52	52
Wycombe Wanderers	46	8	5	10	26	5	7	11	21	32	51	52	-
Oldham Athletic	46	8	4	11	26	31	6	5	12	22	35	51	48
York City	46	6	8	9	28	33	7	3	13	28	47	50	56
Northampton Town	46	4	12	7	26	31	6	6	11	17	26	48	43
Lincoln City	46	9	4	10	27	27	4	3	16	15	47	46	42
Macclesfield Town	46	7	4	12	24	30	4	6	13	19	33	43	43